MIGRANTS AND THEIR MONEY

Surviving financial exclusion in London

Kavita Datta

First published in Great Britain in 2012 by

The Policy Press
University of Bristol
Fourth Floor
Beacon House
Queen's Road
Bristol BS8 1QU
UK

Tel +44 (0)117 331 4054
Fax +44 (0)117 331 4093
e-mail tpp-info@bristol.ac.uk
www.policypress.co.uk

North American office:
The Policy Press
c/o The University of Chicago Press
1427 East 60th Street
Chicago, IL 60637, USA
t: +1 773 702 7700
f: +1 773-702-9756
e:sales@press.uchicago.edu
www.press.uchicago.edu

British Library Cataloguing in Publication Data
A catalogue record for this book is available from the British Library.

Library of Congress Cataloging-in-Publication Data
A catalog record for this book has been requested.

ISBN 978 1 84742 843 1 hardcover

Cover design by The Policy Press.
Front cover: image kindly supplied by www.alamy.com
Printed and bound in Great Britain by MPG Book
Group
The Policy Press uses environmentally responsible print
partners.

MIX
Paper from
responsible sources
FSC
www.fsc.org   FSC® C018575

This book is dedicated to the memory of
Daya, whose loss is immeasurable
and whose support will never be forgotten.

Contents

List of tables, figures and photos

Tables

Figures

Photos

List of abbreviations and acronyms

A2   Ascension 2 countries – Bulgaria and Romania, which joined the EU in January 2007

A8   Ascension 8 countries – Czech Republic, Estonia, Hungary, Latvia, Lithuania, Poland, Slovakia and Slovenia, which joined the EU in May 2004

APR   Annual Percentage Rate

ATM   Automated Teller Machine

BBA   Basic Bank Account

BCSB Banking Codes Standard Body

BME   Black and Minority Ethnic populations

CAB   Citizens Advice Bureau

CDFI   Community Development Finance Institution

CTF   Child Trust Fund

DFID   Department for International Development (UK)

DSS   Department of Social Security (former UK government agency)

DTI   Department of Trade and Industry (UK)

DWP   Department for Work and Pensions (UK)

EPZ   Export Processing Zone

EU   European Union

FATF   Financial Action Taskforce

FDI   Foreign Direct Investment

FITF   Financial Inclusion Taskforce

FSA   Financial Services Authority (UK)

HSMP Highly Skilled Migrant Programme

IDA   Individual Development Account

IMF   International Monetary Fund

IOM   International Organisation for Migration

IPPR   Institute of Public Policy Research (UK)

ISA   Individual Savings Account

KYC   Know Your Customer

MAC   Migration Advisory Council (UK)

MTO   Money Transfer Organisation

NBFI   Non-bank Financial Intermediary

NEET   Not in Education, Employment or Training, describing young
         people
NEF   New Economic Foundation (UK)
NMW   National Minimum Wage
ODA   Overseas Development Assistance
OECD   Organisation for Economic Cooperation and Development
PAT   Policy Action Teams
PBS   Points Based System
POCA   Post Office Card Account
ROSCAs   Rotating Savings and Credit Associations
RSP   Remittance Service Provider
SAFE   Services Against Financial Exclusion
SAP   Structural Adjustment Programmes
SBS   Sector Based Schemes
UK   United Kingdom
UNDP   United Nations Development Programme
US   United States

Acknowledgements

This book is based upon research which was funded by Friends Provident Foundation to whom I am very grateful. I would like to extend a special thanks to Danielle Walker-Palmour for her enthusiasm and support for this project. The research also benefited from earlier financial input by London Citizens and the School of Geography at Queen Mary, University of London. I owe a particular debt of gratitude to Zahra Gibril, Yara Evans and Irina Changerova for their invaluable contribution to this research in conducting interviews with Brazilian, Bulgarian and Somali migrant men and women. Thanks are also due to dedicated researchers and community organisers who participated in London Citizen's Summer Academy including Nil Tuptuk, Olivia Sheringham, Ana-Carla Reis França, Awale Elmi and Michal Garapich.

I would like to acknowledge the support of all of my colleagues at the School of Geography, Queen Mary, University of London, particularly Cathy McIlwaine, Jane Wills, Jon May, Yara Evans and Joanna Herbert with whom my interest in transnational migration has been developed. I am grateful to Alison Shaw, Laura Vickers and Jo Morton at The Policy Press, and their anonymous peer reviewers, for their valuable comments and patience. Thanks to my husband, Priya, as always, for putting up with this book and to my daughters, Aashna and Kinza, for being so very patient. I owe a special thanks to Aashna for her help with the figures, diagrams and photographs.

Finally, and most importantly, I am indebted to all the migrant men and women who participated in this project for their openness in divulging information relating to all aspects of their remarkable transnational lives.

ONE

Migrants, money and exclusion

This book explores migrant men and women's experiences of, and responses to, financial exclusion in London, offering an insight into an aspect of migrants' lives that is often overlooked yet vital for their broader integration. It documents the changing spatial and temporal geographies of financial exclusion in advanced economies such as the UK that are increasingly characterised as finance-led. Drawing on primary empirical research with over 400 migrants, it investigates how men and women from five diverse communities originating in the global South (Brazil and Somalia) and East and Central Europe (Turkey, Poland and Bulgaria), negotiate the complex socioeconomic landscape of London, the financial capital of the world. In particular, it considers how they strategise for their inclusion into financial institutions, which affords them access to banking, savings, credit and remittance services. The book also highlights how migrants cope with exclusion through the crafting of 'diverse' and 'proliferative' financial practices (Stenning et al, 2010a, 2010b). In so doing, the book opens up three areas of inquiry: first, migrants' agency in strategising for inclusion while coping with exclusion; second, the social, economic and financial resources and assets that they are able to draw upon to do so and which shape their financial practices; and third, the scale of these practices, some of which are embedded within local social and economic relations, and others which are more transnational and connect migrants' financial lives across different spaces. The book argues that these 'mix and match' financial practices do not reflect a singular narrative of financial inclusion and that it is essential to re-inscribe the social into understanding the construction of financial relations (Leyshon and Thrift, 1995). It also illustrates the importance of drawing upon cross-disciplinary work on how people have coped with financial exclusion in very different contexts and emphasises the need, as Pollard and Samers (2007: 314) argue to '"provincialize" our understandings of hegemonic economic practices and knowledges' from the perspective of people and places who are located at the margins.

Arranged in three parts, this opening chapter begins with a consideration of the evolution of financial exclusion in the UK from the 1980s onwards and the key processes that have shaped it. It identifies the emergence of distinctive geographies of financial exclusion as well as particular groups at risk of exclusion. It discusses the wide-ranging implications of being at the margins of a financialised economy. Alongside this narrative, the chapter tells the story of growing transnational migration to the UK, and specifically London, detailing the nature of this migration and the forces shaping transnational mobility. It proceeds to identify the factors that place migrant men and women at risk of financial exclusion, highlighting the particular importance of immigration status, labour market position and transnational financial lives. In the third and final section the chapter outlines 'alternative' financial practices deployed by financially excluded individuals and households in a range of different contexts that are not solely shaped by their exclusion from formal financial circuits but also reflect, to varying extents, a preference for different ways of 'doing finance'.

The inexorable rise of finance – and financial exclusion?

The capital instability fostered by over 30 years of neoliberal globalisation is evidenced in the recent financial meltdown which has focused collective attention on financial markets and their ability to generate significant inequalities. Few experts foresaw that what began as a crisis in the US subprime mortgage markets in 2007 would evolve into a global recession (Martin, 2009).[1] As such, the speed at which the crisis spread to, and affected, virtually all parts of the world, including those regarded as being the least integrated in the global economy, took many by surprise (Papademetriou and Terrazas, 2009; Dymski, 2010). Within advanced economies the UK was identified as being particularly at risk of a severe and protracted downturn (Wearden, 2009; IMF, 2010). Here, while the recession occurred after an unusually long period of growth, its onset was very rapid (Rogers et al, 2009; Sumption, 2010). Experiencing a significant contraction of its GDP, the first headline casualty was the financial sector, as evidenced by high-profile redundancies, with employment in finance in London shrinking by a third from a peak of 360,000 jobs in 2008 and a corresponding decline in the sector's contribution to national wealth (Allen, 2010; French et al, 2010). While for some the economic downturn represented an opportunity for radical change that would lead to a dismantling of the neoliberal project, the loss in faith in the financial basis, or the financialisation, of the UK's economy was apparently momentary, with a return to 'business as usual' (albeit with some cosmetic changes) in a short space of time (French and Leyshon, 2010; Helleiner, 2010).[2] For example, in assessing the impact of the downturn on the City of

London, commentators noted that while the crisis led to a thinning-out of financial institutions and capacity, this facilitated a reduction in competition such that the profits of remaining firms recovered rapidly, undoubtedly aided by the £1.3 trillion public money spent on propping up the financial sector (French et al, 2010).

Yet outside of the world of high finance the recession continues to have significant implications, especially for poorer people and places in terms of job losses, income stagnation, rising inflation and public service cuts (French and Leyshon, 2010). Reflecting the experiences of past economic downturns and the tendency of financial capital to go through cycles of exclusion in response to financial crises, one particular implication of the contemporary recession is an intensification of financial exclusion alongside greater financial exploitation (Leyshon and Thrift 1995; French et al, 2009). Indeed, concerns about financial exclusion preceded the downturn in the UK where an estimated 1.5 million households (7 per cent of the population) lack access to any financial services, while a further 4.4 million households (20 per cent of the population) utilise only one or two basic financial services (Kempson and Whyley, 1999; Blake and de Jong, 2008). As financiers seek to avoid risk by removing capital from the poorest in society, there is a danger, as recognised by the UK's Financial Services Authority (FSA) that 'many of those who currently are not considered, and do not consider themselves, to be financially excluded could, because of their economic and financial circumstances, find themselves at risk of slipping into that vulnerable group' (Pond, 2009: 1). This is corroborated by French et al (2009: 295), who identify the emergence of a 'new class of financially excluded'. Recent figures indicate that the numbers of unbanked individuals in the UK, which were showing some evidence of decline, have stalled (FITF, 2010). Furthermore, the current phase of risk aversion and reduced outreach by financial organisations has effectively meant that access to affordable credit has become harder for many, accompanied by a boom in unsecured subprime lending (NEF, 2008). For example, the UK home credit company Provident Financial reported a sharp increase in their customer base, taking the total number of subprime customers to over 10 million in 2008 (Transact, 2008). Correspondingly, levels of (over-)indebtedness have also risen significantly, with the personal debt owned by British households increasing from £370 billion in 1993 to £1.5 trillion in 2010 (Blake and de Jong, 2008; Montgomerie, 2009; Cox et al, 2011).

The term 'financial exclusion' was first coined in the early 1990s by geographers who propelled much of the original thinking around it to broadly denote 'the processes which prevent poor and disadvantaged social groups from gaining access to the financial system' (Leyshon and Thrift, 1995: 312; see also Leyshon and Thrift, 1993, 1994, 1996). Even while economic geographers had largely failed to acknowledge questions related to money and finance up to that point in preference for an emphasis on the 'material landscapes of the economy' (Lee et al, 2009: 724), subsequent work focused upon the reorganisation of finance on the global scale, the emergence of international financial centres, as well as the restructuring of domestic financial systems through processes of re-regulation, bank mergers, establishment of provincial financial centres and employment patterns in the financial services sector (Leyshon and Thrift, 1995, 1996; Dymski, 2005). Much of this research was initially silent on questions of equity and the ways in which individuals and households were negotiating a rapidly changing landscape of credit and debt (Berthoud and Kempson, 1992; Kempson, 1994; Leyshon and Thrift, 1995; French and Leyshon, 2004; Leyshon et al, 2004; Dymski, 2005, 2006; Leyshon et al, 2006). This was partly attributable to the fact that the problem of exclusion was veiled by wider changes that were occurring in the UK, and global economy at large, which have since been described as financialisation (Dore, 2002; Froud and Williams, 2007; Langley, 2007; Erturk et al, 2008).

Interpreted as offering an account of contemporary capitalism, financialisation has been defined as 'the increasing role of financial motives, financial markets, financial actors and financial institutions in the operation of domestic and international economies' (Epstein, 2005: 3). While the pre-eminence of finance is not an entirely new phenomenon, researchers note that it has assumed a particularly dominant position in advanced economies over the last three decades, as evidenced by the significant growth in financial activities, whether this is measured in terms of employment, profits, the size of financial institutions or financial markets (Epstein, 2005: 3; see also Aglietta, 2000; Boyer, 2000; Dore, 2000; Erturk et al, 2007; Montgomerie, 2009). As such, the financial sector has both transformed and come to dominate economic production (French et al, 2008). This rise of finance can be partially traced back to the 1970s and 1980s following the dismantling of the Bretton Woods consensus and the deregulation and abolition of exchange and capital controls, the removal of barriers between different financial competitors and restrictions on the entry of foreign firms, the development of new delivery technologies and a diversification of financial and monetary products (Leyshon and Thrift, 1996; Kempson et al, 2000).

Emerging out of this 'freeing up' of the financial industry, this period witnessed a marked increase in competition between financial firms in the UK due to the deregulation of wholesale (defined as financial and commercial financial services) and retail financial markets (relating to personal and high street financial services). The passing of the Building Society Act and the Financial Services Act in 1986 by the Conservative government made it possible for financial service firms to compete more freely in what had previously been 'product circumscribed markets' (Martin, 1999). Generating fierce competition between financial institutions, this resulted in considerable product innovation, as evidenced by the development of subprime and buy-to-let mortgages as well as the securitisation of consumer debt. At first these changes, which coincided with the greater availability and circulation of capital within and between advanced economies following the debt crisis which gripped much of the poorer world in the 1980s, led to an expansion in the availability of financial services within core economies as finance was pulled back from poor countries (to be discussed later). New clients were actively sourced through easier access to credit associated with the increase in home ownership in the UK which was facilitated by government-backed mortgage interest tax relief and 'right to buy policies' leading to the sale of (better quality) social housing at discounted rates to some 1.5 million tenants (Leyshon and Thrift, 1995). Furthermore, the privatisation of utilities enabled more people to participate in the stocks and shares market with the percentage of people holding these assets rising substantially from 7.8 per cent in 1982 to 22.8 per cent in 1988 (Paxton, 2003).

Yet, as the UK debt crisis of the 1990s began to take hold, a second round of financial retrenchment occurred, this time resulting in the abandonment of poorer people and places located within advanced economies (Leyshon and Thrift, 1995). Explained by increased competition between financial firms, rising operational costs and debts, as well as broader changes to the welfare state (to be discussed later), these events led to a scramble for more affluent and profit-generating customers who came to be characterised by Leyshon and Thrift (1996: 1153) as the 'super-included', who benefited from the shift from credit-related products to the 'growth-orientated investment-related products and services' (Kempson et al, 2000: 17; see also Reagan and Paxton, 2003). These processes had profound implications both for those who found themselves excluded from financial services as well as those individuals and households who were at best marginally included and were increasingly denied the possibility of taking out credit (Leyshon and Thrift, 1995; Leyshon et al, 1998). Thus, importantly, while absolute levels of financial exclusion declined in the UK through the 1990s as more people were afforded access to financial services, *relative* levels of exclusion increased during the same period. Between 1989 and 1994, the number of people with a current account increased from 71 to 74 per cent, but in the same period the number of unemployed people not holding a transactional bank account increased from 79 to 88 per cent (Leyshon et al, 1999).

In attempting to explain these trends, commentators initially focused upon what may be termed as the 'supply' side of finance. Perhaps unsurprisingly, geographers were clearly interested in the rapidly changing spatiality of financial services provision (Leyshon and Thrift, 1995). Building upon research in the US where 'redlining' practices were shown to be wreaking havoc on poorer, and especially African American communities living in deprived neighbourhoods, research in the UK highlighted the importance of place in shaping access to financial products and services and the crucial links between financial exclusion and uneven development (Kantor and Nystuen, 1982; Dymski and Veitch, 1992, 1994, 1996; Dymski, 1999; Pollard, 2003). Investigated primarily within the context of bank branch closures,[3] the geography of financial services withdrawal within the UK was clearly evident, with rural and deprived urban areas facing the greatest threat of branch closures (Leyshon and Thrift, 1995). Even while the Association of British Bankers sought to justify this in terms of the falling demand for face-to-face banking services, with a representative commenting that "banks and building society branches are shops on the high street. If there is not enough business for a shop to stay open, it closes. Banks are no different", it is apparent that these closures were largely attributable to the drive to reduce operational costs through the centralisation of services, the use of new telecommunications technologies and the outsourcing of services to call centres (Drakeford and Sachdev, 2001: 213). Leading to the emergence of a distinct North–South geography of financial exclusion, the lowest use of financial products was recorded in Scotland, Northern England as well as pockets of London (Kempson and Whyley, 1999; Collard, Kempson and Whyley, 2001). This divide was apparent even a decade later with 13 per cent of all households in Scotland lacking access to financial services and products compared with 3 per cent in the South-East (Leyshon and Thrift, 1995; Leyshon et al, 1999; Marshall, 2004). This said, the South-East, and London in particular, was also identified as having a 'hollow centre' with high levels of financial exclusion recorded in parts of inner London (Leyshon and Thrift, 1996). Indeed, it is at the local level that the spatiality of financial exclusion continues to be especially marked with 47 per cent of those in the UK who have no financial products living in the 50 most deprived districts and boroughs of England and Scotland (Marshall, 2004).

In turn, the undeniable spillover effects of bank closure upon local economies and neighbourhoods led to a growing consensus that 'money shapes places' and that a contraction in financial services has an adverse impact upon local economies potentially creating 'finance gaps' and a downward spiral of degeneration (Marshall, 2004: 244). In particular, the withdrawal of banks from poorer urban and rural communities, and the replacement of 'qualitative' or 'soft' assessments of the credit-worthiness of potential customers undertaken by bank staff located in branches embedded within local communities by more distanciated credit scoring had a detrimental impact upon poorer customers' access to affordable credit (Leyshon and Thrift, 1995; Leyshon et al, 1998; Kempson et al, 2000). Creating what Leyshon and Thrift (1994) refer to as 'geodemographies of good and bad areas and customers', the adoption of more sophisticated credit-scoring technologies meant that while interest rates for low-risk (affluent) borrowers could be kept down, high-risk borrowers – identified as those with poor credit ratings derived from a complex interplay of low incomes, ownership of few or no assets, periods of unsecure employment as well as limited engagement with financial services – were pushed into the subprime market (see also Leyshon et al, 2004). This expulsion of the credit excluded to the subprime market was associated with greater financial exploitation whereby higher rates, fees and penalties were attached to the financial products extended to these groups (Dymski, 2006). Thus, as Dymski (2005: 451) argues, 'financial exclusion does not mean the absence of credit for a portion of the population: far from it. Those who are excluded need credit, are provided it and pay much more for it, than the financially included.'

Whereas previous research had predominantly looked at how financial institutions interacted with their customers, this was then accompanied by an investigation of what have come to be identified as 'demand-side' factors. Particular social groups emerged as being disproportionately at risk from being excluded from financial circuits due to an intersection of marginality. This included the unemployed, low paid, elderly, young people not in education, employment or training (NEET), Black and Minority Ethnic (BME) groups and people with disabilities (Kempson and Whyley, 1999; Fine et al, 2005; Treasury, 2007b; Anderloni et al, 2008; Blake and de Jong, 2008; Mitton, 2008). Examinations of the factors shaping exclusion among these groups highlighted the importance of price (whereby some households were priced out of the market), access (shaped by risk assessments), condition (where the conditions attached to financial products made them inappropriate for the needs of some households), marketing (with some households effectively excluded by targeting marketing and sales) and self-exclusion (Kempson and Whyley, 1999). Poverty in particular emerged as a driver of financial exclusion. Data gathered from the Poverty and Social Exclusion Survey in the late 1990s highlighted that within the UK 35 per cent of households had no savings, 14 per cent were in debt, 7 per cent had no bank account, 15 per cent had no insurance, 10 per cent had borrowed more money to pay debts and 5 per cent had experienced their utilities being disconnected. Furthermore, this analysis showed the overlap between financial exclusion and poverty as 88 per cent of those who were financially excluded were also materially and socially deprived (Goodwin et al, 2000). In turn, the interplay between poverty, gender, age and ethnicity also had particular exclusionary repercussions for certain segments of society, with research illustrating that even while the UK's BME population was very diverse it was especially vulnerable to financial exclusion due to interlocking factors such as educational disadvantage, low employment rates and high levels of in-work poverty, as well as a concentration in social housing (Wallace and Quilgars, 2005; Khan, 2008, 2010).

Importantly, for financially excluded people, access to financial services has become progressively more difficult at a time when it has also assumed greater importance as a result of broader changes in the political economy and welfare state (Leyshon and Thrift, 1996). Deeply involved in the neoliberal transformation of the UK economy, the role of the British state in the emergence of a finance-led economy and its penetration into everyday life cannot be understated (Finlayson, 2008). As Finlayson (2008: 403) argues, 'this is not simply a matter of how national governments are complicit with "global capital"… It is also how government reinvents and establishes new roles for itself, in the context of the reallocation of risk from collective to individual and the delegitimisation of interventionism.' The increased appetite for shifting the responsibility of individual wellbeing from the state to the individual has been central to the neoliberal transformation of the UK economy and state (Reagan and Paxton, 2003; Finlayson, 2008). In seeking to distinguish itself both from its predecessor Conservative government as well as 'old' Labour, New Labour's vision of renewing British society on assuming office in 1997 was articulated around 'stakeholder capitalism' that would offer a 'third way' between social democracy and neoliberalism (Prabhakar, 2010). Subsequently refashioned around ideas of asset-based welfarism that were deeply influenced by similar experiments in the US, individual wellbeing was increasingly associated with *both* income as well as the assets that people held in financial, physical, human and social forms (Sherraden, 1991; Reagan and Paxton,

2001, 2003; Prabhakar, 2008, 2010; Appleyard, 2011). The ownership of these assets, it was posited, would enable citizens to participate fully in the economy, capitalise on opportunities and build upon their capacity to cope with periods of change, thus enabling them to become more self-reliant (Paxton, 2003).

As commentators note, there were very clear limitations to the egalitarianism being proposed by New Labour such that 'asset based welfare was not premised upon either an equal share of income or assets, or their redistribution, but rather an equality of opportunity whereby all people would be facilitated in the acquisition of assets' (Paxton, 2003). Ben-Galim (2011: 3) argues that the role of the welfare state was evolving under New Labour so that in addition to providing a safety net it was 'also expected to empower and enable individuals to bring about change themselves'. In its emphasis on 'helping people help themselves', New Labour clearly visualised a reframing of economic agency whereby passive citizens were transformed into 'active-saver-investor' agents who were in charge of managing their own assets (Watson, 2009; Appleyard, 2011). Moreover, as Watson (2009) argues, the changing state–society contract was premised upon a philosophical framework of duty rather than justice, with citizens duty-bound to secure their own futures. In turn, these ambitions hinged upon the twin agenda of 'making work pay', which was aimed at shepherding people back into employment, and a radical shake-up of the welfare state. While the particularities of the transformation of the UK labour market are investigated later in this chapter, it is important to acknowledge here that these structural changes resulted in stagnating and/or declining wages and income that could not keep up with inflation. The combination of this with dropping savings rates effectively meant that individuals and households had to rely upon credit to meet the costs of everyday living, leading to the subsequent normalisation of debt in British society (Thiel, 2006; Ramsay, 2009; Cox et al, 2011). Furthermore, welfare reform initiated by the Thatcher government continued apace under New Labour and had a significant impact upon wide-ranging areas of everyday life including 'the reduction in the state pension and the expansion of private provision; the reduction in student grants and the expansion of loans; the reduction in state mortgage pension support and the (limited) expansion of private mortgage insurance' (Reagan and Paxton, 2003: 13). It also entailed the expansion of complicated means-tested benefits and the movement to automated payments of benefits (Mosley and Steel, 2004; Finlayson, 2009; Watson, 2009). Fundamentally then, both the neoliberal restructuring of the labour market as well as the welfare state relied heavily upon a financially *in*cluded citizenry that had the resources to participate in asset accumulation as well as the wherewithal to understand increasingly sophisticated and complicated financial products (see also Chapter Two).

Within the context of what has come to be termed as 'the financialisation of everyday life and social relations,' the penalties associated with being at the margins of financial circuits are increasingly significant and can be measured on different registers (Martin, 2002; Langley, 2007, 2008). Overall there is a consensus that financial exclusion results in an inability to save, manage money securely and effectively, access credit and build assets, and deal with financial distress (Treasury, 2007b). For example, the consequences of not having access to a bank account are significant resulting in a 'poverty premium' in terms of higher fees and charge rates (Blake and de Jong, 2008; NEF, 2008). Similarly, a lack of savings can render households vulnerable to financial crisis while a lack of access to affordable credit effectively means that people on low incomes have little alternative but to borrow high-interest credit and so accumulate significant debts. Deficits in financial literacy and knowledge have also meant that financially excluded households have found it difficult to understand and, perhaps more crucially, access means-tested benefits. In turn, the costs of financial exclusion clearly extend beyond the economic. Research documents the correlation between financial incapability and psychological stress resulting in higher mental stress, lower life satisfaction and health problems associated with anxiety and depression (Mitton, 2008; Taylor et al, 2009). There is broad consensus that financial and social exclusion are inextricably linked such that financial exclusion can intensify experiences of poverty and inequality while social exclusion has financial costs (see Chapter Two, this volume, and Datta, 2009a). As such, financial inclusion has been positioned as being 'as much a social as a monetary demand' (Fuller and Mellor, 2008: 1512).

A broader debate has also emerged around the changing nature of citizenship in financialised societies whereby exclusion from financial services has been judged as having a detrimental impact upon individuals' ability to participate fully in the economy and to accumulate wealth, with consequent implications for social mobility, inclusion and community cohesion (Leyshon and Thrift, 1995; Dymski and Li, 2004; Dymski, 2005). For some commentators the fact that financial systems, like the state, have clearly demarcated borders, which those on the outside find increasingly difficult to navigate, effectively means that financial citizenship relies upon putting pressure on 'states to reform the financial systems so that they include rather than exclude and putting pressure on financial systems to realize that they have some state-like responsibilities which reach beyond consumer sovereignty into basic human rights' (Leyshon and Thrift, 1997: 259). In sum, the fear is that financially excluded populations will find it increasingly difficult to live and work in what are fast becoming cashless capitalist societies without *some* level of access to financial services (Blake and de Jong, 2008; Mitton, 2008).

Having outlined the broad contours of the simultaneous rise of finance and financial exclusion, the chapter now turns to argue for the imperative to reconfigure these debates around migration and migrants, which have received little attention to date, particularly in the UK (although see Kempson, 1998; Atkinson, 2006; Datta, 2007a, 2009b; Gibbs, 2010; Datta, 2011a, 2011b). This elision is significant in terms of the epistemic limits it places upon debates relating to finance and financial exclusion.

Living on the (financial) margins? Migrants and migration to the UK

Even while the global ebb and flow of finance has crucially shaped uneven development and driven transnational migration, research into the geographies of money and finance has generally marginalised the movement of people while migration and mobility studies usually fail to acknowledge the flows of finance that accompany or shape migration outside of remittances (Li et al, 2009). The International Organisation for Migration (IOM, 2011) estimates that some 214 million people – or 3 per cent of the world population – live outside of their country of birth. While numerous authors dispute the validity of the claim that the contemporary period represents 'an age of unprecedented migration', reporting instead only a modest increase in the total proportion of people living outside of their country of birth, they do acknowledge the growth of migration from the global South, and East and Central Europe to the advanced economies of the global North (De Haas, 2005: 1270; see also Nyberg-Sørensen et al, 2002a; Olesen, 2002; De Haas, 2007; Koser, 2007; Faist, 2008; Datta, 2009a).[4] Given these trends, it is apparent that migrants are a significant new source of demand for financial services in a number of advanced economies even while nascent research suggests that they may be especially prone to financial exclusion (Anderloni and Vandone, 2006). Primarily investigated within the context of immigration to the US, various reports concur that almost half of all migrants suffer from some level of financial exclusion (Hogarth et al, 2004; Paulson et al, 2006; Rhine and Greene, 2006;

Giusti, 2009; Joassart-Marcelli and Stevens, 2010). In the UK, migrant exclusion is placed at between 3 and 10 per cent higher than the UK-born population (Treasury, 2007b).

Importantly, these exclusions arise out of multiple and interlocking factors, some of which are common to all excluded groups while others are migrant specific (Datta, 2007a, 2011a). As such, financial exclusion is attributable to an intersection of migrant status with other cleavages of disadvantage such as gender, ethnic and racial inequalities, as well as immigration status and labour market position. It is increasingly recognised that host country institutions, especially the state, play a vital role in determining migrants' rights to entry and work as well as setting the broad framework within which financial organisations can interact with these populations and vice versa (Li et al, 2009). In turn, the multiple disadvantages that accrue from being located at the margins of financialised societies have far-reaching implications for migrants' broader socioeconomic integration into host countries.

Financial crisis and transnational migrations to London

Fleshing these arguments out further within the specific context of London, migration to the UK was at historically high levels at the eve of the 2008–10 downturn, with the longer-term increase in net immigration dating back to the early 1990s (Datta, 2011b). In fact, much of what has come to be termed as 'new migration' took place under New Labour's 13-year period of government with annual immigration rising by over 50 per cent from just under 300,000 in 1997 to a peak of 600,000 in 2004 following the expansion of the EU (Cavanaugh 2010). Correspondingly, the foreign-born population doubled between 1991 and 2001 when it comprised 8.3 per cent of the total population, with a further 2.5 million being added to the British population between 1997 and 2010 (Finch and Goodhart, 2010). London has historically served as a significant destination for migrants, such that by 2001, 42 per cent of those who had arrived in the UK had settled in the city. By 2006, just under a third (31 per cent) of the city's population and just over a third (35 per cent) of its working-age population were born overseas (Spence, 2006; Fix et al, 2009).

The arrival of these migrants in London is not accidental but the result of a complex interplay of economic, social, political and financial processes that have generated not only economic migration but also mobility related to conflict and displacement. Nearly 30 years ago, the unfolding of another financial downturn – the debt crisis – triggered a rewiring of the international financial system and the economic restructuring of the beleaguered economies of poorer countries in the global South that fundamentally reshaped global migration patterns (Leyshon and Thrift, 1988; Corbridge, 1988, 1992). Announcements by the governments of Brazil, Mexico and Poland in the early 1980s that they could not service their official debts created panic in both transnational banks and Northern creditor governments that had been involved in the recirculation of money deposited by oil-rich OPEC nations to poorer countries in need of finance for development (Corbridge, 2008).[5] Interpreted as a threat to the international financial system, the debt crisis was met by a reversal of net capital transfers from richer countries (in particular North America, Europe and Japan) to poorer nations, compounded by the refusal of transnational banks to lend to heavily indebted nations. Furthermore, this contraction in credit flows was matched by an institutional withdrawal from the same countries, such that within the space of five years between 1980 and 1985 the top 100 international banks shut just under a quarter of their bank branches in the global South (Leyshon and Thrift, 1995).

Notwithstanding the role of Northern governments and transnational financial institutions in precipitating the debt crisis, the responsibility for the crisis was laid squarely on the shoulders of the governments of poorer countries, which were charged with gross domestic mismanagement, bloated and corrupt governance systems and the pursuit of anti-market policies (Corbridge, 1992; Simon, 2008). This paved the way for radical neoliberal economic reform, inspired by earlier experiments in the UK and the US, and exported to the poorer countries of the global South by international financial institutions such as the World Bank and IMF in the guise of Structural Adjustment Programmes (SAPs). Importantly, as May et al (2010) argue, neoliberal reforms fell on fertile ground in some recipient countries where they were mediated through a longer history of domestic reform. Between 1980 and 1989, 171 SAPs were introduced in sub-Saharan Africa alone with a further 57 initiated by the end of 1996 (Simon 2008). Moreover, the transitional economies of East and Central Europe, including Poland, did not escape neoliberal restructuring (De Boreck and Koen, 2000).

The ambition of SAPs to facilitate debt repayment by the stabilisation of these economies was realised through the implementation of significant restructuring packages including reductions in state expenditure, privatisation of state assets, liberalisation of markets and reductions in import tariffs. Considerable emphasis was placed on the development of conditions that would attract private foreign direct investment partly facilitated through the establishment of Export Processing Zones (EPZs), which offered foreign firms favourable tax, trade and labour conditions through the elimination of custom duties on imports, liberalisation of capital flows in and out of EPZs and minimal labour legislation in terms of adherence to minimum wage and working hours (Beazley and Desai, 2008).This neoliberal financial deregulation led to a surge of geographically differentiated capital flows in the 1980s and 1990s that were accompanied by the movement of people. As Elson (1995) points out, hundreds of thousands of young people – and especially young women – migrated locally and regionally to take up the employment offered in EPZs. Furthermore, these migrations subsequently took on a transnational aspect associated with movements to advanced economies such as the UK from the global South as well as East and Central Europe (Massey et al, 1998; De Haas, 2007). Paradoxically, this transnational migration has been associated with both a lack of development, as poorer states have sought to solve their unemployment problems through the export of labour, as well as development itself, as people have moved in search of better economic opportunities due to uneven development processes (De Haas, 2010).

Furthermore, if economic migration has been one part of the story of the financial restructuring of poorer economies, conflict and forced migration is the other. While migratory flows to the UK prior to the 1980s were dominated by economic migrants, subsequent movements have been progressively more diverse, comprised of people seeking asylum and refuge, reflecting continued instability in the post-Cold War world (Wills et al, 2010). Indeed, there is growing academic consensus that it is increasingly difficult to distinguish between voluntary and forced migration given the complex interconnections between poverty, inequality and conflict, such that it may be more appropriate to think in terms of a migration–asylum nexus (Richmond, 1994).This nexus proposes that mobility is shaped by both compulsion (generating reactive migrations) and choice (related to proactive mobilities) (Richmond, 1994). In between these extremes there is a large mass of migration that is shaped by both.

With migrants originating from different parts of the globe, and going to London for various reasons, commentators have pointed to the increasingly 'super-diverse' nature of the city's population (Vertovec, 2007). Labelled as the 'world in one city', London is home to 179 different national groups with some 300 languages spoken in its schools (Baker and Mohieldeen, 2000; Vertovec, 2007). Indeed, its diversity extends far beyond national and ethnic differences, with other important markers of difference including labour market integration, immigration status, and gender, ethnic, religious and class composition (Vertovec, 2007). Importantly these differences underlie the sorting of migrant men and women into distinct hierarchical categories that shape their rights and entitlements to an array of socioeconomic and – crucially in this context – financial services.

Accounting for migrant (financial) exclusion in London

Fleeing economic deprivation and/or conflict in their home countries, migrants have had to negotiate another neoliberalised economy, that of the UK, whose labour market is increasingly characterised by simultaneous professionalisation, economic inactivity as well as the growth of the 'working poor' (May et al, 2010; Wills et al, 2010). Researchers have carefully documented the greater reliance – or as some have termed it 'addiction' – of advanced economies, and global cities in particular, to migrant labour (Sassen, 1991; Finch and Goodhart, 2010; Wills et al, 2010). This dependency has been fostered by over three decades of neoliberal development that has reshaped the nature and politics of work. Wills et al (2010) illustrate the fundamental changes to the British economy, which, in a relatively short time span, has gone from being dominated by heavy industry to being service based. In turn, the 'new economy', which has been associated with the increased dominance of finance as discussed earlier, has also borne witness to escalating polarisation between men and women, skilled and unskilled, old and young, and White and Black and Minority Ethnic workers. These cleavages are especially evident in London's labour market, where the significant increase in the proportion of highly skilled workers employed at the apex of its labour market – many of which revolve around finance in the City of London – has been accompanied by a smaller but still significant rise in the proportion of workers labouring at the very bottom end in sectors such as hospitality and care (May et al, 2007; Wills et al, 2010). In turn, migrant workers have emerged as significant at both ends of London's labour market.

The British penchant for skilled migrant labour was evidenced in a speech made in 2000 by the then Minister for Immigration, Barbara Roche, who signalled New Labour's take on immigration when she emphasised, "the UK is in competition for the brightest and the best talents – the entrepreneurs, the scientists, the high technology specialists who make the economy tick" (Roche, 2000). In turn, London's reliance upon a global market for highly skilled labour is particularly evident in, although not restricted to, the financial and business services sector (Beaverstock and Smith, 1996; Sassen, 2001; Sklair, 2002). Researchers note an increase in foreign-born employees from less than 5 per cent in the early 1980s to over 10 per cent and closer to 15–20 per cent in certain financial service sector occupations by the end of the 1990s (Thrift and Leyshon, 1992; Sassen, 2001; Hamnett, 2003; Jones, 2010). Particularly concentrated in higher order occupations, this increase is partly explained by the fracturing of financial services into ever more specialised activities for which the national pool of labour is limited in any economy (Jones, 2010). Furthermore, international work experience is a desirable attribute among highly skilled workers given that it is potentially linked to a better understanding of diverse business cultures and regulatory environments leading to widespread inter-firm transfers and secondments evident in transnational financial firms (Beaverstock and Smith, 1996; Beaverstock, 2002). Indeed, authors argue that London's position as one of the top three financial services centres in the world crucially depends upon the movement of highly skilled migrant workers in and out of key occupations in the City (Beaverstock, 2010; Jones, 2010). While some dispute that the movements of these transnational social elites are 'seamless' or 'frictionless', it is undeniable that their migration, and broader integration into British society, is facilitated by the fact that they are perceived as being the 'right' kind of economic migrants (Willis and Yeoh, 2002).

As noted above, the professionalisation of London's labour market has also been accompanied by a concomitant growth of low-skilled and low-paid work. Associated with part-time, flexible working and aggressive subcontracting, the bottom end of London's economy has been typified by low and stagnating wages, deteriorating conditions of work as well as an erosion in the bargaining power of workers (Sommerville and Sumption, 2009; Wills et al, 2010). Perhaps unsurprisingly, this labour market has been characterised by a rising number of vacancies as attempts to marshal the long-term native unemployed into these jobs through the twin agenda of a 'work-ethic' mantra and reform of the benefit system have proven to be ineffective (Rogers et al, 2009). This expanded low-wage economy has come to be dominated by migrant workers leading to the emergence of what may be best described as a 'migrant division of labour' (May et al, 2007; Wills et al, 2010). As an illustration, in 2001 it was estimated that 46 per cent of London's low-wage jobs were occupied by foreign-born workers (Spence, 2005). Indeed, this reliance on migrant workers is even more significant in certain sectors of London's economy such that it is clear that some parts of London's low-wage economy could no longer function without the labour of migrants (Wills et al, 2010). Exploring this specifically within recognisable migrant-dependent sectors of the economy, the percentage of cleaners born abroad rose from 40 per cent in 1993/94 to almost 70 per cent in 2004/05. Similar trends were evident in the hospitality industry with 29 per cent of chefs and cooks born abroad in 1993/94 increasing to 76 per cent in 2004/05 (Wills et al, 2010). Furthermore, even while migrants are crucial in lower-end jobs, they also comprise a significant proportion of the unemployed and those working in the informal economy (see Chapter Three).

In part this 'migrant division of labour' has been facilitated by the radical overhaul of the British immigration system over the last two decades, which has entrenched differences between migrants with different immigration pathways carrying discrete conditions of entry and entitlements to work and reside in the UK. Despite the consensus in certain quarters that migrant labour is 'good' for the British economy, the state has been pushed by different interest groups to manage migration to a greater or lesser extent (Wills et al, 2010). Leading in the opinion of some to 'political hyper activism', seven major pieces of immigration legislation were enacted over a 10-year period between 1999 and 2009, with 47 changes to immigration rules occurring in just five years from 2004 to 2009 (Spencer, 2011: 13). In fact, efforts to control immigration into the UK began in earnest almost as soon as migration to the country increased and crystallised in the 1990s around a set of 'managed migration' policies. These reflected three key immigration priorities: first, a cherry picking of the 'right' kinds of migrant – namely the highly skilled – from a global market, which the British economy needed to maintain its competitive edge; second, a clamping down on so-called 'bogus' asylum seekers, refugees and irregular migrants; and third, an encouragement of European migration over and above migration from the global South (Anderson et al, 2006; Markova and Black, 2007; Datta, 2009a; Hopkins, 2010; Wills et al, 2010).[6]

Flynn (2003) argues that the UK's migration regime has been characterised by a liberal approach to certain types of economic migration facilitated by an opening up of borders combined with a harshly repressive and restrictive approach to asylum seekers and irregular migrants, resulting in the development of a 'bifurcated immigration policy'. Taking these in turn, New Labour's immediate priority upon assuming office in 1997 was to address the problem of 'bogus asylum seekers', an ambition developed in response to both an increase in the number of people applying for asylum throughout the 1980s and 1990s with numbers peaking at 80,000 applications in 2000, as well as the inheritance of a considerable backlog involving some 50,000 cases from the outgoing Conservative government (Spencer, 2011). Determined not to appear 'soft' on immigration, the incoming government built upon the Immigration and Asylum Acts passed by its predecessor, resulting in the reorganisation of the UK asylum system, which aimed to reduce the number of asylum applications and fast track the processing of applications of those already in the country with an emphasis on detention and removal. As such, over a period of time, asylum seekers' access to both the UK labour market as well as state support in terms of welfare and housing entitlements has been systematically eroded (Home Office, 2008, 2010).

Forming part of the wider reform of the welfare state already documented, which sought to reduce dependency upon the state, asylum seekers' access to welfare has been particularly curtailed (Geddes, 2000; Spencer, 2011). Building upon the Conservative legislation of 1991, 1993 and 1996, which reduced the number and range of welfare payments asylum seekers were eligible for – including jobseeker's allowance, income support, housing benefit, child benefit and council tax benefit – New Labour went further and made explicit use of 'destitution as a means to both deter new arrivals and encourage refused asylum-seekers to leave…and crossed a line that some will not easily forgive or forget' (Spencer, 2010). These measures included a reduction in the income support available to refugees alongside the introduction of a voucher system redeemable only at certain shops, which was subsequently abandoned. The geographical dispersal of asylum seekers was also pursued and organised by the newly established National Asylum Support Service to alleviate the pressure on local authorities in London and the South-East. In accordance with an increasingly tough stance towards asylum seekers, the UK now has 11 Immigration Removal Centres, which house both asylum seekers awaiting decisions on their applications (including, perhaps most controversially, children) as well as those facing deportation (Home Office, 2010; Wills et al, 2010).[7] Illustrating this emphasis on detention and return, Black and Sward (2009: 2) argue that the 'Foreign and Commonwealth Office team working on promoting return of irregular migrants and failed asylum seekers is currently five times larger than the team focused on migration and development in the Department for International Development'.

While New Labour adopted increasingly restrictive asylum and refugee policies, it sought to partially liberalise immigration into the country via other routes. Here, as Flynn (2010) argues, it was apparent that the government was moving away from the previous Conservative government's priority of 'zero immigration' to managing migration in the interests of the British economy, ambitions that were set out in its second White Paper on immigration published in 2002, *Secure*

Borders, Safe Haven: Integration with Diversity in Modern Britain, which received broad cross-ministerial support (Finch and Goodhart, 2010). In particular, the growing belief in the link between immigration and economic growth was supported by both the Treasury and a powerful business lobby (Spencer, 2010). In keeping with its ambition to maintain its competitive edge in a global world, a proactive immigration policy that sought to address bottlenecks at both the skilled and unskilled end of the labour market made sense (Flynn, 2010). A succession of policies followed to realise these priorities including the Highly Skilled Migrant Worker Programme (HSMP) in 2002, followed by the Sector Based Schemes (SBSs) introduced in May 2003, which collectively aimed to recruit both skilled and unskilled labour, the latter in strictly temporary and limited employment in sectors such as hospitality and food processing. Furthermore, in March 2006 the government also put forward details of the new Points Based System (PBS) that has since been adopted and categorises migrants into five tiers according to skill-based criteria and labour market shortages (see Wills et al, 2010 for further details).

To a large extent these (economic) immigration priorities have been facilitated by the expansion of the EU twice in the last decade: first in 2004 to include the Ascension 8 (A8) countries of the Czech Republic, Estonia, Hungary, Latvia, Lithuania, Poland, Slovakia and Slovenia, and then again in 2007 to incorporate Romania and Bulgaria (the A2 countries). A key concern among the 'old' EU states regarding the enlargement of the Union was its implications for westward migration (McDowell, 2009). As a concession, each state was able to decide upon its own terms for entry, employment and residence for up to a period of seven years. The UK emerged as one of only three EU states, alongside Sweden and Ireland, to permit A8 nationals to take up immediate employment without work permits, which is partly attributed to the Treasury's view that this migration would be beneficial to the UK economy (Finch and Goodhart, 2010).[8] Others argue that this was a pragmatic decision to legitimise an already established flow of particularly Polish workers to the country and served as a form of amnesty for these migrants (Garapich, 2008). Undoubtedly, the decision was also shaped by the significant labour shortages already identified in both skilled and, particularly, low-skilled jobs such as construction, hospitality, transport and public services, as well as care, including nursing (Anderson et al, 2006; McDowell, 2009; Wills et al, 2010). As Spencer (2010) argues, subsequent high employment rates among A8 migrants (81 per cent in comparison with 74 per cent for UK-born workers) support the argument that there were jobs to be had.

This said, the A8 enlargement of Europe brought an unanticipated number of Eastern European migrants to the UK with 345,000 workers registering for employment in the space of just over a year between May 2004 and December 2005 (Anderson et al, 2006).[9] It is estimated that by 2009 nearly 1.5 million A8 workers had migrated to the UK, where they comprised half of the labour immigration flow, with the Polish emerging as the largest migrant community in the UK by 2009 (having been thirteenth in 2003) (Fix et al, 2009; Somerville and Sumption, 2009). This 'invasion from the East', as it came to be depicted in certain segments of the media, had a strong bearing on the UK's position on the subsequent enlargement of the EU in 2007 to admit Romania and Bulgaria, whose nationals received a much more guarded and cautious welcome (MAC, 2008). In particular, the government chose to restrict A2 nationals' access to the British labour market along the lines set prior to their ascension to the EU via temporary worker schemes, including the Seasonal Agricultural Workers Scheme (SAWS) and SBSs, the European Community Association Agreement (which facilitates the migration of self-employed individuals) and the highly skilled migration programme (Simeonova, 2004; MAC, 2008; Markova, 2009). Initially imposed for two years, these restrictions were reviewed and extended at the end of 2008 on the advice of the Migration Advisory Committee (MAC, 2008), a decision that was shaped by the looming economic downturn, the unknown implications of lifting restrictions, as well as the state of these two economies. There was appreciation of the fact, for example, that Bulgaria was and remains one of the lowest income economies in Europe with a GDP per capita just one third of the 15 'older' EU nations, with the economic downturn of 2008–10 leading to further increases in unemployment and a contraction in the country's GDP (MAC, 2008; EUROSTAT, 2009). Even while the number of A2 migrants increased rapidly to 67,000 in 2008, they comprised 1 per cent of the UK's foreign-born population as compared with 11 per cent for A8 migrants (MAC, 2008). Perhaps even more importantly, migrants coming from poorer parts of the world, including Africa, Asia and Latin America, are increasingly only able to gain legal access to the UK through family reunification, as international students, as tourists or as asylum seekers and refugees with all of these avenues being increasingly restricted. It can be argued that alongside skills, race has been significant in distinguishing the 'right' kind of immigrants (McDowell, 2009).[10]

The Coalition government has sought to further restrict these migrations to the UK by raising the bar of the entry of non-EU migrants as well as renewing restrictions on A8/A2 migrants. Reflecting the fact that the PBS was devised, as Spencer (2011) argues, 'during a time of boom but implemented during a recession', a decision was made to raise the minimum qualifications required for a Tier 1 visa from an undergraduate to a postgraduate degree as well as minimum salary levels (Rogers et al, 2009). For those migrants entering the UK under family reunification schemes, the government has introduced a language requirement for spouses, while the fees charged for elderly parents' entry have increased significantly (Sumption, 2010). There has been an extensive review of student entry visas with new limits on the number of hours international students can work. A cap on non-EU immigration has also been implemented. Meanwhile, EU migrants have not escaped from this tightening of the regime. As highlighted above, the restrictions on A2 migrants' access to the British labour market were extended until 2013, with the MAC also recommending that the WRS, on which A8 migrants are required to register, should also be extended until 2011 (Rogers et al, 2009; Angelov and Vankova, 2011). Sorted into these different categories, migrants' access to a wide range of services – including housing, health *and* financial services – is clearly shaped by their immigration status. This is further explored in Chapter Three.

Connecting transnational financial lives: diverse and 'alternative' financial practices

Even while migrants' financial practices are shaped by their exclusion from formal financial circuits and wider socioeconomic marginalisation, there is an appreciation that these are also structured by wider processes. Within the context of broader research undertaken on financial exclusion, critics have noted the undue focus on particular types of formal regulated financial institutions and the representation of financial users as passive recipients of the directives from the financial services industry (Ford and Rowlingson, 1996). Yet, as Ford and Rowlingson (1996: 1347) argue, if 'one starts from a different place, from the perspective of the household, there is evidence that cultural tradition, custom, and practice govern the use of financial resources, as well as evidence of strategic decision making by households as to which institutions provide them with the services they require and in a form which best enables them to enhance their control and management of their resources'. Significantly, these commentators highlight the critical importance of considering individual and household financial practices in the round – or, in other words, both in terms of what individuals and households are excluded from as well as the opportunities open to them, on the grounds that both exclusion and inclusion shape broader financial practices (Ford and Rowlingson, 1996; Leyshon and Thrift, 1996). More nuanced investigations of how financially excluded households manage their money outside of formal banking and other financial institutions, particularly pertaining to credit practices, illustrate that financial practices are grounded in complex social networks and relations and are not simply a response to exclusion from cheaper credit sources (Fuller and Jonas, 2003; Leyshon et al, 2004, 2006; Byrne et al, 2007). These alternative financial practices are perceived as re-evaluating the role of money and finance, and bringing it back into the social and cultural realm (Leyshon and Thrift, 1995).

Variously labelled as 'alternative', 'diverse' and 'proliferative' financial practices, research undertaken in the global South as well as in transitional economies has also paid particular attention to the money management practices of financially excluded individuals and households. Given that financial services only serve a minority of the population in poorer countries, researchers have uncovered the 'mix and match' financial practices deployed by households through the development of relationships with individuals, groups and institutions, and a selection of the financial services offered by institutions ranging from the regulated to the unregulated, and including both market and non-market services (Rutherford, 1999; Matin et al, 2002; Ruthven, 2002; Collins, 2005; UN, 2006; Beck et al, 2007; CGAP, 2009; Stenning et al, 2010a, 2010b).

In turn, there is scope to further investigate these alternative financial repertoires by focusing upon migrant men and women who carry financial habits developed in diverse places and re-created in the financial capital of the world. These practices are undoubtedly shaped by migrants' transnational lives. Increasingly identified as offering a framework through which contemporary international migration can be understood, transnationalism is broadly defined as the networks of ties and associations that bind people, places and transactions together (Glick-Schiller et al, 1992; Vertovec and Cohen, 1999). As such, transnational approaches dismiss the idea of migration as a single, final and rupturing act, whereby migrants are transplanted from the old to the new, with scholars highlighting instead how migrants are able to function and participate in the economic, social and political life of both 'sending' and 'receiving' countries (Levitt and Glick-Schiller, 2004; Lie, 1995). Transnational migrants are envisaged as being situated within 'transnational social fields' or 'transnational social formations', which are comprised of a 'set of multiple interlocking networks of social relationships through which ideas, practices, and resources are unequally exchanged, organized, and transformed'. Multi-sited and multi-scalar, transnational social fields connect migrants to families, institutions and places scattered over transnational spaces (Levitt and Glick-Schiller, 2004: 1009; see also Guarnizo, 1997, 2002; Faist, 2000a, 2000b; Kivisto, 2001; Landolt, 2001; Portes, 2003; Vertovec, 2004).

Taking diverse forms, the links and networks maintained by migrants incorporate social, political, cultural and financial links, with the latter predominantly investigated within the context of migrant remittances (Levitt, 1998; Faist, 2008). Even while the latter focus is understandable given both the volume and potentially transformatory development power of remittances, commentators have begun to note the diversity of transnational financial flows. These flows also incorporate migrant investments in expatriate bonds (issued by home countries to raise finance from their overseas diasporas and often exempt from tax), philanthropic and charitable giving as well as transnational entrepreneurial financial flows (see Chapter Six; see also Itzigsohn, 2000; Portes, 2003; Levitt and Glick-Schiller, 2004; Phillips, forthcoming). Also significant is the fact that if migrants have financial assets and liabilities in more than one place then their 'daily rhythms' and activities are governed and shaped by multiple sets of laws and institutions (Levitt and Glick-Schiller, 2004). As such, the financial practices that migrants pursue in host countries are crucially shaped by their transnational assets and liabilities, the particular sets of financial knowledge that they bring with them, the financial habits that they have developed in other places, the transnational obligations that they bear, *as well as* the financial landscapes that they encounter in host countries and cities like London (Datta, 2011a). Structured as such by the myriad and interlinked inclusions and exclusions that they encounter across transnational spaces, these practices are crucially shaped by migrant agency.

Organisation of book

The book is organised into six chapters. Chapter Two details the evolution of public policy responses to financial exclusion in the UK, highlighting the emergence of key priorities in relation to banking, savings, credit and financial education. It identifies the varied, if limited, impact of these policies upon migrant communities as well as the changing political and economic context within which current financial inclusion interventions are being shaped. Chapter Three provides an overview of the financial practices of the migrant men and women drawn from the five research communities. Focusing specifically on formally provided financial services including banking, savings and credit, the chapter details the levels and nature of exclusion and inclusion migrants experience in relation to each of these financial services. In so doing it identifies the key factors shaping migrants' financial practices including labour market position, immigration status, nationality, ethnicity and gender. Chapter Four investigates the financial strategies that migrant men and women devise in order to access banking services in the city, highlighting both the legal and illegal nature of these, and the diverse local and transnational assets that migrants draw upon to strategise for inclusion. In Chapter Five the lens shifts to consider those migrants who deploy a range of individual and group-based informal financial practices relating to saving, borrowing and lending. These alternative practices illustrate how dynamics of trust and solidarity are reproduced in the financial practices of migrant men and women, and the potential to develop alternative institutions of accumulation. Chapter Six maps remittance flows from London to migrants' home countries, thus graphically highlighting the uneven nature of development in the contemporary world as well as the transnationality of contemporary finance. It considers the mechanisms by which migrant men and women send money back to their home countries, highlighting the continued importance of semi-formal and informal mechanisms that call into question the current drive to formalise remittance sending. Chapter Seven summarises the main findings of the research explored in the book and considers the implications for future migrants.[11]

Notes

[1] As Wright and Black (2011) argue, the subprime mortgage crisis was one of multiple drivers of the 2008–10 global downturn. In turn, this downturn is part of a longer history of financial crises which have threatened the global financial system in the last 30 years including the debt crisis of the 1980s, the global stock market crash in 1987 and the Asian financial crisis of the 1990s (French et al, 2009).

[2] This said, concerns about a potential 'double-dip' recession as well as a protracted recovery period continue to prevail (Datta, 2011b).

[3] Bank branch density is low in the UK at 180 per million population as compared with 435 in France and 940 in Spain (NEF, 2008).

[4] This pattern is observed within the context of both voluntary and forced migrations. Thus, for example, even while the 50 poorest countries in the global South provided asylum to 18 per cent of the world's refugees towards

the end of the 2000s, significant numbers of asylum seekers and refugees have also migrated to the richer nations of the world (UNDP, 2009).

[5] It is important to acknowledge the distinct geography of lending by transnational banks, which was predominantly directed at Latin American countries, with nine US banks owed US$48.6 billion by just five Latin American countries (Corbridge, 2005).

[6] Spencer (2011) argues that the ability of the state to manage migration is itself constrained by a number of factors including political, legal, economic, technical and evidential constraints.

[7] These measures have enabled the provision of accommodation and support directly to asylum seekers *outside* of the welfare system. As such, this support can be withdrawn immediately if asylum seekers leave these institutions (Spencer, 2011).

[8] In an effort to allay public misgivings about this migration, encourage formal labour market participation as well as restrict access to welfare, a Workers Registration Scheme (WRS) was established, which A8 migrants were required to sign up to within a month of starting to work in the UK. A8 migrants were then eligible for certain benefits after a year of being registered on the WRS (Anderson et al, 2006).

[9] Up to 30 per cent of those who registered on the WRS may already have been in the UK prior to May 2004 as undocumented or irregular workers (Anderson et al, 2006).

[10] This expansion of European 'white' migration has led some to comment that migrant integration has slipped off the agenda because European migrants are perceived as facing fewer problems of integration (McDowell, 2009; Denham, 2010).

[11] The methodological approach adopted in this study and details of the research are included in the Appendix.

TWO

Changing financial landscapes: public policy responses to financial exclusion in the UK

"At the heart of all [the Government's] work is one central theme: national renewal, Britain re-built as one nation, in which each citizen is valued and has a stake; in which no-one is excluded from opportunity and the chance to develop their potential; in which we make it, once more, our national purpose to tackle social division and inequality." (Tony Blair, 1997)

Financial *inc*lusion entered the realm of public policy in the aftermath of New Labour's electoral victory in 1997, assuming particular importance in the early 2000s. Coming back to power after 14 years in opposition, and inheriting 'levels of poverty and inequality unprecedented in post war history', the 'renewal' of British society structured around an eradication of social exclusion featured prominently in the incoming government's rhetoric (Stewart and Hills, 2005: 1). Importantly, from a public policy perspective, financial inclusion was identified as one potential mechanism for stitching back a divided society. In part, this reflected an emerging consensus that as one of several expressions of exclusion, financial exclusion was an important manifestation of socioeconomic inequality, inextricably linked to, and indeed exacerbating, broader experiences of social exclusion (Affleck and Mellor, 2006; Edmonds, 2011). As detailed in Chapter One, the inability of individuals and households to participate fully in society was increasingly attributed to an interlocking of marginality deriving from low incomes, poor education, marginal labour market positions, housing situation *and* exclusion from formal financial circuits (Reagan and Paxton, 2003). Furthermore, the public policy focus on neighbourhood and community regeneration also necessitated an emphasis on financial exclusion given the vital role that finance played in shaping places, such that its withdrawal rendered entire communities vulnerable to under-investment and spiralling degeneration (Marshall, 2004: Wallace and Quilgars, 2005). More broadly, ambitions to create an asset-holding citizenry and undertake welfare reform were crucially tied in with increased access to financial services and products (Reagan and Paxton, 2001).

This chapter charts how financial inclusion policy has evolved in the UK within the context of significant political and economic changes. Pursuing three lines of enquiry, it begins by critically identifying the key policies, programmes and partnerships put in place by the New Labour government, focusing particularly upon banking, saving, affordable credit and financial capability initiatives. It then moves on to consider how these have impacted upon migrant communities in the UK. In so doing the chapter highlights that while a plethora of financial inclusion initiatives were operationalised during the New Labour era, and there was some expression of concern about the exclusion of (particular) migrant groups from formal financial circuits, the impact of these programmes on these communities has been limited, if varied. In the third section, and by way of a conclusion, the chapter considers how financial inclusion policy hangs in the balance following both a change in government and a tightening fiscal situation.

From financial exclusion to inclusion in the UK

Reflecting its prioritisation of eradicating exclusion, New Labour established the Social Exclusion Unit[1] within weeks of being elected in 1997 and charged it with the responsibility of spearheading government initiatives and energising public policy around exclusion. In particular, the Unit's brief was to 'develop integrated and sustained approaches to the problems of the worst housing estates, including crime, drugs, unemployment, community breakdown and bad schools' (Mandelson, 1997, cited in Jessop, 2000: 17). The Unit was comprised of several Policy Action Teams (PATs), which sought to address different aspects of exclusion in British society. PAT 14 particularly focused upon the scope for widening access to financial services[2] and identified some 40 recommendations in its 1999 report, *Access to Financial Services*. These recommendations crystallised into three priority areas in the government's 2004 Spending Review: access to banking, affordable credit and money advice, with savings emerging as a focus in subsequent reviews (Treasury, 2004, 2007a; Wallace and Quilgars, 2005; Kempson and Finney, 2009).

Before considering these in greater detail, it is perhaps instructive here to reflect on how these priorities illustrate the evolution of public policy understandings of financial exclusion which over time have shifted from an initial focus on access – and the supply of financial services to excluded populations – to demand-side factors that shape how financial services are used (Datta, 2011a). As such, financial ex/inclusion is commonly understood as referring to the (lack of) access of individuals and households to financial services, which itself can be differentiated in terms of access to various financial products and services (ranging from 'basic' financial products such as banking, savings and credit to more 'complex' pensions, insurance instruments, and financial advice) as well as different levels of access.[3] Furthermore, there has been gradual recognition that access to financial services and products alone cannot be equated with financial inclusion. Given the increased complexity of financial products, financial literacy and capability are increasingly important in ensuring financial inclusion (to be discussed later; see also Chapter One).

Banking inclusion has long been identified as the 'bedrock of financial inclusion', with New Labour's 2004 Spending Review undertaking to halve the 2.8 million people who were identified as unbanked by 2006 (Thiel, 2006; Collard, 2007: 14; FITF, 2010). Importantly, a clear distinction was, and continues to be, made between the unbanked (those without any form of transactional bank account); the marginally or under-banked (those who have a bank account but do not use it regularly or effectively to manage their money) and the fully banked (people who have access to and use a wide range of banking services) (FITF, 2010).[4] The early emphasis on banking inclusion was attributable to a number of imperatives including the growing volume of payments – wages as well as benefits and pensions – being made via bank accounts (to be discussed later; see also Reagan and Paxton, 2003; Carbo et al, 2007). The subsequent emergence of an increasingly cashless society made access to banking services crucial so as to negotiate everyday life and avoid the penalties associated with being unbanked including higher fees and charge rates for the payment of utility bills[5] (Treasury, 1999; Blake and de Jong, 2008; Fuller and Mellor, 2008; NEF, 2008). Arguably, 'banking the unbanked' also afforded a commercial opportunity for the expansion of the banking sector, with bank accounts serving as a gateway to other financial products including formal credit, saving, insurance and investment products (Treasury, 1999; Wallace and Quilgars, 2005).

In turn, the exclusion of certain segments of society from affordable credit ran contrary to the asset-based welfare agenda and was regarded as a particularly important manifestation of financial exclusion (see Chapter One; see also Fuller and Mellor, 2008). The public policy preoccupation with credit reflected a growing consensus in political circles that access to credit, particularly for poorer households, was desirable on the grounds that it played a significant role in smoothing consumption, enabling people to meet their emergency needs as well as acquire assets (see also Thiel, 2006; Blake and de Jong, 2008; Cox et al, 2011). Yet, as critics were quick to point out, and as discussed in Chapter One, there was a lack of public acknowledgement that this dependency on credit to meet the costs of everyday living was shaped by stagnating and/or declining wages and income that had not kept up with inflation and dropping savings rates (Thiel, 2006; Ramsay, 2009). Notwithstanding this, the public policy focus was on those excluded from mainstream credit – estimated at 9 million people by the end of 2006 – who comprised both unbanked as well as banked individuals, with the latter predominantly owning entry-level bank accounts that did not afford access to credit cards or overdrafts (to be discussed later; see also Thiel, 2006). Served by a highly diverse subprime credit market including regulated and unregulated credit providers such as home credit companies, payday lenders, sale and buy back shops, mail order catalogues, pawnshops and money lenders, there was increased alarm about the prevalence, precarity and rising levels of indebtedness and particularly over-indebtedness (Drakeford and Sachdev, 2001; Kempson and Paxton, 2003; Reagan and Paxton, 2003; Collard and Kempson, 2005; Carbo et al, 2007; Cox et al, 2011).

Photo 2.1 Cheque casher and pawnshop in London

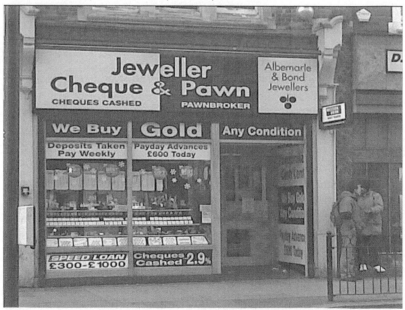

Furthermore, the growing expectation that people would assume greater responsibility for securing their immediate and long-term futures led to public policy interest in savings opportunities. Again evidence pointed to a significant 'savings gap' in the UK whereby a quarter of all households were identified as having no savings at all, while half had savings of less than £1,500. In addition, close to 10 million people were reported as either not saving at all or not saving enough for their retirement (Collard et al, 2003; Collard and McKay, 2006). Highlighting a mismatch between financially excluded households' savings patterns (saving small amounts over short periods of time) and formal savings products, the key obstacles to formal saving were identified as bank branch closures in deprived areas, minimum savings thresholds and the lack of tax relief or higher interest rates available to higher income savers (Collard et al, 2003; Kempson et al, 2000).

As noted above, the initial focus on widening access to financial services evolved into a growing recognition that the depth of integration into financial circuits was of equal importance (Blake and de Jong, 2008; Mitton, 2008; Datta, 2011a). Reflecting the 'quiet panic' around financial illiteracy in both national and international circles, the role of financial education – composed of financial literacy (an understanding of financial concepts) and capability (the skills and motivation to plan ahead and seek financial advice) – became increasingly central to a whole raft of financial inclusion policies (OECD, 2005; Froud et al, 2007). The government set out its own understanding of financial capability as encompassing 'people's knowledge and skills to understand their own financial circumstances, along with the motivation to take action. Financially capable consumers plan ahead, find and use information, know when to seek advice and can understand and act on this advice, leading to greater participation in the financial services market' (Treasury, 2007c: 19). In part, the imperative to intervene in financial literacy was borne out of the 'big bang' reforms detailed in Chapter One, which led to the emergence of increasingly complex financial markets and sophisticated products (Williams, 2007). Coinciding with the identification of fairly significant levels of financial illiteracy in the UK, the Department for Education and Employment (DfEE, 2000: 2) argued that 'the nature and delivery of financial services have changed dramatically over past years with new technology and the introduction of numerous more products. If adult financial literacy is to be resolved in a real attempt to empower the individual and allow them to become truly self-reliant, then financial skills and understanding need to be improved across most of the population.' These sentiments were reinforced by the charity Citizens Advice (2001: 1), which pointed out that financial literacy was not just 'a desirable trait' but 'an essential requirement [for consumers] to play an informed role in today's 21st century market'. Within this context, financial education was perceived as facilitating individuals to make the 'right' choices regarding the selection of financial products and services that suited both their immediate and long-term needs; to manage their debts; and to negotiate their transition back to work by taking advantage of tax and benefits that would ensure that work really did pay (Treasury, 1999; Kempson et al, 2000; Reagan and Paxton, 2003; Wallace and Quilgars, 2005; Mitton, 2008).

'The Acid Test': financial inclusion programmes and partnerships

> In politics, the acid test is what you end up achieving. I say to the doubters, judge us after 10 years of success in office. For one of the fruits of that success will be Britain will be a more equal society. (Mandelson, 1997: 7)

The above government priorities were executed through the development of specific programmes implemented through partnerships forged between public, private and third sector organisations. In contrast to some of its European counterparts, the UK government was identified as engaging in 'strong government action' incorporating elements of 'coercion' and 'moral persuasion' in furthering its financial inclusion agenda (Carbo et al, 2007: 23). In recognition of the fragmentation of financial inclusion initiatives and funding following the 'disappearance' of PAT 14's recommendations into relevant government departments and agencies,[6] there was an attempt to create greater coherence across government, which was clearly part of the agenda of 'joined-up government' (Vass, 2007). In turn, the Treasury assumed the centre stage in determining the course of financial inclusion strategy (Treasury, 2007a, 2007b). The Financial Inclusion Taskforce (FITF), an independent cross-cutting body, was set up in 2005 to monitor and coordinate the government's progress in reaching its goals (Wallace and Quilgars, 2005). Comprised of representatives drawn from the financial services industry, third sector, local government and customer advocacy, FITF was initially commissioned for a period of four years, and then granted a second term, which extended to 2011. A Financial Inclusion Growth Fund was placed at its disposal to pump prime financial inclusion initiatives. Set at £120 million in 2004, a further £130 million was allocated to this fund for FITF's second term; this was designed, in the words of the then Chancellor of the Exchequer, Gordon Brown, to 'tackle financial inclusion, including more face-to-face money advice, supporting local citizens advice bureaux, support for not-for-profit lenders' (Edmonds, 2011: 4).

Assuming the role of mediator, the government set about creating an enabling environment and coordinating public, and particularly private and third sector institutions, which were charged with the responsibility of delivering financial inclusion projects (Collard et al, 2003; Carbo et al, 2007). Part of this centred around prompting the UK's financial sector, which *had* illustrated considerable innovation in creating and sustaining wealthy niche markets, to focus more attention upon creating products and services that would meet the needs of excluded groups (see Chapter One; also Atkinson, 2006). Stopping short of implementing a universal service obligation (an idea briefly floated by New Labour in its election campaign of 2010), the government pressured the financial services industry to bear some of the responsibility to increase inclusion under the remit of Corporate Social Responsibility (Wallace and Quilgars, 2005; Carbo et al, 2007; Collard, 2007; NEF, 2007). Even while there is a tension between the public policy financial inclusion agenda and the financial services industry's search for profits and profitable customers, the latter's participation was evidenced in the development and extension of several banking and savings instruments (as discussed below). In turn, the involvement of third sector organisations or community-based intermediaries that were trusted by individuals and communities was clearly important. Comprising a diverse range of organisations, including most prominently Citizens Advice, housing associations and other third sector organisations, the development of specific programmes to tackle financial exclusion in deprived communities, such as Toynbee Hall's 'Services Against Financial Exclusion' (SAFE), was also evident (Clark et al, 2005). These various organisations came together to offer a range of delivery mechanisms including direct provision, community partnership and limited ad hoc partnerships (Wallace and Quilgars, 2005).[7]

The key programmes and products designed to address financial exclusion revolved around facilitating access to banking via Basic Bank Accounts (BBAs)[8] and Post Office Card Accounts (POCAs), promoting savings through the Child Trust Fund and the Savings Gateway, the provision of affordable credit by increasing the capacity of third sector lenders and the Social Fund, and building financial literacy and capability. Considering these in turn, the pledge to halve the number of families without access to transactional bank accounts led to a joint government and banking sector initiative which saw the emergence of two entry-level basic money management banking products: BBAs and POCAs (Toynbee Hall, 2005).While all the high street retail banks developed their own versions of these accounts, they were guided by general principles that stipulated that BBAs had to accept income paid in by automated credit transfer, and cheques and cash paid in by account holders; allow cash withdrawal at convenient access points; and sustain bill payment by direct debit. Further, customers could not be charged for everyday account usage or entail any risk of unauthorised overdrafts (Clark et al, 2005; Fuller and Mellor, 2008; FITF, 2010). For the most part, high street retail banks developed these new accounts voluntarily, although the Chancellor of the Exchequer imposed a deadline of October 2001, by which date they were expected to create these accounts (Atkinson, 2006).

In turn, the POCA was primarily designed to serve as a delivery mechanism for welfare payments following the government's decision to move to automated credit transfers. Driven by a desire to both address benefit fraud as well as realise important savings, automated credit transfer cut the cost of social security administration from 68 pence per transaction for order books to 1 pence per transaction for direct payment, potentially saving the public purse around £400 million each year when fully implemented (Treasury, 1999; Wallace and Quilgars, 2005; Herbert and Hopwood Road, 2006; Collard, 2007).[9] The transfer to automated credit transfer was completed between 2003 and 2005, when an estimated 96 per cent of welfare payments were being paid directly in accounts, with 40 per cent of recipients preferring to receive these in POCAs (Atkinson, 2006; Herbert and Hopwood Road, 2006). Exclusively designed for benefit recipients, POCAs do not support any of the facilities generally associated with a card account, including debit card payments. Instead, its main functionality is a swipe card that enables cash withdrawal over post office counters (Reagan and Paxton, 2003). Banks contributed £180 million to the cost of developing and running the POCA scheme while also providing access to BBAs at post office counters (FITF, 2010).

Both BBAs and POCAs were designed to 'bank the unbanked' by addressing the barriers which prevented access to the banking system, with particular attention paid to identification verification processes (FSA, 2005). Guided by anti-money laundering legislation, banks are required to carry out customer identification checks whereby prospective clients need to produce primary documentation, including passports, drivers licences and/or national identification cards to verify their identity, as well as secondary documentation to prove their current address via gas, water, electricity or landline telephone utility bills (Toynbee Hall, 2008). In recognition of the fact that the unbanked struggled to produce some of this documentation, the Financial Services Authority (FSA) provided guidance on alternative ways by which financially excluded individuals could provide relevant information including letters from the Benefits Office, employers or persons of 'good repute' (FSA, 2005). Furthermore, identification checks could be conducted within bank branches thus speeding up the process of opening accounts (Blake and de Jong, 2008). There is some evidence that these initiatives were successful in extending the reach of banking institutions. A recent review undertaken by the FITF (2010) reported that over 3 million new accounts have been opened since April 2003 of which 2.4 million are accessed via local post offices, while the remainder are provided by 17 major retail banks in the UK.[10] This in turn has contributed to a steady decline in the number of adults living in households without a transactional bank account from 3.57 million in 2002–03 to 1.54 million in 2008–09 (DWP, 2009). Constituting a reduction of 57 per cent, the unbanked comprised 3 per cent of the population in 2008–09, as compared with 8 per cent in 2002-03 (FITF, 2010).

Yet, this said, POCAs and especially BBAs have both attracted some criticism. Most importantly, not all individuals who are eligible for BBAs have been successful in opening such accounts. This is partly due to the fact that retail banks, which stand to make little profit from these accounts, and indeed may incur costs associated with serving poor customers who prefer physically accessible bank branches, have not marketed them widely (Collard, 2007; FITF, 2010). BBAs rarely feature in the centrally set sales targets for banks, with the result that bank branch staff have few incentives to sell them (FITF, 2010). There are also significant differences across banks, and bank branches, in the criteria used to open these accounts. Despite guidance from the FSA that identification procedures could be relaxed, high street banks have interpreted this differently, resulting in considerable uncertainty among both bank staff as well as customers (Reagan and Paxton, 2003; FITF, 2010; see also Chapters Three and Four). This has led to calls for an appropriate balance to be struck between the need to protect against money laundering while expanding access to banking services as part of the effort to promote financial inclusion (Toynbee Hall, 2008). Research undertaken by Citizens Advice uncovered that while potential customers had been refused BBAs on the grounds of poor credit scores even though these accounts do not support credit facilities, others had been sold inappropriate banking products in lieu of these (Herbert and Hopwood Road, 2006; see also Collard, 2007; FITF, 2010).

Furthermore, while those who have been successful in opening these accounts made savings of between £125 and £215 per annum on utility payments, these were offset by an average loss of £140 per annum in penalty charges for failed direct debit payments, which was most evident in the poorest households and resulted in a high rate of account failures (Herbert and Hopwood Road, 2006; FITF, 2010). Despite the fact that bank charges have declined in recent times from £25 to £10, even one failed direct debit payment can have severe financial repercussions for such households (Herbert and Hopwood Road, 2006; FITF, 2010). This said, there *is* an important market for BBAs among people who have multiple debts, especially those whose income would otherwise go into an overdrawn current account and be offset against debts leaving them with insufficient income to meet their essential needs and/or service their multiple debts (Herbert and Hopwood Road, 2006). Even while they remain excluded, BBAs would potentially enable such individuals and households to manage their money and deal with their debts without compounding their indebtedness (Herbert and Hopwood Road, 2006).

A two-tier service culture also appears to have evolved across banks such that BBA customers are likely to be discouraged from using counter services, with cheque clearance also taking appreciably longer (Herbert and Hopwood Road, 2006; Mitton, 2008). Not surprisingly then, there have been calls for a 'cultural change' among bank staff, who are not used to dealing with people who have no history of financial usage. More importantly perhaps, even while the public policy expectation was that having got their foot in the door newly banked individuals would become more confident and knowledgeable in their usage of financial services such that BBAs would act as a conduit to 'Citizen Banking Products' including savings, credit and mortgages, recent evidence suggests that this may not be the case. While the newly banked can cite several advantages of being banked including security, convenience and ready access to cash, a significant number still continue to manage their everyday living costs in cash because of a perceived lack of transparency and flexibility in the banking system and the ever-present threat of bank charges (FITF, 2010). As a result, a sizeable proportion of these individuals are at best marginally banked (OFT, 1999a, 1999b; Wallace and Quilgars, 2005). Furthermore, despite the introduction of entry-level bank accounts, a number of individuals and households *still* remain unbanked. The majority of these individuals are concentrated at the bottom end of the income distribution, in single headed and lone parent households, in social housing, benefit dependent, with health-related conditions and numeracy or literacy problems (FITF, 2010).

Financial inclusion initiatives related to savings include Individual Savings Accounts (ISAs), stakeholder savings and investment products. In addition, two specific programmes introduced by the New Labour government – the Child Trust Fund (CTF) and the Savings Gateway – aimed to address both inter- and intra-generational inequality in the ownership of assets (Collard and McKay, 2006; Paxton, 2009). The development of the CTF was deeply influenced by New Labour's centre-left think tank, the Institute of Public Policy Research (IPPR), which helped to stimulate government interest around a 'new politics of ownership' (Kelly and Lissauer, 2000). Drawing heavily upon the experience of the US and the Individual Development Accounts (IDAs), their arguments were bolstered by a report by the Fabian Society that also advocated the use of capital grants to engender an asset-owning society (Sherraden, 1991; Le Grand and Nissan, 2000). Linking asset ownership to the achievement of individual equality, autonomy, responsibility and opportunities, these ideas were picked up by the government and developed in two consultation documents: *Savings and Assets for All* (Treasury, 2001a) and *Delivering Savings and Assets* (Treasury, 2001b), with the CTF being rolled out in January 2005. As Finlayson (2008) argues, there was no political pressure on New Labour to develop these programmes, the benefits of which would be realised over several electoral cycles. Thus, given that it did not stand to win favour with the electorate in the short term, the CTF in particular is held as being illustrative of New Labour's thinking on asset-based welfare and its approach to social policy (Finlayson, 2009). It also fostered interest in other advanced countries, with the US experimenting with 'baby bonds' and the emergence of 'nest-egg accounts' in Australia (Finlayson, 2008; Prabhakar, 2010).

Primarily aimed at facilitating inter-generational social mobility, the CTF opened up savings opportunities to families with young children. With all children born after September 2002 deemed eligible for the scheme, the fund was initiated by a government endowment of £250 to £500, with the higher payment reserved for children from lower-income families, defined as those in receipt of Child Tax Credit and annual incomes below £13,230 (Finlayson, 2008). Issued in the form of vouchers that parents could invest in shares or cash in a range of banks and building societies, further endowments were made when a child reached the age of seven. Parents, family members, and friends could make tax-free contributions to these accounts up to an annual limit of £1,200. No withdrawals were allowed until the account matured when a child turned 18, at which point the money could be spent as the child saw fit (Paxton, 2009). Designed to ensure that all children reached adulthood with a financial asset that would help them improve their life chances, the CTF occasioned some debate revolving around the universality of the fund, the age at which it should start, and the uses to which it could be put (Paxton, 2009). In particular, a strong argument emerged on whether the CTF could be more progressive and better targeted at lower-income families (to be discussed later). The ultimate decision to retain the universal element of the CTF was based upon an appreciation that the financial circumstances of families could change over time as well as the need to ensure wider public support (Paxton, 2009).

In contrast to the CTF, the Savings Gateway was much more focused on the asset excluded and aimed at facilitating intra-generational mobility. Involving two pilot runs (the first rolled out over five areas and involving 1,500 accounts, the second extended to six locations and including 22,000 accounts), the Savings Gateway sought to encourage low-income working age adults, identified as those on income support, jobseeker's allowance, severe disability allowance and/ or working tax credit, to save formally by offering the incentive of government-matched savings (Harvey et al, 2007; Prahbhakar, 2009). Savings Gateway accounts were offered by banks and building societies with savings matched by government contributions when the accounts matured. Furthermore, while savers could withdraw their own deposits during the two-year period, it was only upon maturation that they would have access to the matched contributions (Paxton, 2009). A limit was set for the amount of matched funding with no prescriptions on how the fund was spent when it matured (Paxton, 2009). Some adjustments were made to the Savings Gateway programme after the first pilot. Reflecting the twin ambition of both increasing asset holding among poorer households as well as inculcating a habit to save, there was some experimentation with the level of matched funding deployed, with the first pilot using a 1:1 ratio (with every £1 saved receiving £1 in matched funding) and the second using a spectrum of matched funding ranging from 20 pence to £1. The final decision, determined by the potential cost of extending the programme nationwide, as well as a consensus that the actual level of matched funding did not appear to have a significant bearing on incentivising saving, was that the matched funding would be less than the ratio of 1:1 (Paxton, 2009). Furthermore, while the initial pilot in 2002 was implemented in partnership with community organisations, including Toynbee Hall in East London, on the premise that it required considerable explanation and advice, best offered by trusted intermediaries, the subsequent role of community organisations was scaled down even while the importance of financial advice was recognised.

Assessments of both the CTF and Savings Gateway are mixed (Kempson et al, 2005). For some the key achievement was that the 'plumbing' had been laid for both intra- and inter-generational mobility (Paxton, 2009). Even while the initial take-up of the CTF was slow, particularly among lower-income families, by 2007, 75 per cent of parents had opened accounts and active saving for children had risen from a pre-CTF level of 18 per cent to over 50 per cent (Paxton, 2009). The average amount of additional contributions was £200, although there was considerable variation, with the majority of accounts *not* receiving any additional payments. Evaluations of the first and, particularly, the second Savings Gateway pilot reported some evidence that, given the right incentives, people on low incomes exhibited a capacity both to save and to save regularly: participants noted that the programme had enabled them to feel more financially secure while also improving their money management skills (Collard and McKay, 2006; Harvey et al, 2007).

Yet, critics have raised broader concerns. Prabhakar (2009) argues that while the CTF was a 'hybrid' policy, at least in its planning stages, such that it comprised elements of inculcating savings habits and advancing financial literacy *as well as* boosting citizenship and tackling wealth inequalities, the actual policy that emerged was heavily biased towards the former. Indeed, even the IPPR recognised that compromises had had to be made to the overall asset-based welfare approach in order to win favour with the government, appeal to a wide range of stakeholders and translate into large-scale policies (Paxton, 2003; Ben-Galim, 2011). Yet, in making these compromises, the CTF failed to realise its full potential and emerge as a 'citizen-stake', such that 'what began as a contribution to the reworking of the social democratic tradition, via an embrace of asset-based welfare, became a tool for changing the behaviour of the poor rather than a challenge to prevailing patterns of ownership' (Finlayson, 2008: 95). There was also sustained criticism of the CTF with regards to the size of the endowments made by the government, which were dismissed as being too small to create a substantial asset at maturity, as well as criticisms of the Fund being regressive and potentially exacerbating wealth inequalities between rich and poor households and their offspring. The fact that richer parents and families could potentially afford to contribute the maximum amount permitted would result in a fund worth £31,750 upon maturity, as opposed to the £2,270 saved by those who only received government funding (Maxwell and Sodha, 2006).

Moving on to consider public policy interventions relating to the provision of affordable credit, three priorities were particularly pursued by the New Labour government: reducing the cost of commercial credit; increasing the availability, capacity and sustainability of alternative not-for-profit lenders via the support for Credit Unions and Community Development Finance Institutions (CDFIs); and extending access to the Social Fund administered by the Department for Work and Pensions (Collard and Kempson, 2005; Collard, 2007; Appleyard, 2011). The cost of commercial credit, and the lack of an interest rate ceiling[11] in the UK, which was abolished by the Conservative government's Consumer Credit Act of 1974 (making it one of a select group of European countries to do so), has generated a great deal of debate in the UK (Thiel, 2006; Fuller and Mellor, 2008; Ramsay, 2009). While the 1974 Act facilitated the expansion of both consumer and mortgage credit and the subsequent growth of the 'alternative' credit market, growing disquiet about the subprime credit market was reflected in New Labour's election manifesto promise to 'tackle loan sharks' in 1997 (Ramsay, 2009). A strong anti-poverty lobby campaigned for the reintroduction of interest rate ceilings as a mechanism of tackling over-indebtedness and reducing the charges of commercial lenders in the run up to the Consumer Credit Act of 2006 (Collard, 2007). In part their case was based upon the high interest rates evident in the subprime industry, which started at 180 per cent APR, averaged at around 600 per cent APR, with some loan and credit companies charging annual interest rates equivalent to 2500 per cent APR (Thiel, 2006; Cox et al, 2011). This was rejected on the basis of a government-commissioned Department of Trade and Industry study (the evidence base of which has been heavily criticised) on the grounds that interest rate ceilings promoted less product diversity and would potentially result in raising access hurdles to high-risk borrowers, a growth of the unregulated informal credit market and even fewer credit options for poorer households (Policis and DTI, 2004; Collard, 2007; Ramsay, 2009). There was also a fear that financial institutions such as banks would find a way of circumventing these caps with interest rates potentially becoming a less important component of the total price of credit (Policis and DTI, 2004).

In place of interest rate ceilings, the government's affordable credit initiatives focused more substantively on the potential role that locally embedded 'alternative' organisations like Credit Unions and CDFIs

Photo 2.2: 'Coming to a high street near you': advertisements for unsecured loans in London

could play in addressing financial exclusion (Drakeford and Sachdev, 2001). Recognised as bolstering anti-poverty initiatives, political support for Credit Unions can be traced back to the late 1980s, when local authority funding led to a rapid expansion of Credit Unions across the UK from 94 organisations in 1986 to almost 700 in 2000 (Jones, 2006). Perhaps contradictorily, with some exceptions, this expansion was not matched by a concomitant rise in membership, which was attributed to restrictive legislation, insufficient support from the national trade association, and the internal organisational and financial structure of Credit Unions (Jones, 1999, 2006). This in turn paved the way for significant reforms including legislative changes and the move from 'social development' inspired Credit Unions to 'New Model' or 'Quality Credit Unions' with radically reformed financial, organisational and operational structures (Fuller and Jonas, 2002; Jones, 2006; McKillop et al, 2007). Commentators note that the linking of Credit Unions with financial inclusion initiatives meant that these organisations came under considerable pressure to reassemble themselves as financially viable and sustainable organisations (Richardson and Lennon, 2001; McKillop and Wilson, 2003; Collard and Kempson, 2005). Inspired by the global reform of credit unions, legislative changes within the UK facilitated this change in culture, with the FSA assuming responsibility for Credit Unions in 2002, the lifting of limits on membership, relaxation of loan balance requirements and diversification of funding sources. Credit Unions were encouraged to include not only the poor but a more diverse (and profitable) membership and offer a range of financial services. Despite these changes, the membership of Credit Unions outside of Northern Ireland remains low (Byrne et al, 2007; McKillop et al, 2007).

CDFIs were also part of the bid to extend affordable credit to the financially excluded and emerged as a policy response in both the UK and the US following the sociospatial withdrawal of banks and affordable credit (Rogaly et al, 1999; Mosley and Steel, 2004; McGeehan, 2006; Thiel and Nissan, 2008; Appleyard, 2011). Comprising personal, civil society and business lending organisations, CDFIs focus on those who are excluded from mainstream credit, lending to individuals, social enterprises and businesses through a variety of loan products including personal, bridging and working capital loans. Perceived as being part of a more 'socially responsive economics', the development of this sector was influenced by broader experiments with microfinance in the poorer countries of the global South (Affleck and Mellor, 2006: 304). As such, the twin ambitions of CDFIs were not only to fill finance gaps and recirculate finance in local economies but also to 'democratise economic involvement' through the promotion of enterprise development and regeneration of local communities (McGeehan, 2006: 85; see also Mosley and Steel, 2004; Appleyard, 2011). CDFIs were therefore identified as working towards a 'double bottom line' comprising both social and economic objectives linked to job preservation and creation, supporting environmentally and ethically sound businesses and affording equal opportunities to the credit excluded (Appleyard, 2011: 250). McGeehan (2006) documents three broad 'waves' of CDFI development in the UK, the first dating back to the 1960s, which led to the establishment of a community development fund that inspired a second wave of initiatives in the 1990s. The third and most recent period of growth is partly attributable to the linking of CDFIs with financial inclusion policies by the New Labour government (Appleyard, 2011). An umbrella organisation was created in 2002, the Community Development Finance Association, to coordinate and strengthen this sector (Collard, 2007).

Assessments of this sector were fairly sanguine in the mid 2000s, partly due to the development of specific funding streams such as the Phoenix Fund and additional support from the FITF Growth Fund, with the number of CDFIs increasing from six in 1994 to 80 by the end of the 2000s (Drakeford and Sachdev, 2001; Thiel and Nissan, 2008; Appleyard, 2011). Furthermore, there was also a diversification of products being offered, evidence of some sectoral maturity and the inclusion of hard to reach customers. By the end of the 2008–09 financial year, the CDFI sector had lent £492 million and created or preserved 96,000 jobs located in 17,000 businesses (Appleyard, 2011). Despite these advances, however, broader evaluations of CDFIs were less sanguine, with commentators noting that political and financial support for these organisations was waning through the New Labour reign (Thiel and Nissan, 2008; Appleyard, 2011). In contrast to the US experience, the UK CDFI sector remained small, offering limited types of finance (due to their own funding restrictions), with patchy geographic coverage (Appleyard, 2011). Furthermore, the fact that both Credit Unions and CDFIs came under increased pressure to 'scale up' their interventions and become financially sustainable led some to argue that their ties with local communities, and social agendas, were largely being 'watered down' as they searched for more profitable customers and financial sustainability (Fuller and Jonas, 2002; Brown et al, 2003; Affleck and Mellor, 2006).[12] Such concerns are summed up in research that has questioned the extent to which Credit Unions and CDFIs can be considered as 'alternative'. Identifying three types of 'alternative' organisations, namely 'alternative-oppositional', 'alternative-additional', and 'alternative-substitute', Fuller and Jonas (2003) argue that far from offering a radical alternative to mainstream financial organisations, the latter two types of organisations simply substitute for, or extend the reach of, hegemonic finance.

The exclusion of lower-income groups from affordable credit was also explored within the context of the expansion and reformation of the Social Fund administered by the Department for Work and Pensions. Set up to provide interest-free loans and grants to people on income-related benefits, the Social Fund comprises six grants and loans: Sure Start maternity grants, community care grants, cold weather payments, funeral payments, budgeting loans and crisis loans. Under increased pressure caused by the adverse impact of the economic downturn on lower-income households, a tightening of the home credit market and rising inflation, there have been recent calls to reform the Social Fund, particularly in relation to the oversubscribed crisis loans and community care loans (DWP, 2010). It has been proposed that the administration of these loans should also be passed over to local authorities (DWP, 2010). Third sector organisations have strongly opposed these proposed changes arguing that they would have severe repercussions for many of the most vulnerable people in society as well as being endangered by local council spending cuts in the aftermath of the 2008–10 downturn.

Enhancing financial literacy and capability clearly runs through all of the above initiatives (Reagan and Paxton, 2003).[13] Two sets of consumers were identified as being particularly in need of advice within the context of the complex financial market in the UK: those with sizeable assets (who were generally able to find asset managers), and those with few resources, who were unaware of their rights and the least likely to seek advice (NACAB, 2005a, 2005b; Wallace and Quilgars, 2005; Gloukoviezoff, 2006). In turn, the FSA assumed strategic control of financial education policies, with one of its key remits being to improve public understanding of the financial system through the provision of adequate information and advice and heightening awareness of risks and benefits of financial products (Williams, 2007).[14] The *National Strategy for Financial Capability* set out the government's ambition to provide all adults with high-quality 'generic' financial advice to enable them to make effective decisions about their money, to ensure that children and young people had access to personal finance education and to develop a range of government programmes to improve financial capability among vulnerable groups (Gibbs, 2010). Supported by the Financial Capability Innovation Fund, seven target areas were identified relating to schools, young adults, the workplace, consumer communication, on-line tools, new parents, and money advice. These were then developed into a range of projects including those that specifically targeted children and young people via the integration of financial education into the school curriculum (Learning Money Matters),[15] those aimed at so-called NEET youth (Young Adults Make Sense of Money) as well as programmes which sought to target a broader population including 'Money Box', 'Make the Most of Your Money' and 'Now Let's Talk Money' campaigns (the latter partly sustained by Financial Inclusion Champions). In April 2010, the FSA's Financial Capability Division became the Consumer Financial Education Body (CFEB), which was charged with the responsibility of setting up a new national financial advice service, and which launched a new service, Money Made Clear.

Again, there have been some criticisms of financial education initiatives. While the introduction of financial skills in the national curriculum was an important first step, the focus was on basic numeracy and literacy skills, whereas it was recognised that individuals needed fairly sophisticated skills in order to be effectively integrated in financial circuits. The provision of financial education via schools was also uneven, with commentators suggesting that financial advice would be potentially more effective if it were less generic and offered in relation to specific financial events such as opening bank accounts

(Treasury, 2007c). Furthermore, the FSA was criticised for reaching out to more accessible mainstream groups rather than the financially excluded. More broadly, financial education policies continue to be premised upon an identification of a *lack* of knowledge and learning that must be compensated for, and a subsequent validation of particular forms of financial literacy over others. Yet, financial illiteracy is not necessarily related to incompetence on the part of customers with low incomes, but rather a mismatch between their particular know-how and that required to use financial services (Gloukoviezoff, 2006). As such, even while individuals and households may have developed fairly complex ways of managing their money, their budgeting skills have been challenged by the introduction of increasingly complex financial products that require 'dematerialized management' involving the use of bank accounts, cheque books, debit, and credit cards. Thus, they now have to acquire a new set of financial skills so as to be able to get by in a cashless society (Gloukoviezoff, 2006).

Within this context, New Labour's financial literacy and capability programmes have been critiqued for being driven by a narrative of responsibility rather than empowerment (Williams, 2007; Fuller and Mellor, 2008). Thus, while financial literacy education could potentially empower consumers by addressing the barriers that prevent their participation in financial markets and improve their decision-making skills, within the UK the provision of this education has been explicitly tied to an 'agenda of responsibilization' (see Chapter One; also Williams, 2007). As such, the provision of financial education has been interpreted as being driven by the interests of the financial services industry to expand their markets, and the desire of the state to transfer the responsibility of personal economic security to individuals (Froud et al, 2006; Williams, 2007). Framed in this way, it is financially capable citizens who can access their rights while also fulfilling their responsibilities in terms of looking after their own long-term futures and welfare by making the right choices based upon a realistic and informed assessment of their circumstances (Reagan and Paxton, 2003).

Migrants and financial inclusion policy

Public policy interest in financial exclusion among new and more settled migrants has grown in recent years, both in the UK and other advanced economies. From the 'supply-side' this has been fuelled by an appreciation of a large and growing demand for financial services from an increasingly diverse migrant population and a particular interest in the global remittance market (see also Chapter Six). Anderloni and

Vandone (2006) point out that the financial services industry in a number of European countries – including the UK, Netherlands, Spain and Germany – is beginning to show an interest in serving migrant communities as part of a strategy to increase their share of this market segment. 'Demand-side' initiatives have been led by an appreciation that not only are migrant populations particularly susceptible to financial exclusion, but also, as discussed in Chapter One, that at least some of the factors shaping this exclusion are likely to be specific to them (Datta, 2007a, 2011a). Furthermore, where once migrants' access to employment, housing and social and economic integration were afforded greater priority, there is a growing consensus that access to bank accounts is also of vital and immediate importance in financialised economies (see Chapter Three; also Isaacs, 2008).

Yet, despite this interest, the impact of the government programmes and policies outlined above on migrants has been limited, if varied, across different financial services as well as across different migrant communities. While migrant men and women are eligible for BBAs, which potentially afford them access to entry-level banking products, they encounter a number of barriers in doing so such that access is slow. As discussed further in Chapter Three, a key obstacle is the documentation required to open accounts, which foreign-born populations including migrants, refugees, asylum seekers and international students are particularly likely to struggle to produce and which banking staff may struggle to recognise (see Chapter Three, also Herbert and Hopwood Road, 2006; Gibbs, 2010). Migrants' usage of and participation in formal savings instruments and programmes is also restricted (Gibbs, 2010). Research suggests that nearly twice as many Black and Asian groups have no savings when compared with the White population, and they are also less likely to save in mainstream saving products such as ISAs and Premium Bonds (Khan, 2008). Furthermore, non-EU migrants were specifically excluded from the Savings Gateway Scheme, even though those who had had children while in the UK were eligible for the Child Trust Fund.

A similar picture emerges in relation to migrants' access to affordable formal credit, which is particularly circumscribed by non-existent or thin credit histories that translate into poor or negative credit ratings (Appleseed and Community Resource Group, 2004). There is some evidence which suggests that 'alternative' credit initiatives may be more suited to (some) migrant communities with, for example, membership of Credit Unions relatively prevalent in the African Caribbean community. Thus, while one per cent of the British-born adults were members of Credit Unions in 1998, the comparable figure among African Caribbean migrants was 38 per cent (Kempson and Whyley, 1999; Atkinson, 2006). This said, even within this community, membership has declined due to the preference of second and third generations to save in more mainstream products (Atkinson, 2006). Furthermore, other new migrant populations have typically shown little interest in Credit Unions. In Northern Ireland, where 50 per cent of the population belong to the 600 or so Credit Unions, research highlights that new migrants have shunned these organisations (Byrne et al, 2007). Gibbs (2010) attributes this to a lack of understanding and knowledge of how they operate, poor English language capability and the fact that Credit Union accounts are seen as being 'too local', hence constituting a risk to migrants who only intend to stay in Northern Ireland for a short period of time. This said, other Credit Unions that are located in diverse ethnic areas, such as Tower Hamlets Credit Union in East London, have attempted to cater for their clients through the provision of an Islamic Fund (Isaacs, 2008). In addition to Credit Unions, CDFIs such as Fair Finance in East London and Oakham in South London have also taken a lead in interacting with (new) migrant communities, particularly in relation to the provision of finance for small businesses.

Research also documents a dearth of financial advice programmes specifically directed at migrants (Gibbs, 2010). Citizens Advice Belfast (2010) reported that over 70 per cent of new migrant clients using their services were seeking financial advice relating to the opening of bank accounts, acquiring credit, accessing debit cards and transferring money home. While public interventions such as Money Made Clear may be beneficial to some migrants, this is only likely to be the case if information is provided in relevant languages. On the basis of their own research, Citizens Advice Belfast (2010) recommended that the development of tailored financial education programmes utilising advisors from migrant communities, who would have greater awareness of the needs of new migrants as well as the products and services such as welfare benefits which they are eligible for, was crucial to the provision of effective financial advice to migrants. In the absence of such services, and predominantly due to language difficulties, many migrants rely upon their family, friends and own migrant communities for advice, which they may or may not be able to provide (Gibbs, 2010; Mawhinney, 2010). Even while trust plays a vital role in determining where advice and information is sourced, language-specific facilities in bank branches may enhance financial literacy and capability among migrant men and women (Mawhinney, 2010).

Evidently then, these 'first generation' programmes and policies that have, by and large, tended to subsume migrant communities within broader excluded populations, including those with few and basic financial needs, have not been effective in reaching out to migrants (to be discussed later; see also Anderloni and Vandone, 2006; Datta, 2011a). Within this context there have been calls for the development of targeted and tailored financial products and services for migrant communities (Gibbs, 2010; Datta, 2011a). Even while Rahim et al (2009) argue that the financial services sector in the UK has been slow to supply specialist products for new migrants, it is important to acknowledge that there is some evidence of product innovation. Particular (global) banks have taken the lead in developing banking products designed for migrant clients although this is clearly mediated by nationality and class. Both the HSBC's Passport Accounts and the NatWest's 'Welcome' accounts have specifically targeted migrants through the simplification of documentation requirements (see Chapter Three). Customers wishing to open a HSBC Passport Account are also able to access a 'red24' service that provides multilingual information on a range of relocation issues including advice on banking services. Other more wealthy segments of the migrant market have been targeted by initiatives such as the Barclays Bank service for Non-Resident Indians (NRIs). Through these services, NRIs can initiate the process of opening accounts before they have left their home country by completing documentation formalities. Linked to free remittance transfers, the accounts offered are a version of basic bank accounts with an associated cash card, capable of sustaining direct debits and standing orders (Isaacs, 2008). This said, the financial services industry has shown little enthusiasm for developing products for more marginalised communities including Somali migrants (Isaacs, 2008).

Product innovation has also not necessarily been accompanied by sufficient investment in human resources, which are critical in the delivery of these products (Appleseed and Community Resource Group, 2004). Besides locational inconvenience and banking service hours, research particularly highlights the importance of addressing language barriers and cultural differences in relation to the development of financial services for migrant populations. Customer relations in particular have been identified as being critical in moving migrants from entry-level products to more profitable higher-end products such as mortgages, pensions and insurance. Critics have argued that this is best achieved through a broader understanding of 'KYC' (know your customer) procedures, which extend beyond identification to relationship building with migrant clients (Appleseed and Community Resource Group, 2004). Again, there are some examples of innovation, with a number of UK high street banks expressing a particular interest in the 'Polish pound', as evidenced by the employment of Polish-speaking staff as well as training staff to deal with the needs of Polish customers. In reaching out to these communities, it is apparent that a certain amount of innovative experimentation is taking place in terms of the use of multilingual staff, appreciation of cultural difference, location and banking services (Anderloni and Vandone, 2006). However, a key hurdle in developing migrant-specific products and services is how to scale up such initiatives, which have predominantly remained confined to a handful of banks and targeted at a narrow range of migrant communities. For example, economies of scale have meant that it is essentially the larger and more visible migrant populations that have benefited from multilingual staff (Sumption and Somerville, 2010). The ability to replicate these services and products across a highly diverse migrant population within the context of a tightening fiscal and changing political environment situation is highly debatable (Appleseed and Community Resource Group, 2004).

The way forward: cuts, cuts and more cuts?

In May 2010 the Coalition government assumed power in the UK. With many of the projects and programmes initiated by New Labour due to end in 2011, financial inclusion policy was seen by many as hanging in the balance, partly as a consequence of the economic downturn. This apprehension was further attributable to the fact that while financial inclusion initiatives featured quite prominently in the budget New Labour produced in the run-up to the 2010 election, both the Conservative and Liberal Democrat party manifestos identified limited financial inclusion priorities. Thus, while New Labour promised that if re-elected it would impose a Universal Banking obligation, create a People's Bank at the Post Office, implement a levy on the banking industry to fund the expansion of Credit Unions and CDFIs, disclose bank lending practices and clamp down on the high interest rates endemic among instant loans, payday and doorstep lenders, the Conservatives only pledged themselves to limiting excessive charges specifically in relation to store cards and establishing a free national financial advice centre funded by a levy on the financial services industry, whereas the Liberal Democrats proposed to promote smaller and regional financial organisations to provide 'local finance' and to clamp down on bank charges (Rahman, 2010).

Despite reassurances by the Coalition's Financial Secretary to the Treasury that the '[g]overnment remain committed to helping poorer households to access appropriate financial services, to improve their financial resilience and to avoid falling into unsustainable levels of debt', since assuming power the Coalition government has gradually wound down or abruptly terminated New Labour's financial inclusion programmes (Edmonds, 2011:22; see also Ben-Galim, 2011). The FITF was asked by the Coalition government to continue its work on banking, savings, insurance and access to affordable credit until the end of its term in March 2011, at which point the Financial Inclusion Growth Fund, which had been crucial in funding many of the above financial inclusion programmes, also came to an end. The latter termination posed a particular risk to debt advice, which had been built up over the previous five years, supported by a fund of £27 million, with 500 trained specialists in England and Wales providing free debt advice through the Citizens Advice offices. The savings programmes set up by New Labour have fared particularly badly under the Coalition government. Indeed, concerns about the fate of these initiatives were raised prior to the election in the light of the changing economic climate. In particular, the universality of the CTF was seen as being at risk in a tightening fiscal situation. Furthermore, while the outgoing government had legislated for the national roll-out of the Savings Gateway, the final date for this was set as 2010, with an unclear identification of both the pace of the roll-out and the number of people who would be eligible for it (Paxton, 2009). In the event, the Savings Gateway was quietly dropped by the Coalition government, with the Chancellor, George Osborne, stating in his budget speech of 2010 that 'we have decided that we simply cannot afford to extend the Savings Gateway' (Osborne, 2010). The CTF suffered from a similar fate (Ben-Galim, 2011). Even before joining the Coalition, the Liberal Democrats had strongly opposed this initiative on various grounds, including a perception that it was not the best use of public funds, that the take-up of this Fund among lower-income households was poor and thus exacerbated inequality, and also that the endowment was too small. Indeed, the Liberal Democrats had pledged to scrap the CTF if elected in its 2010 election manifesto (Ben-Galim, 2011). More broadly, the Liberal Democrats were perceived as articulating a critique of the wider assets-based welfare policies of New Labour that were shying away from addressing wealth inequalities and promoting citizenship (Prabhakar, 2009). Even while the Conservatives had been broadly supportive of the CTF, in the closing days of the election campaign, they undertook to restrict it to the poorest third of families, thus attacking the universal element of the fund (Prabhakar, 2009). Once in government, the decision to scrap the CTF altogether was attributed to the savings of £500 million that would be made for the public purse. In the event, there was very little resistance to the abrupt termination of these programmes, partly attributable to the fact that there were no direct losers, the failure of the outgoing New Labour government to generate cross-party political support, but also due – perhaps more importantly – to the lack of support for these initiatives from child poverty lobbies (Ben-Galim, 2011).

Yet, financial exclusion, and particular manifestations of it such as over-indebtedness, continue to be highly significant issues facing British society. As highlighted in Chapter One, the personal debt owed by British households has risen significantly, especially in recent years, partly as a result of the 2008–10 downturn (Cox et al, 2011). Perhaps somewhat ironically, and reflecting the 'privatisation of public debt', this debt liability is set to increase further as a consequence of the economic recovery plan put in place by the Coalition government, which is premised upon significant reductions in government spending. Cox et al (2011) report that the Coalition government's Emergency Budget and Comprehensive Review herald a number of policy changes that, while purportedly tackling the public debt, will have severe consequences on those who are financially excluded, especially those on low incomes. This includes cuts of around £7 billion to welfare benefits, reduced support of local authorities, thus putting pressure on particular services such as money and debt advice services, and the capping of housing benefit. Furthermore, it is clear that individuals and households will be expected to continue to contribute towards social care and pensions as well as to cope with higher tuition fees (Ben-Galim, 2011).

Partly in recognition of this, several – as yet – short-term initiatives have been created to keep afloat those financial inclusion programmes that have aspects resonating with the Coalition government's elusive 'Big Society' agenda. This move has included a specific focus on private consumer debt, as evidenced by the creation of a contingency fund to continue debt advice initiatives for a limited period, albeit framed within the context of a more cost-effective and sustainable service (Edmonds, 2011). To this end, the former Consumer Financial Education Body was re-launched as the 'Money Advice Service' in April 2011 and charged with the responsibility of playing a central role in coordinating debt advice across the nation. The new body has been funded for the 2011–12 financial year by a budget of £43.7 million raised from financial services firms regulated by the FSA (www. moneyadviceservice.org.uk). The Coalition government also replaced the CTF with 'Junior ISAs' from November 2011, positioning the latter as a more 'cost-effective replacement for the CTF' (Ben-Galim, 2011: 13). These have a maximum £3,600 annual contribution with government contribution reserved only for children in care (with £5 million set aside for this). Six million children have been identified as being eligible for Junior ISAs, and if parents were to contribute the maximum amount, then funds at maturity would contain between £70,000 and £80,000 (Lodge, 2011). Within the field of affordable credit, the government has expressed an interest in supporting both Credit Unions and Post Office branches by affording the former the opportunity to scale up their operations through the Post Office network while also supporting an ailing Post Office sector. Funded through a 'modernisation fund' worth some £73 million over the next four years, the bolstering of Credit Unions has been linked once again to welfare reforms, making work pay and reforming the Department for Work and Pensions crisis loans.

This chapter has detailed the evolution of public policy on financial exclusion over a period of significant upheaval that has witnessed both a change in government and the formation of the first Coalition government in the UK, as well as a global and national economic downturn. While the Coalition government's financial inclusion agenda is still taking shape, the chapter argues that the plethora of policies, programmes and products that have been implemented to date have failed to focus substantively on migrant communities, which have remained largely peripheral to these initiatives. It is within this context that the next chapter details the financial lives and practices of migrant men and women in London.

Notes

[1] Within the lifetime of the New Labour government, the Social Exclusion Unit was subsumed into the Social Exclusion Taskforce in 2006, which was, in turn, abolished by the Coalition government in 2010, with its functions being absorbed by the Office for Civil Society.

[2] Other PATs focused on children and young people; crime; employment and opportunity; health and care; homes and neighbourhoods and transport.

[3] Access itself comprises of 'no access', 'insufficient access' or 'inappropriate access' to financial services and products. While 'no access' is self-explanatory, 'inappropriate access' refers to individuals who are sold products that are unsuited to their needs and/or who do not understand all the intricacies of the products that they have acquired (Gloukoviezoff, 2006). In turn, 'inappropriate access' can be as problematic as 'no access', particularly within the context of credit, and can result in over-indebtedness if a borrower lacks financial capability (Mitton, 2008).

[4] The term 'marginally banked' is used throughout this book to refer to those who are neither unbanked nor fully banked.

[5] It is important to acknowledge that even while prepaid meters entail higher utility bills, low-income households may express a preference for this because it enables them to keep in control of their budgets (Collard et al, 2003).

[6] The New Labour government's departments and agencies involved in financial inclusion initiatives included the Financial Services Authority (FSA), Department for Work and Pensions, Office of Fair Trading, Ministry of Justice, Cabinet Office, Department of Innovation, Universities and Skills, Department for Business, Enterprise and Regulatory Reform, Legal Services Commission, and Department of Trade and Industry (Wallace and Quilgars, 2005).

[7] Examples of partnerships include those between the FITF, banks and the Post Office to increase access to banking services; between the Treasury and the Bank of England in conjunction with the umbrella organisation of CDFIs to look into credit for entrepreneurs; while the Treasury also piloted the Savings Gateway accounts in conjunction with Halifax Bank (Wallace and Quilgars, 2005).

[8] Similar entry-level banking products have also been introduced in other advanced economies including France, Denmark, Germany, Belgium and the Netherlands (Thiel, 2006; Anderloni et al, 2008).

[9] Importantly, the POCA was also introduced to compensate local post offices for the loss in income they incurred following the payment of welfare through automated credit transfer (Collard, 2007).

[10] The inclusion of POCA account holders in estimates of banked populations is debateable given the limited functionality of these accounts (see also Chapter Three).

[11] Interest rate ceilings specify the maximum rate of interest that lenders may charge for different types of loans. The main determinants shaping these are loan size (with small loans typically attracting higher interest rates) and whether the lender is regulated or not (Policis and DTI, 2004). The only cap which survived the Consumer Credit Act 1974 was on Credit Union interest rates, which were capped at 26.8 per cent APR or 2 per cent per month (Policis and DTI, 2004).

[12] Similar concerns are also evident in the microfinance industry in terms of the relative merits and importance of 'finance-only' and 'finance-plus' programmes with the former often resulting in weakening ties with local communities (Kabeer, 2003; Copestake, 2007; CGAP, 2009).

[13] While concerns about financial illiteracy predated the new Labour government, earlier efforts were marked by a focus on the suppliers of financial products rather than consumers (Williams, 2007).

[14] The New Labour government's decision to create the FSA was in part borne out of an assessment that the existing regulatory environment was not effective in the face of a rapidly changing and sophisticated financial services industry. It also signified a movement from sectoral to a single statutory regulator of the financial services industry (Williams, 2007).

[15] This programme was explicitly linked to the CTF, with a significant proportion of the funding devoted to the development of CTF-specific teaching resources (Treasury, 2007c).

THREE

Mapping migrants' financial lives in London

"I took money from my father, 100 Euro, for my ticket, and I had £300 in my pocket, and that is how I arrived in London in August 2007." (Asen, Bulgarian man)

Having outlined the broad contours of financialisation, transnational migration and financial exclusion, and public policy responses to these, this chapter provides a first detailed insight into the formal financial practices of migrant men and women drawn from the Brazilian, Bulgarian, Polish, Turkish and Somali communities in London. With varying levels of resources at their disposal, migrant lives are initially played out on the fringes of formal circuits, which different men and women are able to maintain for different lengths of time. Yet, given the financialisation of the British economy which renders living on the margins increasingly difficult, the majority have to engineer some level of access to formal services, particularly banking in the first instance, but also savings and credit instruments over a period of time, as they seek to navigate their (working) lives, provide for their children and households in London as well as fulfil their transnational obligations to families left behind in home countries. Furthermore, access to savings and particularly credit is recognised as crucial for asset accumulation, whether in the UK or more usually in home countries, and is often, although not always, a driving force behind migration.

Utilising understandings of financial in/exclusion expanded upon in Chapter Two, and focusing upon the core services of banking, savings and credit,[1] this chapter details the differential access that migrant men and women have to the formal financial sector in London, and the financial practices that they develop around these services. In so doing the chapter extrapolates the 'demand-side' factors that shape migrants' financial practices, paying particular attention to labour market participation, immigration status, the intersectional location of migrants in relation to gender, nationality and class hierarchies, as well as transnational financial practices. As part of London's 'super-diverse' population, earlier discussion has highlighted that migrants enter the UK with very different entitlements in relation to their right to live and work here, and also occupy distinct segments of the UK labour market. Furthermore, they originate from countries with diverse levels of financial services infrastructure and development and have complex transnational financial histories, assets and liabilities that shape their practices in London. These are further mediated through gender, nationality and class cleavages. Collectively, these factors have a significant bearing upon migrants' formal financial lives in the city. The chapter draws upon the narratives of migrant men and women based on 319 questionnaires, 81 in-depth interviews and three focus group discussions.[2]

Settling in London: the importance of banking

Migrant men and women identified banking as the most important financial service that they required access to in London, thus confirming its status as both a basic yet essential 'gateway' financial service and on par with migrants' broader immediate needs relating to employment and housing (see also Isaacs, 2008). In turn, this research uncovered relatively significant levels of banking *in*clusion, with 87 per cent of migrants interviewed being categorised as banked.[3] Disaggregating the banked population by nationality and gender further revealed that inclusion ranged from a high of 100 per cent among Turkish participants to 98 per cent of Bulgarian, 85 per cent of Somali, 83 per cent of Brazilian and 75 per cent of Polish migrants (see Figure 3.1). In turn, banking inclusion among men and women was fairly even with 87 per cent of all male migrants and 86 per cent of all female migrants owning bank accounts across the five communities although the female banked population within the Somali community fell to 77 per cent in comparison to 91 per cent of their male compatriots.

These patterns of inclusion can be read against two registers: first in relation to the total un/banked population in Britain and second in comparison with migrant banking in/exclusion in other advanced economies. Taking the latter first, migrants' access to banking in London compares favourably with the situation in countries like the US, where much higher levels of migrant banking *ex*clusion are identified, ranging from 35 per cent of Ecuadorians, 64 per cent of Salvadorans and 75 per cent of Mexican immigrants (Kennickell et al, 2000; Hogarth et al, 2004; Paulson et al, 2006; Rhine and Green, 2006). This said, a relatively higher proportion of migrants are unbanked in relation to the comparable British-born population, which recent studies place at 3 per cent (FITF, 2010). In seeking to understand these patterns of banking in/exclusion, this section begins by focusing on banked migrants and extrapolates the factors that account for relatively high levels of banking inclusion. It then distinguishes between different 'types' of banked migrants separating out men and women who may be more accurately categorised as 'marginally banked' on the basis of the kind of bank accounts they hold and the range of banking services that they utilise. The emphasis then shifts to unbanked populations in order to understand why (albeit a minority of) migrants are unable to access banking services.

Figure 3.1: Levels of banking inclusion, by nationality and gender (%)

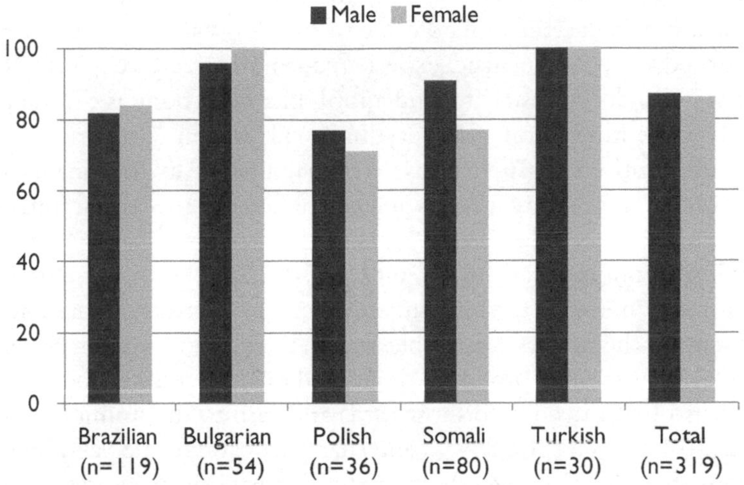

Source: Questionnaire surveys

Accounting for banking inclusion

A number of factors explain migrants' banking inclusion in London including labour market participation, access to, and dependency upon, state welfare, and the economic and social costs of being financially excluded, with the latter identified as hindering broader integration into British society. Particularly important, as evidenced in the narratives of many migrant men and women, was the link between banking access and labour market participation, which is itself attributable to the increased incidence of the payment of wages directly into bank accounts. In order to better understand this, three points need to be elaborated upon here: the centrality of employment for migrants, the particular importance of formal sector employment, and the link between formal sector employment and banking access. It was apparent that almost irrespective of why migrant men and women came to London – as students, tourists, asylum seekers or nationals of the expanded EU – the search for employment consumed many within days of their arrival in the city (see also Wills et al, 2010). While many anticipated that they would be able to find jobs easily, partly due to (mis)information being relayed by family and friends already resident in the city, the reality was somewhat different and shaped by their immigration status, routes into the UK and networks in the city. Thus, while Veronika, whose husband had migrated from Bulgaria prior to her arrival, was able to find a job "during the first week after my arrival," Rosana, a Brazilian woman who came to London via Italy, where she had worked as a chambermaid, experienced an unanticipated delay: "I thought it would be easier [to find a job], like everybody is deluded, like, 'I'll arrive in London and everything will happen'."

The implications of such delays were significant as the financial resources that migrant men and women mobilised to meet their initial living expenses in London began to run out. These resources consisted of varying amounts of cash and credit cards, the latter being sometimes explicitly acquired so as to satisfy immigration authorities that migrants could support themselves during their stay in the UK. Josana from Brazil recounted that she had brought several credit cards with her "because I had heard that I needed to show cards and cash to the immigration officers, so I applied for a few ... international cards, to be valid here although they did not have much credit, like American Express, and I also brought around £500 cash on me." In contrast, those who had moved to London as asylum seekers often carried very little money with them, having exhausted most of their resources on migration-related costs. In the opinion of one such migrant, Jibril Osman, from Somalia: "I don't think anyone from Africa [can afford to] bring money from Africa to Europe." The majority, in turn, had underestimated how expensive London was, particularly in relation to accommodation and transport costs, which they attempted initially to offset by living with family, kin and friends, who provided free or cheap accommodation (see also Datta et al, 2007a). Matuez, a Polish man, recalled that he had even packed "food from home" in a bid to keep expenses in London at a minimum. Others still had little choice but to turn back to family in home countries to help tide them over until they had secured jobs, a practice that is sometimes referred to as 'reverse remittances' and that is dependent upon the capacity of families to extend this support to their migrant relatives (see also Datta et al, 2007b).

Given this context, employment assumed a particular importance for many: 82 per cent of all migrant men and women were employed, ranging from all of the Polish and 96 per cent of Bulgarian and Brazilian migrants, respectively, to 60 per cent of Turkish and 50 per cent of Somali migrants (see Table 3.1). These employment patterns are supported by research that documents high employment rates among A8 and, to a lesser extent, A2 migrants, both in relation to the UK-born population and other migrant communities, as well as the lower rates of employment associated with asylum seekers and refugees (Sumption and Somerville, 2010). Found by design in low-paid sectors of London's economy, just under 60 per cent of the participants worked in the hospitality, construction, care and cleaning sectors, which are recognised as 'migrant-dependent' sectors. This said, there were intra- and inter-community differences in the labour market positions occupied by migrant men and women, reflecting both gender and racial divisions in London's labour market that interrelate with a migrant division of labour (see Chapter One; also Wills et al, 2010). Correspondingly, the majority of Brazilian women were domestic cleaners and/or nannies, while their male compatriots tended to work in catering, construction and office cleaning. While only half of all Somalis interviewed were employed, they all worked in low-paid jobs in home care (predominantly women), as taxi drivers (predominantly men), kitchen porters and in administrative jobs. The Polish and Bulgarian respondents were concentrated in the building/construction trades (dominated by men), followed by retail, cleaning and hospitality (in kitchens, and as bar tenders). All but two of the Turkish migrants were employed in an ethnic economy working for Turkish employers in a variety of low-paid and low-skilled occupations ranging from cashiers and general shop assistants in Turkish supermarkets, in pitta bread factories, as butchers and as cooks in Turkish takeaways. As set out in Table 3.1, wages earned from these occupations were generally low. Over half of migrants (54 per cent) were earning £1,000 or less a month, with low wages being particularly endemic in the Turkish and Somali communities.

Wider research documents that low-paid workers adopt a 'portfolio of employment' in order to ensure their social reproduction (Stenning et al, 2010b; Wills et al, 2010). This was evidenced in this study through practices such as working long hours and holding down two or more jobs (14 per cent of all migrant workers), with additional jobs also frequently located in the low-wage economy. Reflecting the demands that this entailed, Jacinto, a Brazilian man, recounted that he had worked a seven-day week holding down three jobs in the cleaning sector for six months. As such, "my life was to [go to work], get home, have a shower, eat something, then call my family in Brazil, every day, and then go to bed, to start all over again the next morning". Furthermore, just under a quarter of the migrant men and women lived in dual-income households where income was pooled.

Table 3.1: Employment rates, wages and payment mechanisms of migrants, by percentage

	Brazilian	Bulgarian	Polish	Somali	Turkish	TOTAL
Employment status:	(n=119)	(n=54)	(n=36)	(n=80)	(n=30)	(n=319)
Employed	96	96	100	50	60	82
Unemployed	4	4	0	50	40	18
Wages per month:	(n=114)	(n=52)	(n=36)	(n=40)	(n=18)	(n=260)
Less than £200	2	0	0	5	0	2
£201–£400	5	0	0	18	6	5
£401–£600	11	4	6	5	17	8
£601–£800	8	12	17	17	32	13
£801–£1,000	29	26	22	20	27	26
£1,001–£1,200	18	23	19	22	0	19
£1,201–£1,400	10	23	3	2	0	10
£1,401–£1,600	7	10	8	5	6	7
£1,601–£1,800	2	0	3	3	6	2
£1,801–£2,000	4	2	14	3	0	5
£2,001–£2,200	0	0	0	0	0	0
More than £2,201	3	0	0	0	0	1
No response	1	0	8	0	6	2
Payment mechanisms:	(n=114)	(n=52)	(n=36)	(n=40)	(n=18)	(n=260)
Cash	30	2	42	17	100	29
Personal cheques	3	0	0	8	0	2
Automatic deposit	58	90	25	40	0	53
Payroll/company cheques	1	4	8	0	0	2
Cash and automatic deposits	5	0	8	0	0	4
Combination of above	3	4	17	35	0	10

Source: Questionnaire surveys
Note: In all cases, 0 indicates there were no cases in the sample.

These employment portfolios also highlighted the importance of informal sector employment. Contrary to an expectation that employment conditions have progressively standardised in advanced economies, it is generally accepted that the informal economy has survived, and indeed even flourished, which is sometimes erroneously attributed to a 'swelling' immigrant population (Sassen, 1994; Gibson-Graham, 1996; Samers, 2005; Iskander, 2007; Pfau-Effinger, 2009). Defined as economic activities undertaken by workers and/or firms that are not recognised, regulated or protected by existing legal or regulatory frameworks, the diversity of the informal economy is well documented and includes both paid and unpaid work, 'cash in hand' employment, volunteering, mutual aid, subsistence production and informal micro-enterprises (Gibson-Graham, 1996; Becker, 2004; Marcelli et al, 2009). Within the context of this research, informal work predominantly manifested itself as 'cash in hand' work with just under a third of migrant workers identifying that they received cash wages (see Table 3.1). Again, the incidence of this varied across different national groups, with all the Turkish workers receiving their wages in cash followed by 42 per cent of Polish (mainly labourers working in the building trade) and 30 per cent of Brazilian workers (predominantly in domestic cleaning and child care). Furthermore, the employment trajectories of a number of migrant men and women highlighted that initial employment was often found in the informal economy, which was partly attributable to English language competency, immigration status and migrants' social networks. These jobs were then either replaced or supplemented by formal sector employment, with the latter reflecting a straddling of the two sectors. For example, some Brazilian migrant women who worked as cleaners combined office and domestic cleaning, with the former employment being organised via agencies and the latter informally.

Even while commentators argue that there has been an erosion of the distinction between formal and informal economies – which they attribute to 'a new dynamic of informalization' in advanced economies arising from neoliberal restructuring and associated processes of outsourcing, as well as the 2008–10 economic downturn that has exerted downward pressures on formal sector wages and working conditions – migrant workers themselves continued to make important distinctions between these sectors (Sassen, 1994; see also Marcelli et al, 2009; Rogers et al, 2009; Datta, 2011b).[4] Three interrelated complaints about working in the informal economy emerged that revolved around low wages, exploitation and insecurity. Men and women argued that 'decent' wages, which were represented as the National Minimum Wage (NMW), were only available in formal sector employment. In contrast, and by way of example, cash wages in the informal Turkish economy ranged from £1.54 to £3.75 per hour at a time when the NMW was £5.35 per hour, leading to women like Ayse commenting that the latter was a mere "ideal", at least for her husband and herself. Reflecting the exploitation that this entailed, her compatriot Ali complained:

> "Do I work? Forgive me, but I work like a dog. All I do
> is work. That is all I do. In this god forsaken country that
> is all I have done ... At the moment I am working for my
> nephew. Don't let that mean that 'Oh he is family, you must
> be getting paid good money.' I work like a dog for him –
> hope he hits the other world soon. You must think that I
> am a cruel man. I work 12 hours a day in my nephew's
> meat warehouse – don't even ask me where he got all the
> money to get that place. He pays me £220! £220! Is that
> fair for what I do, working long hours in the cold doing
> back breaking work? [I] am not a young man as I once
> was. My own nephew pays me £220! What can I expect a
> stranger to pay me?"

Migrants from other communities highlighted interrelated vulnerabilities associated with informal work. With employers often associating cash wages with irregular immigration status, Jacinto recounted that while his Brazilian employer had initially promised him wages of £8 an hour, "in the end he wanted to pay me £2.50 an hour, because he thought I did not have papers. It is the old story, they presume that and then they exploit you." Other informal workers such as Andrzej, a Polish man, spoke about the insecurity and irregularity of building work in the construction industry, which meant that he was often unsure whether a job would last for a day, a week or a few months.

Given these experiences, formal sector employment assumed a particular importance for many, which, in turn, made banking access critical because of employers' preference to pay wages on a monthly basis and then directly into bank accounts (see Chapter Two, see also McKay and Winkelmann-Gleed, 2005; Atkinson, 2006). The corresponding decline in cash wages is highlighted by the fact that while 1 in 8 workers in 1999 received their wages in cash, this had declined to 1 in 20 workers in 2009 and is predicted to fall further to 1 in 50 workers by 2018 (Payments Council, 2009). The observation of Celina, a Brazilian woman, that "the siege is tightening" and that it was increasingly difficult to obtain cash-in-hand employment unless one wanted to work in "home-cleaning" was borne out by the fact that 53 per cent of all migrants received their wages via automatic deposit, with a number of others also reliant upon bank accounts to access their wages (see Table 3.1). Significantly, even while migrant workers show a definite preference for formal sector employment, it is *employer* rather than migrant choice that has driven banking inclusion (see also Atkinson, 2006). This was corroborated by the narratives of migrants who concurred that access to formal sector employment hinged upon bank account ownership, with Abdi, a Somali man, commenting that "the first thing that you get asked when you [go for an interview] is [do you have] a bank account, therefore it is very important that you have one, otherwise you can't have the job. It is the first question you get asked, 'Do you have a bank account?'." Indeed, Llander from Brazil, who had been in London for six years and identified himself as an irregular migrant, commented that while it was possible to secure employment in the UK without a visa, it was impossible to do so without a bank account. Drawing attention to his own employment history, he attributed periods of unemployment not to his irregular status but to employers who were not willing to be "flexible" and pay his wages in cash. Reflecting the 'catch-22' situation that this entailed, Rita from Brazil, argued that:

> "[A bank account] is essential, because without one you won't be able to [do] anything, you can't get a job. I find it very interesting here. In theory one arrives here without much money and needing to work, but then you need to have a bank account first, otherwise you won't work. But then what if you don't have money to open an account? I think one [should be able to] have a job first and then open an account. [But] without a bank account, employers won't even talk to you."

Where migrants are unable to secure access to transactional bank accounts, employment may continue to be found on the margins (McKay and Winkelmann-Gleed, 2005).

Access to banking also emerged as important for those who were unemployed and reliant upon state support, again because of the payment of benefits directly into bank accounts (see Chapter Two). With a quarter of all migrant men and women claiming benefits, this particularly explained banking inclusion among Turkish and Somali migrants, whose employment rates were lower in comparison to the other three communities, and where correspondingly welfare dependency was higher (see Table 3.2). Men and women in both communities were in receipt of various benefits including job seekers allowance, working tax credit and child benefit, with average monthly benefit income ranging from £451 in the Somali community to £629 in Turkish households. The latter was partly determined by household composition, with 30 per cent of Somali and 80 per cent of Turkish participants living with between one to four dependent children in the UK.

Table 3.2: Benefit take-up in Turkish and Somali households, by percentage

	Somali	Turkish
Number of households in receipt of benefits:	(n=80)	(n=30)
Claimed benefits	54	93
Did not claim benefits	43	7
Not sure*	3	0
Average monthly benefit income	£451	£629
Benefit income range	£100–£1,000	£120–£1,400

Source: Questionnaire survey

Note: * Includes participants who reported that other members of their household may be claiming benefits

In order to contextualise these findings, it is important to acknowledge the interplay between welfare and migration, and the changing position of the welfare state vis-à-vis migrants (Spencer, 2011). As detailed in Chapter One, the overhaul of the welfare state from the 1990s onwards has entailed significant reductions in the access to benefits of migrants, and especially asylum seekers, partly motivated by public policy belief that people were choosing the UK as a destination because of 'easy' access to welfare. While this has been widely disputed by research that has pointed to the more complex motivations shaping both forced and voluntary migrations, this study uncovered how the access of both those who have migrated voluntarily as well as those whose migrations were forced has been progressively curtailed (Van Hear, 2004; Collyer, 2005). Indeed, important differences exist between migrant communities in terms of access to welfare: while Polish immigrants can access (some) benefits after they have been in continuous employment and registered on the UK's Workers Registration Scheme for a year, the eligibility of Bulgarian and particularly Brazilian migrants is severely constrained. In turn, only a handful of the men and women (10 participants in total) from these communities claimed benefits, with Kremena, from Bulgaria, reporting that she had been cautioned by her financial advisor against applying for benefits on the grounds that this would render any future applications for British citizenship unsuccessful.

Furthermore, even the access to welfare of asylum seekers and refugees has been progressively eroded (see Chapter One). The Turkish and Somali households who were in receipt of benefits had predominantly entered the UK in the 1990s, when their applications for asylum were accepted. This included Amina, who came to the UK having spent six years in a refugee camp in Kenya after leaving her native Somalia and who was brought to the UK by her father's friend. Recalling her experience, she said: "He [took me] up to the immigration point [at Heathrow] and then left me. They [the immigration authorities] said 'How did you get here?' I said a man brought me and he had left me. They took me in. From the airport, they took me to a town, then moved me to London for a while. After two years they gave me the right to stay." Similar stories were recounted by Turkish migrants like Hatice, whose husband had been arrested and tortured on numerous occasions by the Turkish authorities because of his political beliefs. Explaining why they had chosen to move to England, she said: "There are other political immigrants [here] so that's why we came ... England has been much more accommodating than Turkey could ever be." Following changes to both the immigration and welfare regimes, more recently arrived men and women in these same communities did not exhibit similar levels of access to welfare, while even those who had received benefits for a number of years were being pressured to rejoin the workforce. For some, like Lula, from Somalia, whose children were growing up, letters from the DSS informing her that she "must go to work" were particularly worrying as she had made little progress in learning English over the three years that she had been enrolled on a language course, which she attributed both to the trauma of having lived through a war as well as a prior lack of formal schooling.

As highlighted in Chapter Two, benefit recipients have had to open accounts in order to access their payments since 2003, with the transfer to automated transfers completed in 2005 (see also Chapter Two). As a Somali woman, Asha Abdillahi, remarked:

> "Even benefit needs an account, so if you cannot work for whatever reason, still you need an account, including post office account. Even if you are old and cannot go to the toilet on your own [you] need an account. ... This is the 21st century. No one pays cash any more."

Reinforcing again how banking inclusion has been driven by broader changes to payment mechanisms, Hafsa, Asha's compatriot, revealed that she had opened an account seven years after she had arrived in the UK and then only because "the DSS sent me a letter saying this was the only way to receive benefit and [the] system was changing and there will be no more benefit books". This said, there were significant differences between Turkish and Somali migrants in relation to the kinds of accounts that were opened in order to access benefit payments. While all the Turkish men and women had opened accounts in a range of high street banks, just under half of Somali migrants (48 per cent) accessed their welfare payments through POCAs, which is corroborated by wider research (Herbert and Hopwood Road, 2006). The popularity of POCAs among Somali men, and particularly women, was linked to a number of factors. Raaxo, a Somali woman, who had been informed of changes to benefit payment mechanisms, had been considering opening a "normal bank account" for some time, during which "the government opened a post office account for me". Furthermore, a prior familiarity with post offices where benefit cheques had been cashed, a perception of banks as alien and unwelcome places as well as difficulties in opening accounts (see also Chapter Four) had resulted in a preference for POCAs. In contrast, among Turkish migrants the decision to deposit welfare payments in bank accounts rather than POCAs was driven by a desire to escape the perceived surveillance of the latter by the government. This also explained the concentration of Turkish workers in the cash economy, which enabled them to keep wages and benefits payments separate (see below).

The discussion now moves on from factors that have, to some extent, forced migrants to open bank accounts to those that are more reflective of migrant agency. Men and women across the five communities explained the importance of banking access in relation to facilitating economic and social integration into British society. This was most succinctly expressed by Rosana, a Brazilian woman, who remarked that "[bank accounts are] very important because it makes you feel like a citizen, you can do a lot of things". For a start, there was an appreciation that accounts enabled banked populations to keep their money both safe as well as easily accessible in comparison with, for example, cash savings that were held at home as well as money deposited in POCAs, given that post offices were closed in the evenings and on weekends. Other advantages that accrued from being banked were lower utility bills through direct debit payments (although see Table 3.3, on p 70), as well as facilitating consumption in what some migrants depicted as an increasingly cashless society. To this end, Rosana went on to say, "Well, if you don't have a bank account, well, it makes it all much more difficult, to work, to buy, to travel. You want to buy a ticket on the internet, then you need a debit card, so all depends on having an account."

Men and women further reflected that being located outside of the formal banking system eroded social standing both within migrant but also host communities. Highlighting this, Ahmed, from Somalia, commented that: "I like it [having a bank account]. It is nice, when you are with your friends, getting your [ATM] card out and taking your money out. If you don't have an account you will be a little bit jealous." Others went so far as to link banking access with citizenship rights, which echoes wider debates about the nature and importance of *financial* citizenship in advanced financialised economies, enabling individuals to fully exercise their rights and participate in society (see Chapter One). Rosana (introduced earlier) argued that access to banking potentially bestowed the same privileges that citizens had on migrants, a point that her compatriot, Marcia, further developed. In her opinion, not only did banking access "open doors", affording entry into the world of work as well as financial resources such as affordable credit, but also the power of banks was such that they were critical in establishing the credibility or reputation of a person:

> "If you don't have a bank account, you won't be able to work, because they won't take you in without one, because if you don't have a bank account, they will presume that you are here illegally or that your name is on a credit blacklist .... It is a little discriminatory, but it has got more weight than having your name in the police books, so it is really the bank that determines whether you are a person of good character or not. It is ridiculous, but that is how it is."

Having identified the key factors that shape banking inclusion across the five migrant communities, the discussion now turns to a more nuanced investigation of banked migrants' financial practices, which determine the extent to which they may be classified as fully banked or, as was more usually the case, marginally banked.

Identifying 'marginally banked' migrants

Commentators note that simple access to banking services 'fails to address the full breadth and depth of the experience of financial inclusion: it is not just about access to products but also the quality of engagement with those products and the need for individuals to develop skills and confidence to make informed decisions' (Reagan and Paxton, 2003: 1; see also Chapter Two). It is this quality of engagement – shaped by the kinds of bank accounts that banked populations own, the services that these enable them to access as well as the financial practices deployed by account holders – that delineates those who may be categorised as 'fully banked' from those who are 'marginally banked'. In turn, the banking practices of migrant men and women illustrated considerable diversity, such that while some had multiple bank accounts (albeit a minority, comprising 7 per cent of all migrants) and utilised a range of banking services from internet banking to money transfer services, others had much more limited interactions with banks (see also Gibbs, 2010).

Beginning with the type of bank accounts owned by banked migrants, Figure 3.2 illustrates the predominance of current accounts followed by current and savings accounts held in a range of high street banks. This said, 15 per cent of banked migrants were served by basic entry-level accounts including BBAs and student accounts. Among the studied communities the proportion with entry-level accounts ranged from nearly a third (32 per cent) of Polish migrants to 19 per cent of Somali, 12 per cent of Brazilian and 8 per cent of Bulgarian men and women. This finding is significant in that it indicates that policy interventions to address banking exclusion via basic bank account initiatives are having some impact on the researched communities, particularly those who may be loosely categorised as recent arrivals in the UK (see also Chapter Two).

Figure 3.2: Types of bank accounts held by banked migrants

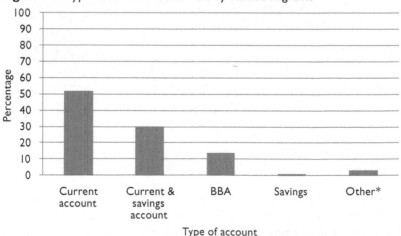

Note: *This category includes those migrants who identified the institutions in which they held accounts rather than types of accounts, including the Islamic Bank of Britain and Tower Hamlets Credit Union.

Source: Questionnaire survey (n=277)

In turn, the kinds of bank accounts held determine the range of services available to account holders. All migrants were asked to identify the banking services they used relating to credit and savings (to be discussed in greater detail later) as well as ATMs, internet banking and direct debits. The main banking service accessed and highly valued by migrants was the provision of debit cards that could be used to withdraw money from ATMs. Nearly three-quarters of all banked migrants used ATMs, ranging from a high of 87 per cent among Bulgarian participants to 63 per cent of Somali men and women. Within this context, the recent decision by some high street banks to start charging BBA account holders for the usage of ATMs is highly problematic. Reflecting the continued importance of face-to-face banking, internet banking facilities were only used by a handful of migrants, predominantly by migrants from Poland, Bulgaria and Brazil, who had prior transnational experiences of using these services in their home countries.

Banking practices related to the payment of utility bills further reflected the fact that, for many, bank accounts functioned primarily as a vehicle for receiving wages and/or benefits. As such, just under half (47 per cent) of banked migrants paid their household bills in cash, with a further 11 per cent using a combination of cash and direct debit and 10 per cent a combination of other payment methods including cash (see Table 3.3). In fact, the use of direct debits was most prevalent among Brazilian migrants, accounting for a quarter of participants; this was again partly attributable to a continuation of transnational banking practices. Marilena explained that she had set up direct debits to pay bills in both her native Brazil and in London because "it is difficult to be handling cash, and then you feel tempted to spend, although with the debit card is the same, perhaps a little less. I myself don't use cash much. I use a lot of direct debit and then the debit card. [I also used these] in Brazil." At the other end of the spectrum, the majority of Turkish migrants (94 per cent) preferred to pay household bills in cash, which, in the opinion of some, afforded them greater control over their household budgets (see Table 3.3).

Broader explanations for the limited usage of accounts and associated banking services centred around three factors. Household poverty emerged as particularly significant, especially in the Somali community, with migrant women like Fardiuso arguing that once all her living expenses were put together she had little if anything left in her account to manage:

"I get DSS money. I don't have any other income, so I just use that every two weeks and spread it till the next payment.

Table 3.3: Payment of household bills by banked migrants, by percentage

	Brazilian (n=99)	Bulgarian (n= 53)	Polish (n=27)	Somali (n= 68)	Turkish (n=30)	TOTAL (n=277)
Cash	42	21	70	46	94	47
Direct debit	21	13	11	8	0	13
Cash and direct debit	19	17	0	4	0	11
Cheque	3	2	0	1	0	2
On-line bill payment	3	2	4	0	0	2
Pay point at shops or Post Office	0	2	11	21	0	6
Key payment/ top up payment	0	0	0	9	0	2
Combination of above, including cash	6	30	4	8	3	10
Combination of above, excluding cash	6	13	0	3	3	6

Source: Questionnaire surveys

> When my money comes through, I take it out on the day. I take out all the money. The first thing I always do is pay off any debt I owe, for example the electricity/gas card. Top them up, get bus pass, and then do the house shopping. I try and get all the essentials, and if I have anything left over I bring it home and keep it at home, using it as and when I need it. Usually there is just change left. Most of the time, there is nothing left and I go into negative with my top-ups or end up borrowing on them."

A lack of proficiency in English further prohibited more effective usage of banking services (see also McKay and Winkelmann-Gleed, 2005:Atkinson, 2006). Again, taking the Somali community as an example, migrants were asked to identify their language skills at the time when they arrived in the UK and at the time of the research. The corresponding figures for the two time periods were as follows: 57 per cent and 6 per cent identified their English language as non-existent, 38 per cent and 36 per cent as basic, 4 per cent and 28 per cent as adequate, and 2 per cent and 30 per cent as fluent. Lula, a Somali woman who held a current account, said that she hardly ever used it because: "I don't know the language and I would face difficulties when making deposits and transfers, so I don't use it. When I go to the bank, I can't even tell them what I want from them, so that's why." It is apparent that learning a new language is a long and arduous process, especially for those who are juggling multiple responsibilities, as highlighted by the experience of Lula above (see also Chapter Four).

Limited interactions with banks were also attributable to what may be best described as a fear of surveillance. It is important to acknowledge that while many migrants focused on the advantages of banking inclusion, some argued that bank accounts were another instrument to keep them under surveillance. Stories of banks being patrolled by immigration officers abounded in the Brazilian community. In turn, a number of Somali participants argued that it was important to withdraw all benefit payments as soon as they arrived in accounts not simply so as to be able to meet everyday living expenses, as discussed above, but also because if too much money accumulated in these accounts then "the government" would reassess the amount of welfare people needed to get by. In the opinion of Awale, from Somalia: "The government calculates how much you need to live on, with all your expenses, and there is nothing left over." Similar opinions were evident among Turkish participants and explained a commonplace practice whereby wages received in cash were kept at home, while benefit payments were deposited in bank accounts (as discussed earlier). Many attributed the desire to keep the two separate because of fears of being "found out" and being questioned about their eligibility to claim these benefits, given their participation in the wage economy. As Hatice acknowledged, "I get cash in hand. The benefits go into my account. And when we need that we go to the cash point and withdraw it. What's left stays in the account and what's left in our hand [from our wages] stays at home."

Unbanked migrants

A minority of migrants – comprising 13 per cent of all men and women – were unbanked, with Brazilian migrants making up the bulk of this population (see Figure 3.3). These migrants included both those who had never attempted to open an account and could be classified as the self-excluded (91 per cent) and those who had been refused accounts (9 per cent). This said, it is important to bear in mind that those who identified themselves as falling into the former category often self-excluded because of a perception that their applications to open bank accounts would be rejected. Immigration status emerged as a significant explanatory variable, in addition to the highly mobile and transient nature of migrants' lives in London and their stage in the migration cycle, in explaining the unbanked status of some migrants.

Figure 3.3: The composition of unbanked migrants by nationality

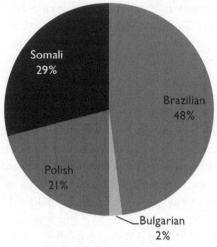

Source: Questionnaire surveys (n=42)

Taking these in turn, the immigration statuses of the men and women across the five communities were remarkably diverse. They included those who had claimed asylum upon arrival in the UK, some of whom had subsequently been afforded refugee status (comprised mostly of Somali and Turkish participants), those who had entered as students and tourists (predominantly Brazilian migrants), and those who as nationals of the (expanded) European Union could live and work in the UK (mostly Polish and Bulgarian migrants but also including Somali and Brazilian migrants who had acquired European nationality prior to moving to London) (see Chapter Four). Furthermore, an unverifiable number were irregular, primarily because of expired tourist visas or the non-renewal of student visas, but also those who had entered the country using false passports and documents (to be discussed later). Indeed, it is important to be aware of the diversity of immigration status that exists within specific communities. Thus, for example, Van Hear (2004) documents that Somalis have been the third most numerous African nationality to apply for asylum in Britain since the 1970s, such that by 2000, the UK received nearly half of all Somali applications for refuge in Europe. Reflecting the tightening of British asylum and refugee policies, the tendency to grant refugee status to Somali applicants in the 1980s was replaced by temporary status in the early 1990s and a refusal of asylum status by the late 1990s (Sporten et al, 2006). As a result, the immigration status of the UK Somali community ranges from British citizens, refugees and asylum seekers, persons granted exceptional leave to remain, undocumented migrants and people granted refugee status/dual nationality in a European country who have subsequently moved to the UK (Vertovec, 2007).

Within the context of banking access, the main obstacle that irregular migrant men and women faced was a lack of appropriate identification documents, a finding corroborated by wider research (see Chapter Two; see also Herbert and Hopwood Road, 2006). As highlighted in Chapter Two, the main forms of identification required by banks are proof of identity and address (Toynbee Hall, 2008). Focusing on the former first, it seems counter intuitive perhaps that migrants would not possess passports given that they cross international borders to enter the UK. Yet, as Spencer (2011) argues, changes in immigration policies and border control relating to the implementation of visas and carrier sanctions have effectively made it more difficult for some groups including asylum seekers to get to the UK without recourse to forged documentation and/or the use of smugglers. Thus, while some asylum seekers arrive without any kind of photographic identification, or dispose of it at the port of entry, others purchase false documents. For example, a Turkish migrant, Ayse's husband, purchased a false passport and visa to migrate to Germany, having been refused a Turkish passport because of his failure to complete mandatory military service. He was then smuggled into the UK from Germany in 1999 "on the back of a lorry". In turn, while a number of Somali men and women did hold passports, these were not internationally recognised, given the categorisation of Somalia as a stateless nation. Reflecting on the different value attached to different passports, Dirive Adnan, a Somali man, recounted that his applications to open a bank account in "several banks" were unsuccessful partly because he was presenting his Somali passport, which was rejected as having "no value" (see also Chapter Four; Vasta, 2008).[5] Furthermore, despite public policy initiatives for unbanked populations to use alternative identity documents to open bank acocunts – including travel documents issued to refugees which bear a photograph and copy of the holder's signature as well as the official stamp of the Home Office – these are not universally accepted by all banks/bank branches (see Chapter Four; see also Herbert and Hopwood Road, 2006). This was evident in the case of a Somali man who participated in the questionnaire survey who had had his application to open an account turned down on the grounds that his papers were insufficient proof of his identity despite bearing, in his words, "pictures" or his photograph. Importantly for other (predominantly Brazilian) migrants who *did* possess internationally recognised passports and had entered the country legally, but who had since become irregular, the demand for passports was often interpreted as a verification of whether they had the right to remain and work in the country (see also McKay and Winkelmann-Gleed, 2005; Vasta, 2008). The fear of detection and deportation was strong enough to deter them from even approaching banks, while others engaged in a range of strategies to procure appropriate documentation (see Chapter Four).

In turn, irrespective of immigration status, the transience of migrant populations, as well as their living arrangements, proved to be problematic in terms of providing proof of address. The majority of migrants in this study lived in rented accommodation accessed directly from landlords (51 per cent), from local councils (22 per cent) or through an agency (18 per cent). Those who rented directly from landlords (comprising 64 per cent of Polish and 40 per cent of Brazilian migrants, for example) reported that tenancy agreements that could be used to verify their address were rare (see also McKay and Winkelmann-Gleed, 2005). For other migrants who were sharing accommodation with (usually co-national) non-family (accounting for a quarter of all participants), providing proof of address was difficult as rent payments often included utility bills. Indeed, a common sentiment expressed by Amaldo, a Brazilian migrant, was that the demand made by banks for proof of address made little sense given the high levels of residential mobility among migrants:

> "... the banking system here needs to be improved. Like, they collect a lot of data, and a lot of useless data, such as ... for instance, some will ask for your last three addresses, and in a city where you move houses often, where you share accommodation and move out every three months, and you can use other people's address then. So they give too much importance to something that is easily forged."

Stage in migration cycle was also important in explaining banking exclusion and emerged as particularly important in understanding banking exclusion among Polish migrants, which was perhaps surprisingly high given both their status as EU citizens as well as the banking initiatives put in place specifically to attract this clientele (see Chapter Two; also Anderloni and Vandone, 2006). While banking exclusion was partly attributable to the fact that a significant number of Polish migrants earned their wages in cash (as discussed earlier), which was quickly spent on everyday living expenses – Andrez, for example, admitted that "I spend my money as soon as I earn it" – others were unsure about their future plans and how long they would stay in London. As such, they were ambivalent about the importance or relevance of banking services for them, as articulated by one young man: "I don't need it [a bank account] really. I arrived recently so it's a bit early to decide for me ... I still don't know how long I will be here." These findings are corroborated by the prevalence of temporary and circular migration among A8 migrants as well as uncertainty about the duration of stay (Sumption and Somerville, 2010). This may suggest that, as relatively mobile migrants, these men and women do not value financial integration into British society as highly as other migrants.

Surviving the city: the importance of savings and credit

Having detailed migrants' access to, and usage of, banking services, the focus now shifts to savings and credit. Migrant men and women's financial needs change over the migration cycle such that while the initial preoccupation may be to secure access to banking services, subsequent phases are associated with more diverse financial needs related to opportunities to save and access affordable credit (Anderloni and Vandone, 2006; Rahim et al, 2008). Dependent upon the cultivation of more complex relationships with financial institutions, these financial resources are critical to wealth building and asset accumulation (Rhine and Green, 2006). This said, it is clear that in comparison to banking, the saving and credit-related practices of individuals and households were simultaneously shaped by both greater exclusion from formal services as well as personal choice, need and/or preference and reflect a more varied interaction with formal financial services (Leyshon et al, 2004; Atkinson, 2006; Byrne et al, 2007).

Saving practices

"I am saving to have enough to pay for my and my wife's coffin. [I] don't want my family to borrow money from others to cover my funeral expenses – it would hurt my pride that I have worked for ages and yet do not have enough to cover expenses arising from my death." (Ali, Turkish migrant)

Almost irrespective of whether they were able to save or not, the majority of migrant men and women emphasised the importance of saving. Furthermore, and despite the economic marginalisation noted earlier, 59 per cent presented themselves as savers, which reflects the adoption of strategic money management practices by these men and women, who effectively chose to save rather than to spend or consume (Rutherford, 2002). As highlighted in Table 3.4, the ability to save varied along both nationality and gender cleavages. Turkish, Brazilian and Polish migrants exhibited the highest propensity to save (87 per cent, 73 per cent and 64 per cent, respectively), with the rate falling to 54 per cent of Bulgarian and just over a quarter of Somali participants. While roughly the same proportion of male and female migrants saved (58 per cent and 59 per cent, respectively), women emerged as being more likely to save in all but two of the communities. This may be explained by gendered (financial) norms whereby women are expected to engage in prudent and less risky financial behaviour, which is cognisant with the fact that they bear primary responsibility for social reproduction. Thus, unlike men such as Jibril Osman from Somalia, who argued that "I've never really respected money to save, I like to worry about today rather than tomorrow", female migrants emphasised the importance of saving. Indeed, Celina, who had married in London, felt that her ability to save was being compromised by her husband:

> "Before my lifestyle was that I was on my own and was my only expense. I would eat at work, I would go to bed early to wake up early to do cleaning, so I had one rhythm. Today I have another. I pay for two people's expenses because my husband is studying. He is doing a degree at university. My rhythm has adapted to his, so I spend a lot more. He does not contain his wish to have things, and I think that is a cultural thing, so I am spending more now."

Broader research suggests that savings patterns are shaped by a complex interplay between motivations for saving, types of savers and savings, as well as the mechanisms used to save (Rutherford, 2002; Kempson and Finney, 2009). A common typology used to study savings practices sorts individuals and households into three categories, namely rainy day, instrumental and non-savers (Rowlingson et al, 1999; Kempson and Finney, 2009). Rainy day savers are identified as being 'dedicated savers', who save actively and regularly, and can build fairly substantial levels of savings that are not earmarked for any specific expense. Instrumental savers are more 'circumstantial savers', who save to spend for specific purposes and engage in saving-up practices, whereas non-savers do not perceive themselves as savers, have little or no savings and no plans of saving (Rowlingson et al, 1999). This said, non-savers may engage in activities such as putting money aside for regular household expenditure including bills (Kempson, 1998).

Table 3.4: Savings profile of migrants, by percentage

	Brazilian	Bulgarian	Polish	Somali	Turkish	TOTAL
	(n=119)	(n=54)	(n=36)	(n=80)	(n=30)	(n=319)
Can save	73	54	64	28	87	59
Cannot save	24	46	28	72	3	38
No response	3	0	8	0	10	3
Gender and savings:	(n=87)	(n=29)	(n=23)	(n=22)	(n=26)	(n=187)
Male savers	66	54	59	40	87	58
Female savers	81	53	71	11	87	59
Savings per month:	(n=87)	(n=29)	(n=23)	(n=22)	(n=26)	(n=187)
Less than £100	17	31	35	45	73	33
£101-£200	9	31	13	5	27	15
£201-£300	14	17	4	18	0	12
£301-£400	39	14	48	18	0	28
£401-£500	2	7	0	5	0	3
£501-£600	7	0	0	5	0	4
£601-£700	1	0	0	0	0	0.5
£701-£800	7	0	0	5	0	4
£801-£900	0	0	0	0	0	0
£901-£1,000	2	0	0	0	0	1
More than £1,000	1	0	0	0	0	0.5

Source: Questionnaire surveys.

Deploying this framework, and using levels of saving as a proxy, a minority of the migrant men and women who classified themselves as savers could be identified as rainy day savers. These predominantly comprised Brazilian migrants, who saved relatively larger sums than migrants from the other four communities (see Table 3.4). This was perhaps best exemplified by a young Brazilian man who participated in the questionnaire survey who was saving £220 a week out of a total wage packet of £300 earned by working a six-day, 65-hour, week. Clearly, saving such a significant proportion of weekly or monthly wage packets required careful management of household economies, which was achieved through both the intensification of work (working longer hours, having more than one job, living in dual-income households) as well as cutting back on consumption (in relation to, for example, food, accommodation and transport costs) (see Chapter Four; also McIlwaine et al, 2006; Datta et al, 2007a). It was evident that migrants who were determined to save were deploying both sets of strategies. As highlighted earlier, 14 per cent of migrants had additional jobs while a quarter lived in dual-income households. This included men like Asen, from Bulgaria, who regularly managed to save more than half of his weekly wage packet of £300 by holding down two jobs as a porter and a cleaner (and indeed a third job before the 2008–10 economic downturn), as well as cutting back on his expenditure. As he went on to say: "I [have] very simple needs, really. And my accommodation fee is very reasonable, as I live with other Bulgarians and pay for my bed and the price for the bills is included in my rent." Other strategies revealed shopping around for the best deals, including those related to food. Turkish migrants, for example, preferred to shop in Turkish shops or "warehouses", which were cheaper "than the big English supermarkets", in the opinion of Ali. The imperative to save also impacted upon the social life of migrants, with younger migrants in particular complaining that it was so expensive to socialise in London that they had had to restrict themselves to "living the good life", as Carina from Brazil put it, on weekends (see also Datta et al, 2007a).

The majority of savers, in fact, fell into the instrumental savers category and included those who saved small amounts of money as and when their circumstances permitted. With the exception of Brazilian migrants, significant numbers of men and women from the other four communities saved less than £100 per month, ranging from around a third of Bulgarian and Polish (31 per cent and 35 per cent, respectively), just under half of Somali and three quarters of Turkish migrants (see Table 3.4). The latter, in particular, attributed their inability to accumulate significant savings to low household incomes, which were derived from a combination of wages and/or benefits, as well as household composition. To this end, Ayse, a Turkish woman, reported that:

> "We save small amounts of money and that is spent pretty quick. The children go on school trips, there are birthdays and festivals that we have where I have to get presents for the family, and in the new year I want to send a little money to family in Turkey, so at the end of the day, what little is saved is spent. That is how it is, honestly. The savings are just kept at home. It's so little, it is not worth the trip to the bank."

Furthermore, notwithstanding efforts to save, instrumental savers commented upon the fragility of their savings, such that money which had been carefully accumulated could be spent on unexpected expenses. While Lucila from Brazil was proud of her ability to carefully plan her monthly expenditure and aimed to save between £100 and £150 per month out of wages earned looking after two young children, she often spent her savings, with the result that "I rarely get to the end of two months having saved £300. I always end up using it." In fact the only time that she was able to accumulate savings was if the children she looked after fell ill and she was required to work longer hours.

Those migrants who categorised themselves as non-savers, including nearly three quarters of Somali men and women, attributed this predominantly to unemployment and benefit dependency.[6] Presenting an overview of the Somali community in London, Dirive Adnan argued that: "the community can save when someone has a surplus in money, but most of our people do not work, they get benefits instead … Somalis cannot save because … they just live on benefits and I don't think that this is enough to save … if they get £40 a week or £50, this will maybe cover their transport, and bills and living expenses, there would be nothing remaining to save." Corroborating Dirive's account is the fact that even while a number of Turkish households were also in receipt of benefits (see Table 3.2), significantly more Turkish participants identified themselves as savers in comparison with Somali migrants (87 per cent as opposed to 28 per cent). This may be explained by the fact that in the former community, benefits were supplemented by wages earned in the ethnic economy. In turn, the struggle of making ends meet in Somali households that relied solely upon benefit income was evident in Asha Addillahi's and Lula's accounts of how they managed on meagre resources. Both women commented that they withdrew all their benefit income the day it arrived in their POCAs and spent the bulk of their money on the same day. For example, Lula used her money to "pay the outstanding bills, make top-up for mobiles for kids, get them their bus pass. It is £10.30 a week for the girl. When the kids come home every kid goes into a room, turns on the lights to study, so the bills are high. In the winter we always have the heater on all the time. I don't like for them to feel disadvantaged." In her opinion she would only be able save when her children grew up and got jobs themselves.

The motivations to save among all migrant men and women revolved around life cycle expenses, emergency as well as investment opportunities that are also identified in broader research (Rutherford, 2002). It is important to acknowledge that while many of these needs can be anticipated, they can nonetheless be a source of great anxiety and worry (Rutherford, 1999). Instrumental savers in particular saved in order to meet both living costs, as identified earlier, as well as saving up for significant life course events. Saving for children emerged as particularly important in a number of migrant households. For some, like Ali, this related to paying for the education and upkeep of his three daughters, who were living with him in London, whereas others were saving to send money back home to their children, highlighting their own transnational parenting practices and the sacrifices that they made in order to support their children (see also Datta et al, 2007b). Just under half of all participants (46 per cent) had dependent children; 85 per cent lived with their children in the UK while 15 per cent had left their children behind in their home countries. A transnational father, Andrzej, a Polish man, said: "tell me about it [how hard it is to save] … you heard of squats? It's a good way to save money [which would otherwise be spent on rent] … anyway, I cope, even when I am out of job … and I have to send money to [my] kids, so I know how to cope." Similarly, Valerio, a Brazilian man, "always sent £300 on average per month to my family in Brazil, to support my two children, a daughter from the first marriage, and a son from the second. So I do not lead a life of luxury here. I support them, and I save to go to Brazil for visits." The practice of saving for others also included saving for other family members, particularly parents, who were often the recipients of remittances (discussed in greater detail in Chapter Six).

Wider research recognises that savings are critical in enabling individuals and households to avail themselves of investment opportunities and wider asset accumulation that facilitate social mobility. In this study, where migrant men and women were accumulating significant savings, these were earmarked for the acquisition of financial and physical assets either in London or more usually in their home countries (see Chapter Six). Indeed, savings made in London potentially enabled migrants to rebuild transnational assets that had been eroded to fund migration. Rita, who had "basically spent savings of a lifetime to get here [to London]" remarked that she would be "happy if I manage to recoup the money I spent coming over here, like, to take it back, even if it is through an investment, such as in a laptop, or a very good mobile phone." The acquisition of other physical transnational assets was also important, such that savings remitted back to home countries were invested in the acquisition of property, land or businesses (see Chapter Six). This was especially relevant for migrants like Pepa, who planned to return to Bulgaria and was in the process of purchasing a flat there because she did not want "to clean houses forever, that is why I have a back-up [plan] … I bought this flat I am paying for now." Furthermore, other migrants like Kat, a Polish woman, reflected a desire to invest in the UK. In her case, she wanted: "to buy some property here, like you know … for my pension … I will have a pension in Poland also, but here it is much better of course, the pound is very strong … it could work like this: I will be living in Poland but earning money here… that would be good".

While the preceding discussion has highlighted types of savers and motivations to save, the availability of accessible and flexible savings opportunities for poor households is crucial both in terms of inculcating the habit to save formally as well as enabling savings to grow (Vonderlack and Schreiner, 2001). This said, the transaction costs associated with utilising particular (formal) saving instruments can structure the take-up of these opportunities, including arranging and paying for child care, the transport costs incurred in travelling to the saving organisation, and the cost of photocopies, which may be required to open accounts (Vonderlack and Schreiner, 2001). Atkinson (2006) argues that the demand for formal saving mechanisms is driven by choice and shaped by both past savings histories as well as present circumstances. As set out in Chapter Two, the predominant formal savings instruments in the UK range from limited-access bank and building society accounts, National Savings bonds and equity-based products, which may not necessarily suit those on low incomes or those who prefer more sociable forms of saving (Atkinson, 2006). While informal saving methods were evident in the five communities (see Chapter Five), more formal savings instruments included saving in (predominantly) current but also savings accounts (accounting for 60 per cent of savers), with savings deposited in individual, joint and shared accounts (see Table 5.2). None of the migrant men and women interviewed reported having access to Child Trust Fund or Savings Gateway accounts (see Chapter Two). Importantly then, even while a significant proportion of migrants were accumulating savings in bank accounts, the bulk of these were being built up in current accounts (with limited opportunities for growth) with a far smaller number depositing these in dedicated savings accounts.

Credit and debt management

"But without credit, if you don't have credit, no matter where you are, there is no way you can improve your life, because you won't achieve much just by working. To work today is simply to keep alive, to survive. You can't take that step forward without having credit. It is very difficult,

> impossible really, to save money to buy a car or a house, or
> to pay for your education. If you have credit that makes it
> a little easier for you. Of course, you'll have to pay interest,
> but it helps you, credit makes life easier for anyone." (Mario,
> Brazilian man)

In contrast to views expressed about both banking and savings, migrants' views about credit were ambivalent. Some, like Mario, valued access to credit on the grounds that it facilitated consumption, an opportunity to build a credit history in the UK and the acquisition of assets; others pointed to the risk of accumulating significant debts that they would subsequently struggle to pay. In so doing the latter group often presented themselves in a favourable light in comparison with the British-born population, which was characterised as being excessively dependent upon credit. To this end, Kremena, a Bulgarian woman, argued that: "We did not have to borrow any money here and I pray we do not to have to do it in the future. I know this is how we [Bulgarians] are different from them [the British]. This is their asset, lightness of being ... to live on credit." Importantly, the native population was also characterised as using loans for non-essential purposes. For example, Mario related that one of his British co-workers at a restaurant had a credit card ("despite being less educated than me") that he had used to buy a car. He argued that "I'd use the money to improve my life, to study, rather than going round spending this money".

In turn, an examination of migrants' credit-related practices revealed that just under half of the migrant men and women (47 per cent), with some differences between the migrant communities, had taken a loan in the year preceding the research (see Table 3.5). A disaggregation of 'credit' revealed three main types of formal credit: overdraft facilities, credit cards and personal loans. Furthermore, while just over half of the Polish migrants had been successful in acquiring credit from banks in the UK (57 per cent), this was far less evident in the other communities. Correspondingly, none of the Turkish migrants had acquired loans from banks, while 5 per cent of Somali, 17 per cent of Brazilian and just over a quarter of Bulgarian migrants (28 per cent) had done so. As such, loans acquired from informal sources assumed a particular significance in these communities (this is further elaborated upon in Chapter Five). Only two migrants, both Somali, had received loans from the DSS (possibly through the Social Fund) to refurbish their houses.

It is important to acknowledge that the credit-excluded migrants covered by this study comprised both banked and unbanked populations. While unbanked populations have particular difficulties in establishing that they are credit-worthy, banked populations lack access to formal credit that may be attributed to the kinds of bank accounts that they hold (Rhine and Green, 2006). While BBAs support a number of functionalities including debit cards, standing orders and direct debits, the majority offer only limited (up to a maximum of £10) or no overdraft facilities.

Table 3.5: Credit history of migrants, by percentage

	Brazilian (n=119)	Bulgarian (n=54)	Polish (n=36)	Somali (n=80)	Turkish (n=30)
Proportion of migrant men and women who had loans	51	67	19	48	30
Loan size range	£1,500– £20,000	£200– £15,000	Not specified	£150– £5,000	£1,000– £80,000

Source: Questionnaire surveys

Credit-worthiness, in turn, depends on proof of income (as discussed earlier) as well as a credit history, both of which recent migrants may struggle to produce.

It is important to acknowledge that the financial histories of migrant men and women are effectively truncated by transnational migration and that the subsequent interpretation of these 'thin' or non-existent credit histories as a bad credit risk by financial institutions has damaging consequences in terms of access to affordable credit (to be discussed later; see also Theil, 2006). As such, the recreation of financial histories is vital and dependent upon the regular movement of income through bank accounts (McKay and Winkelmann-Gleed, 2005; Atkinson, 2006). Manuel from Brazil pointed out that bank accounts functioned as a sort of "historical record of your life", while his compatriot, Valerio, commented that, once banked:

> "You can build your credit record, a history of movement in your account [that is, transactions made], because here they pay a lot of attention on account movement. It is important because then you kind of account yourself to the state and institutions of how much your financial turnaround is."

Although migrants attempt to create credit histories by means of the movement of income through bank accounts (as described by Valerio), banks may treat certain migrants with suspicion in cases where they are paid informally and therefore put irregular amounts of money in their accounts.

In turn, there was also a perception among the migrant communities studied that the availability of formal credit depended upon the reputation of their community. Wider research suggests that popular perceptions that the majority of migrants are undocumented may mean that banks are reluctant to deal with migrants (Appleseed and Community Resource Group, 2004). Within this research, while European migrants from Poland and Bulgaria commented upon the (at times excessive) availability of credit opportunities in London, Brazilian migrants argued that formal credit opportunities were withheld from them. Taking these in turn, Yana from Bulgaria argued that "everybody uses the credit system here. In London ... there are a lot of possibilities. As for credit, you can take what you need despite the crunch", while Marcin, a Polish migrant, argued that while his bank was not willing to "open a savings account [but] they were pushing me to get a credit card". Having availed himself of a credit card, he then went on to comment that he had been given insufficient explanation of how to use his card, with the result that "I got this credit card from them [his bank] but I'm still not sure when do I pay. All the time or just when I take some shopping on it? I'm not sure how does it work." In contrast, Brazilian migrants argued that banks actively excluded them from credit because of high rates of default within the community, such that banks could not "tell the good ones [credit-worthy Brazilians] apart from the bad ones". Rosana from Brazil, who had been refused a bank loan on two occasions, admitted that this had made her feel like "I am not a good client if the bank won't give me a loan".

The need for credit arose out of expenses incurred in the UK and migration-related expenses, as well as a desire to capitalise on investment opportunities. Partly as the result of the nature of employment in London's low-wage economy, migrant workers often complained that low and (in some cases) irregular wages combined with living in an expensive city often resulted in economic precarity. In such cases, the availability of credit enabled men and women to meet their daily expenses. To this end, Anastas, a Bulgarian man, attributed his debt of £2,500 to period when "I couldn't work – there was no work – that's all. I am on the edge. If one day I do not work, I am under the survival minimum. The minimal payment here is really the minimum. If you do not have that amount, you just cannot survive." Credit acquired in London also enabled the repayment of transnational debts, a significant proportion of which were directly related to migration. As has been hinted at earlier, migration to London was often financed through a combination of savings and sale of assets, as well as loans acquired from a variety of sources. Importantly, the actual cost of moving to London varied in accordance with both the distance travelled as well as the immigration routes into the country. With regard to travel costs, while travelling to London was relatively cheap for European migrants arriving from Poland (often by coach) and Bulgaria, the cost of an air ticket for those from Somalia and Brazil was considerably higher. Yana, who had come to London from Bulgaria related:

> "The initiative to come to London was not very expensive in my case. My ticket was 300 leva (about 150 Euro). I had about £100 spending money.... I paid from my savings, my own savings."

The cost of migrating to the UK also depended upon the immigration routes available to migrants. As citizens of an enlarged EU, Polish and Bulgarian migrants faced no or limited restrictions on their entry to the country. In contrast, Brazilian migrants either had to acquire tourist or student visas to come to the UK, or else acquire European nationality, which then facilitated their entry to the UK. Furthermore, applications for student visas had to be supported by an upfront payment of school fees as well as evidence of financial independence. Counting up all these costs, Josana had accrued a fairly significant debt:

> "I think that despite that I had my friend here and might have had less expenses than others, I think I spent around R$10,000 [£3,000] on my ticket, accommodation, English course and money to live on."

And yet these costs were significantly less than those incurred by migrant men and women who had arrived as asylum seekers, where it was evident that migration led to an erosion of household assets held in home countries. For people like Hatice, who had to acquire false documents in addition to all the other expenses associated with migration, the cost of moving to the UK was £10,000. Given that Hatice and her family had to leave Turkey in a hurry, they borrowed money from her father-in-law and transferred the deeds of their property to him so that he could dispose of it to recoup this expenditure.

Finally, along with savings, credit acquired in London also facilitated the acquisition of transnational assets in native countries. This was especially evident in the Brazilian community, where loans were seen as being a financially astute way of buying property or setting up a business in Brazil, given the relatively lower interest rates charged in the UK in comparison with Brazil. Doing his sums, Jacinto, a Brazilian man, argued that:

> "The interests here are good. They are not that exploitation that we find in Brazil, something like 157% a year, whereas here it is 16% or 17%, so it is very high. Here you borrow £10,000 to pay in seven years, and you'll repay around £12,000, whereas if you borrow R$10,000 in Brazil you will repay R$80,000 or R$90,000. So that's what people do, they borrow money here to invest it in Brazil, to do businesses or buy upfront [rather than on credit/instalments], so best to work and earn here and then have your debts here and then buy and pay for in cash in Brazil. That is what people do, that is what they plan themselves for. I have colleagues at work who have already bought their small farm in Brazil, or a plot of land, or set up a business this way, they'll send the money to their parents' accounts and they will do the business of buying and administering the property. So it is very important to have access to credit, not only in England but the whole of Europe."

Conclusion

The formal financial lives of migrant men and women reflect considerable variation in relation to both different financial services, as well as across and within migrant communities. Banking inclusion was perhaps surprisingly high in all five migrant communities and driven by imperatives such as accessing formal sector employment and benefit payments as well as facilitating consumption. Importantly, a number of migrant men and women also raised the significance of banking in terms of citizenship, such that the ownership of bank accounts not only facilitated access to wider services and resources but also enabled migrants to establish their legitimacy within both migrant as well as host communities. For some migrants at least, banking inclusion has been facilitated by public policy intervention in the form of entry-level bank accounts. This said, a closer inspection of the banking practices of migrants highlighted the prevalence of marginally banked men and women. This was evidenced by the type of accounts that they held, the ways in which these accounts were used, and their everyday financial practices, which, for a significant number, continued to reflect a continued preference for the cash economy.

In contrast to banking, the savings and credit-related practices of migrant men and women were more diverse and at times reflected a more limited interaction with formal financial services providers. Taking these in turn, savings were clearly important to many migrants, although this did not necessarily translate into a capacity to save, given their low incomes and/or benefit dependency, the costs of living in an expensive city, their household composition as well as obligations to families left behind. Identifiable as rainy day, instrumental and non-savers, migrants' motivations for saving were diverse, including everyday expenses and saving for children as well as investment in either the UK or in home countries. While a fairly high proportion of migrants held their savings in current accounts, fewer deposited these in dedicated savings accounts, which meant that opportunities for augmenting savings were not necessarily available. Importantly, financial exclusion among migrant men and women particularly manifested itself in terms of access to formal credit opportunities. While attitudes towards credit were more ambivalent than those relating to banking or savings, and many men and women expressed a desire to avoid getting into debt, other migrants rued their constrained access to formal credit.

This chapter has also illustrated that the take-up of formal banking, savings and credit services varied across and within migrant communities, thus reflecting important inter- and intra-community cleavages. These diverse financial practices were shaped by a number of key and interrelated factors including immigration status, labour market position, transnational financial lives and practices as well as the gender, national and class positions of migrants. Importantly, while some men and women faced exclusion for short periods of time as they navigated the complex financial landscape that they encountered in London, others remained on the margins years after arriving here. Somali men and women emerged as the least well integrated in the formal financial system in terms of banking, savings and credit, which was attributable to lower labour market participation, immigration status, welfare dependency and household composition. Yet, this said, the same community also contained migrants who had arrived in the UK as young children, or from other European countries, and who had integrated far more successfully into the formal financial system than their co-nationals.

It is important to acknowledge that migrants' interactions with formal financial services only provide a partial account of their broader much more diverse and proliferative financial lives. Hidden by the narratives set out in this chapter was the active strategising that was going on behind the scenes, as it were, to both engender inclusion but also cope with exclusion. These strategies were themselves premised upon the ability of migrant men and women to mobilise a range of assets at both local and transnational scales. This is investigated in greater detail in the next chapter.

Notes

[1] Migrant men and women's remittance-sending practices are considered separately in Chapter Six.

[2] Further details of the methodological framework deployed in this study are included in the Appendix.

[3] Given the limited functionality of POCAs (see Chapter Two), POCA account holders are not included in figures on banked populations in this research.

[4] Rogers et al (2009) identify workers employed in food processing, hospitality and low-wage manufacturing as being particularly at risk of worsening conditions due to the high levels of subcontracting, small workplaces, basic contracts and high turnover endemic in these sectors (see also Datta, 2011b).

[5] Turkish participants like Ayse commented on the particular value attached to British passports such that: "people in Turkey and [Turkish migrants in] Germany are awestruck – it is seen as a very big thing there. We have not been back home yet [since acquiring their British passports] but the neighbours say that a red [British] passport is seen as a big thing, men and women want their children married to people with red passports as it is thought to guarantee residence in Britain."

[6] Wider research points to the fact that non-savers may in fact be misrepresenting themselves as they do not recognise the small everyday practices that they engage in as savings (Kempson and Finney, 2009).

FOUR

Strategising for banking inclusion

"I started at the xxxx [high street retail bank]. [I told] a woman at [the] reception ... I needed an account [in order to receive] benefits. First thing she asked was if I had British passport. I told her I only have a travel document. She told me no, case closed, would not even let me go further. I went to a few others, for example, xxxx [second high street retail bank] and xxxx [third high street retail bank]. I got the same response. They did not even pass asking me the first question." (Hafsa, Somali woman)

Despite interventions that have sought to simplify and speed up the process of financial and particularly banking inclusion, many migrants face considerable difficulties in accessing these services, which is attributable to a number of interrelated factors. For a start, the majority of migrants are both unfamiliar with the financial landscape that they encounter in London as well as the particular importance of banking access in negotiating everyday life in the city. While difficulties in both understanding English as well as making themselves understood present further obstacles, undoubtedly the main challenge that some men and women face relates to their immigration status. Within the context of this study, the experiences of migrants such as Hafsa were commonplace, with many men and women approaching two or more high street banks before some were successful in gaining access to banking while others remained unbanked. Significantly, success was clearly dependent upon migrants' agency and their ability to strategise and mobilise a range of financial, social, civic and human assets at both local and transnational scales. Depending on the kinds of obstacles that men and women faced, these strategies also entailed different kinds and levels of legality and illegality and ranged from the use of family and friends to access financial information and provide translation services to activities such as purchasing false identification documents and bank accounts (see also Vasta, 2006, 2008). While illegal strategies exposed migrants to significant risks, potentially leading to a loss of financial resources as well as erosion of social assets, these dangers had to be balanced against the costs associated with banking exclusion, particularly in relation to restricted access to the formal labour market and welfare (see Chapter Three).

This chapter begins by theorising financial inclusion strategies by drawing upon wider debates which have sought to explain how transnational migrants mitigate against the multifaceted and interrelated socioeconomic and political exclusions that they encounter in host societies through the crafting of diverse survival and coping tactics. Utilising these frameworks, it details the strategies that migrant men and women deploy to facilitate access to banking services, highlighting the material and non-material assets or resources that are mobilised to do so. Here, the chapter distinguishes between those strategies that are designed to 'speed up' the process of banking inclusion and those that predominantly arise due to irregular migration status. These are investigated in turn. In the final section, the chapter identifies the risks that some of these strategies entail for migrants, such that even while banking inclusion may be achieved, this may be temporary and exacerbate vulnerability and marginality among migrants. More broadly, these risks highlight the limitations of migrant agency and the fragility of some of their strategies.

Theorising strategies, assets and capitals

Commentators have increasingly drawn attention to the complex 'alternative economic repertoires' crafted by households to ensure their survival in the aftermath of neoliberal restructuring and financial crises across the globe (Leyshon, 2005: 858; Stenning et al, 2010b). Primarily investigated in poorer and transitional economies, these debates on how households have coped in marginal situations by managing their resources in innovative ways provide a framework to theorise the strategies that migrant men and women devise to engender banking inclusion in London. Research emerging from the global South from the 1980s onwards particularly documents the adverse, if spatially varied, impact of neoliberal restructuring upon poorer households, and especially poor women (see Chapter One; see also Stack 1974; Sparr, 1994; Mohan, 2000; Wallace, 2002). Deeply influenced by feminist scholarship, the interrelated economic and social repercussions of these reforms have been shown to be countered by the adoption of both positive 'income-maximising' strategies achieved through the generation of additional sources of earnings, as well as negative 'consumption-minimising' strategies relying upon a reduction of expenditure on food and utilities (see also Chapter Three, this volume; Datta et al, 2007a). Depending upon households' reproductive needs in relation to care, these strategies may be supplemented by the contraction or expansion of households as well as the development of social networks (Gonzáles de la Rocha, 1991; Chant, 1996; Datta et al, 2007a). In turn, research on post-Socialist economies illustrates how the hardships engendered by wider economic and social transformations in Central and Eastern Europe have led to the crafting of alternative market and non-market economic practices by marginalised households as they seek to cope with transition (Piirainen, 1997; Clark, 2002). Predominantly explored within the theoretical framework of 'diverse economies', these strategies comprise a range of activities from formal and informal work to domestic food provisioning as well as activities undertaken in the 'black' or 'grey' economies as households seek to actively 'domesticate neo-liberalism' (Stenning et al, 2010b; see also Gibson-Graham, 1996; Smith, 2000; Neef, 2002).

A key finding across much of this work is that individuals' and households' ability to cultivate repertoires to cope with socioeconomic change is crucially shaped by the assets or capitals at their disposal (Nee and Sanders, 2001). In particular, earlier research on 'positive' and 'negative' strategies has been critiqued for its simplistic conceptualisation of poverty as well as homogenisation of people derived from singular understandings of ethnic, gendered and class identities (Chambers, 1995; Rakodi, 1999). Centred upon a recognition that households and, indeed, individuals rarely rely upon one form of income-earning activity, and that access to income is only one factor influencing wellbeing, the more sophisticated livelihoods framework recognises how poor households obtain as well as command resources in order to withstand short-term shock and longer-term trends, suggesting that those able to access entitlements during times of crisis are often better placed to guard against deprivation (Moser, 1998; McIlwaine and Moser, 2003). Defined as consisting of 'capabilities, assets (stores, resources, claims and access) and activities required for a means of living', the livelihoods framework positions poor households as actors imbued with agency who can potentially mobilise a range of material and non-material assets to secure both their families' and their own futures (Chambers and Conway, 1992: 7). These resources include financial (liquid and non-liquid capital), human–cultural (education and language skills), civic and political, physical (land, housing, businesses) and social (most commonly identified as social capital) assets, which are operationalised at individual, household, family and community scales (Carney, 1998; Bebbington, 1999; Rakodi, 1999; Moser, 2007, 2008).

While Datta et al (2007a) argue that the prominent focus of investigation has been on in situ populations, emerging research on the coping strategies of transnational migrants has developed along three primary lines of enquiry. First, migration is itself conceptualised as a livelihood strategy used by poor households to secure their future through the generation of remittance income. Second, migrants, as embodied beings, are a significant asset in global care chains, potentially enabling better-off native populations to balance the demands of domestic reproduction with economic survival through the employment of predominantly female migrant care workers (Gregson and Lowe, 1994; Cox, 2005; Hochschild, 2000; Datta et al, 2010). Third, and perhaps most importantly, researchers have observed how transnational migrants combine the different forms of assets that they both bring with them *and* accumulate after migration to navigate the multiple exclusions that they face in host countries (Nee and Sanders, 2001; Kelly and Lusis, 2006). Significantly, within the context of transnational migration the focus has been on diverse *capitals* and capital negotiation practices rather than assets per se, even while there are close synergies between these theorisations (Bourdieu, 1983; Kelly and Lusis, 2006; McIlwaine, forthcoming). Primarily explored within the context of various aspects of migrants' integration into the US economy and society (Menjívar, 2000; Hondagneu-Sotelo, 2001), research on transnational migration to Europe has investigated the ways in which migrants accumulate, exchange and transform different forms of capital in response to their exclusion from labour markets, housing, and immigration status (Zontini, 2004; Andreotti, 2006; Evergeti and Zontini, 2006; Datta et al, 2007a; McIlwaine, 2010; Bloch et al, 2011). In so doing, this body of work has been critical in highlighting that, far from being a passive process, integration or accommodation processes are actively contested, resisted and shaped by migrant agency (Vasta, 2008).

In turn, material and non-material financial, social, human and civic assets or capitals are clearly critical in shaping transnational migration outcomes. Exploring some of these in greater detail here, while in its narrowest form, human–cultural capital has been defined in relation to educational qualifications and language competency, it is also more broadly conceived as comprising wider understandings of a society's norms and values, and competence in its culture (Bourdieu, 1983). Both embodied and institutionalised, human capital is particularly important in structuring migrants' access to better paid and valued employment and is therefore an important contributory factor in facilitating social mobility (Nee and Sanders, 2001). Furthermore, human capital can potentially 'continue to accumulate as [migrants] become more familiar with the "ways things are done" in their new home country, [and] therefore take advantage of mainstream economic opportunities' (Vershinina et al, 2011: 107). The financial capital that migrants possess also mediates the speed and extent of their integration into mainstream societies (Nee and Sanders, 2001). Indeed, as discussed in Chapter One, even while the predominant perception has been that migrants and money flow in opposite directions, transnational migrations are increasingly diverse, including people who move with significant financial assets (Li et al, 2009). For others, financial assets may be released through the conversion of non-liquid assets (through the sale of transnational assets such as land, housing and/or businesses) as well as capital payments for investments held in home countries (in the form of rent, for example).

Undoubtedly, social coping practices, or social capital, have absorbed most attention both within wider research on survival and coping strategies as well as work pertaining to transnational migrants in particular (Bourdieu, 1983; Massey et al, 1987; Putnam, 1993, Vershinina et al, 2011). Defined as the 'the networks, norms, and trust that facilitate coordination and cooperation for mutual benefit', a distinction is commonly made between different forms of social capital, including assistance based on shared values, reciprocity, bounded solidarity (through which members of a particular group support each other) and 'enforceable trust', which is backed by certain sanctions (Putnam et al, 1993:167; see also Harris and De Renzio, 1997; Portes, 1998). Importantly then, apart from potentially enhancing individual wellbeing, social capital also incorporates notions of altruism and reciprocal obligation that operates within communities (Olejarova et al, 2003). Thus, while social capital is firmly embedded within family units where high levels of solidarity and trust are evident, it also links families to wider kin, ethnic and non-ethnic communities (Nee and Sanders, 2001; Al-Sharmani, 2010). As such, it is visualised as operating at different scales: 'bonding social capital' is the strongest, connecting family, friends and co-ethnics; 'bridging social capital' refers to the weaker ties that bring together individuals who occupy the same socioeconomic positions; and finally 'linking social capital' affords access to influential people, organisations and associations (Wills et al, 2010). Highlighting the interconnections between different types of capitals or assets, Nee and Sanders (2001) argue that social capital can be conceptualised in much the same way as financial capital in that it potentially generates profit that can be measured in economic, social, and human skills terms.

In relation to transnational migration, social capital is identified as a particularly significant resource given both its potential availability to all migrants as well as being a form of 'capital that is spontaneously produced and reproduced within the institution of the family and the extended family group, and through recurrent social exchanges within the immigrant community' (Nee and Sanders, 2001: 407; see also Hagan, 1998; Poros, 2001). In turn, it is transmitted through networks that operate at three distinct scales: namely, localised connections used to secure economic and social wellbeing within a host country, global connections with diasporic communities living elsewhere, and networks with communities 'back home' (Nee and Sanders, 2001; Mohan, 2002; Collyer, 2005; Wills et al 2010). Broad-ranging support accrues to migrant men and women via these networks from the informational and instrumental, which is usually provided by contacts who have knowledge of host societies and can impart information on how to navigate its socioeconomic and financial institutions, to emotional support, which may be largely derived from families located in home countries (Nee and Sanders, 2001; Castles and Miller, 2003; Ryan et al, 2009). In sum, the mobilisation of social capital is critical in both reducing the cost and managing the risks associated with migration (in terms of gaining entry into host countries, the range of destinations available) as well as subsequent settlement and integration (by providing information and assistance in relation to accessing labour and housing markets) (Massey et al, 1993).

A key debate regarding the capitals that migrants possess relates to how these travel. Broader research details that although assets can be stored and converted, these processes can have negative outcomes. Moreover, migrants' networks are themselves dynamic, becoming both depleted and bolstered over time (Bourdieu, 1983; Hagan, 1998; Vershinina et al, 2011). As discussed in Chapter Three, transnational migration is financed through a complex mixture of savings and loans as well as the disposal of physical assets, such that it potentially entails an erosion of physical and financial transnational assets. Human capital in the form of educational credentials is particularly likely to be devalued upon migration, as evidenced by the widespread deskilling and de-professionalisation that migrants, and particularly asylum seekers and refugees, face in host communities (Wills et al, 2010; Spencer, 2011; Vershinina et al, 2011). Again, the dissipation of social capital is especially debated given that it is embedded both in specific places and communities, with commentators further noting that the ability to mobilise social assets must not be confused with the resources themselves (Coleman, 1990; Putnam, 1996, 2000; Portes, 1998; Olejarova et al, 2003; Collyer, 2005). The availability of both bonding and bridging social capital, for example, is shaped by immigrants' individual connections with their respective communities in host countries, which itself is structured by the size and growth rate of these communities as well as the diversity and scale of their institutions (Nee and Sanders, 2001). Illustrating this, Sumption and Somerville (2010) argue that in the UK migrants drawn from A8 countries may lack support networks if they are recruited directly from their home countries by employers or agencies and are then dispersed in rural locations with little prior knowledge of local labour markets and the availability of services. Their isolation is further exacerbated by poor language skills that limit access to information (although see Ryan et al, 2009; Sumption, 2009; Gill and Bialski, 2011). In addition, neither family-based nor ethnic social capital is necessarily a panacea in terms of shielding migrants from exploitation (Nee and Sanders, 2001). Stressful demands may be made on household members in terms of providing unpaid labour in family businesses, while wider migrant communities may be as much a source of exploitation as support. This was clearly evidenced in this research in terms of the exploitation encountered by Turkish workers in the ethnic economy at the hands of their co-nationals (see Chapter Three). More broadly, the utilisation of familial and/or friendship networks to source employment can narrow the options available to migrant men and women, thus potentially excluding them from more stable, better-paid jobs (Reingold, 1999; Charsley, 2007; Sumption and Somerville, 2010).

Importantly, the coping strategies adopted by migrants are also shown to be refracted through gender, class and ethnic positions as well as being shaped by structural factors including immigration status, length of residence in host countries and language skills. Immigration status is of particular relevance here with commentators highlighting that the increasingly restrictive migration regimes prevalent across a number of advanced economies have exacerbated differences between and within migrant communities (Datta et al, 2009; McIlwaine, 2009; Spencer, 2011; Sigona, 2012). Reflected by both 'civic stratification' as well as a 'hierarchy of citizenship', particular groups of migrants are afforded greater value, freedoms and rights at the expense of others (Morris, 2002; Castles, 2005; Vasta, 2008). As discussed in Chapter One, transnational migrants are sorted into a variety of categories in the UK, with varying rights associated with each in relation to access to work, welfare and social services. Irregular migrants are especially identified as being pushed to the margins of socioeconomic life, and indeed constitute a distinct social class in themselves. The matrix of vulnerabilities that irregularity generates is illustrated by the fact that 'immigration status not only influences where migrants move to in the first place, where they live and their experiences in the labour market, but it [also] affects who they are, how they live and who their friends and colleagues are' (McIlwaine, 2009: 5). Within the specific context of coping strategies, irregular immigration status can deplete social capital, even though undocumented migrants are especially dependent upon this resource, as their access to essential services is increasingly constrained. As such, Engbersen et al (2001:706) argue that 'immigration policy has effectively devalued the social capital of new migrants by increasing the burden that they impose on social networks'. In particular, it is the inability to engage in *reciprocal* activities that is critical in the maintenance of social capital, which can result in the informal exclusion of irregular migrants from their wider communities (Collyer, 2005; Engbersen, 1995; Engbersen and van der Leun, 2001). Far from engendering inclusion, intra-community divisions arranged around immigration status can lead to activities such as the reporting of irregular migrants to the authorities; the 'selling' of employment between co-ethnics and the collapse of a sense of community (Garapich, 2008; Wills et al, 2010; see also Chapter Three). In return, migrants may adopt what have been termed 'counter-strategies', which involve the use of both 'bastard institutions' and a manipulation of identity as they seek to manage their irregular immigration status (McIlwaine, 2010; see also Putzel, 1997; Engbersen, 2001; Broeders and Engbersen, 2007; Vasta, 2008). These strategies entail significant risks that have to be actively managed by migrant men and women, as will be discussed later.

Strategising for banking inclusion

An important elision in debates on how migrants strategise to counter socioeconomic, cultural and political exclusion relates to the strategies that they construct to ensure their inclusion into the financial circuits of host countries. This is the next focus for this chapter. As discussed in Chapter Three, banking exclusion exacerbates and intensifies the wider socioeconomic exclusions that migrant men and women encounter, particularly in relation to securing formal employment and accessing welfare payments, as well as their broader integration into a financialised economy. Thus, migrants have to deal with the obstacles that surround banking access, which primarily revolve around immigration status, language competency, and unfamiliarity with London's financial landscape, quickly and effectively. They do so through the crafting of diverse (counter) strategies and the mobilisation of a range of local and transnational capitals, which they both bring with them and accumulate in London. These include financial, civic, human and social assets in the form of bonding, bridging and linking social capital. The discussion below considers migrants' strategies, turning first to those initiatives that aim to 'speed things up', and second to those strategies derived within the specific context of the management of irregular migrant identities.

'Speeding things up'

> "I had no idea about finances and the banking system. It was not something I thought of. I never thought of this ... anyway I was coming from a third world country, so it is the last thing people care about."(Deeqa, Somali woman)

The difficulties that many migrant men and women face in relation to accessing banking derives from a variety of factors including, most significantly in this context, the human–cultural capitals that migrants possess, both in relation to their language skills as well as their (prior) experiences and knowledge of dealing with financial institutions. Taking these in reverse order, the latter are largely determined by migrants' transnational financial practices, because individuals who are financially excluded in their home countries often underestimate the importance of financial access in the societies to which they migrate (Atkinson, 2006). In this research, transnational banking *in*clusion was particularly low in the Somali community, where only 11 per cent of men and women reported that either they or their families had bank accounts in their native country. The explanations for this were fairly obvious, as explained by Mohammed:

> "Somalia is a broken country. It is too busy fighting to operate banks or any organisation. In Somalia, no one has a bank account. It is a cash society, and there [has] never really been need for bank accounts, additionally this is not helped by the level of corruption among government officials."

While transnational banking inclusion among migrants drawn from the other four communities was more significant, ranging from 78 per cent of Brazilians, 77 per cent of Turkish, 75 per cent of Polish to 74 per cent of Bulgarian men and women, men and women's individual interactions with these institutions varied based upon low incomes and varying levels of trust. The latter was particularly evident in the Turkish, Bulgarian and Polish communities, where migrants reflected ambivalent attitudes towards banks shaped by past experiences of the collapse of major banks in their native countries (see also Atkinson,

2006). Reflecting on the banking crisis in Bulgaria in the late 1990s, which resulted in the loss of household savings, precipitating both a banking collapse as well as a change in government, Asen stated that he, along with most of his compatriots in his opinion, did not "trust institutions, including banks. There were a lot of banks which collapsed, it seems safer now" (see also Gercheva, 2007; Rodrigues de Paula, 2008). It was clear that Polish migrants like Andrez and Marcin shared the same opinion, with the former arguing that while people had no choice but to use banks in Poland, "they don't trust them". Furthermore, even where migrants had extensive previous knowledge and experience of banking, many had underestimated the *particular* importance of banking access in London (see Chapter Three). It is important of course to bear in mind that these experiences were not shared by all migrants, some of whom possessed high levels of human–cultural capital in relation to financial knowledge, having managed complex financial assets in their home countries (Datta, 2011a).

While a lack of prior knowledge of the importance of financial access delayed the process of opening accounts in London, this was further compounded by poor English language skills. Just over half of all participants reported that they could not speak any English at all when they first arrived in the UK while a further 35 per cent had only 'basic' language skills (see also Chapter Three). Indeed, for a number of men and women, the decision to move to London was explicitly linked to a desire, as expressed by Marila, a Brazilian woman, "to [learn] English and speak it with the British accent". However, given the pressures of working long and irregular hours, progress in learning English could be painfully slow, as confirmed by Veronika, a Bulgarian woman, who acknowledged "my English was not very good ... I was attending some English courses for £10 per hour at Earl's Court. But I couldn't go there for long, my work is very scattered during the week and during the day, I could not commit to anything." Wider research identifies three further points regarding language competency in relation to financial inclusion. First, people are just as keen to be understood as to understand, so that even where account holders can speak English they are likely to be worried about their own accent. Second, the technical language of banks and other financial services may be problematic (Atkinson, 2006). Third, where migrants become eligible for more complex financial services such as savings and credit, a lack of competency or confidence in speaking English can become an even more significant barrier (Gibbs, 2010).

These difficulties necessitated the strategic mobilisation of both social and financial assets as migrants attempted to access banking services.

Social capital was a particularly important resource, with the majority of migrant men and women acknowledging the vital role that family members and friends played in mediating the process of opening accounts. Accessed through networks that predominantly functioned at local scales, social capital enabled migrants to obtain information pertaining to the financial services industry, translation services, as well as recommendations of specific bank/branches/tellers known to be sympathetic to migrant clients. Given the dearth of migrant-specific financial advice initiatives (see Chapter Two), it is not surprising that over a third (34 per cent) of all men and women identified family and friends as their main source of financial advice, with a further 10 per cent highlighting the importance of "other people", who included co-nationals as well as employers. Kremena, a Bulgarian woman, spoke at length about the network of friends that she had developed in London, some of whom were her housemates:

> "We had the financial information we needed because we have friends here. I am here because a friend of mine encouraged me. She told me everything will be OK, that she would help and she really did help me. It is difficult to get the right information ... everybody wants money for everything, this is ugly. [But] once you settle, you have a circle, a network, so everybody knows everything the same ... [but] there is a fear to cross borders [seek information outside of immediate circle]."

Given the varied language competencies detailed above, family and friends also provided crucial translation services. Here there were some inter-community differences in terms of whom migrants turned to for help, with some Somali migrants, like Asha Sureiye and Oraji, asking their children to accompany them to banks so as to provide translation services. As corroborated by wider research, children who are born or raised in the UK, and whose language competency far exceeds that of their parents, perform a vital role in negotiating their parents' access to a range of social, economic and political resources even while this may result in an inversion of inter-generational relations (Atkinson, 2006; Bloch et al, 2009). In the other four communities, friends, house-mates and/or other co-nationals provided translation services. Jacinto, a Brazilian man, related:

> "My flat mate helped me. She made an appointment with the bank. I went along and the bank staff checked all my

documents. I showed her the Brazilian passport. I had a letter from the school. It was all OK. She [the bank teller] explained to me all in English and I pretended that I had understood. I signed a paper and she gave me a student account with an overdraft limit of £200."

Besides accompanying new migrants to banks, members of local social networks built up by migrants in London were also instrumental in directing men and women to particular bank branches and indeed even identifying bank tellers who would be sympathetic to their situation. Just under half of all participants (47 per cent) reported that their decision to open an account in a particular bank/branch was shaped by recommendations by family and friends (see also Atkinson, 2006). To this end, Hafsa, a Somali woman, who had initially attempted and failed to open a bank account herself (as described earlier), later relied upon the information relayed to her by her community:

"I finally went to xxxx [high street retail bank]. There was an Asian lady at the Brixton branch. I think she met people like me before and I was told before by people in the community, when I told them the problems I had, to go there as they are understanding people, who will look at you as an individual and check what you have, your situation and then assist you. So I went to them. The lady just asked me why I wanted an account and when I told her [she needed a bank account to receive her benefits], she said OK, just get me proof of your income, utility bill and something with your photo. I showed all this to her and she opened an account for me. So the process of opening an account was not hard, once I found someone willing to hear my case."

Similarly, Soraya, a Brazilian woman who had unsuccessfully tried to open an account with a particular high street bank heard through "word of mouth" that "in Streatham Hill there was this Portuguese staff that would open accounts, and there they accepted the letter and my passport and opened the account for me".

While the above strategies evidenced the mobilisation of bonding social capital, both bridging and linking social capital were also important in facilitating and speeding up banking inclusion. For a limited number of migrants across all five communities, 'contacts' who were loosely defined as friends of friends or co-nationals proved to be useful, particularly in situations where they worked in banks. Asha Abdillahi, a Somali woman, recalled the assistance given to her by a friend who worked in a bank:

> "Her manager went away for three weeks for holiday and she called me and said 'I am managing new accounts while he is away, come and open an account, [it will] not [be] difficult and [not] too much questions would be asked, even without your passport'."

Chance encounters with co-nationals could also work to the benefit of migrant workers, reflecting the existence of bridging social capital. As Lula recounted:

> "When I went to the bank to open an account at xxxx [high street retail bank], I did not know the language, so I was just standing there, looking around and I saw a Somali lady. She had finished doing her business at the bank and was leaving, she knew the language [English] well. I asked her to help me open an account and she interpreted for me, filled out the forms and told me what was going to happen next. Obviously as I did not know the language I could not do anything myself. I had to go back another day to take them some letters they asked for and bills. After a while, like the Somali lady said, they sent letters to my home and [informed me that they had] opened an account for me."

Beyond family and friends, contacts with employers and schools – a form of linking social capital – also enabled banking inclusion. As noted in Chapter Two, letters from employers and schools are important documents that can facilitate banking inclusion. For example, a number of Brazilian employees working for Pizza Express in Central London had been provided with letters of recommendation by their employer that enabled them to open accounts in a high street bank.

Moving on from the social assets mobilised to speed up banking inclusion, for those who were unable or unwilling to enlist the help of family or friends, the availability of financial advisors proved to be important. Commentators have noted the growth of a diverse and flourishing 'migrant industry' both from within as well as outside of migrant communities. This is composed of different actors including recruitment agencies, travel agents, money transfer operators, tax refund offices, ethnic media and food industries, immigration lawyers, advisors and smugglers, who provide services ranging from the licit to the illicit (to be discussed later; see also Garapich, 2008; Spencer, 2011). One subset of this industry focused upon the provision of financial advice that Polish and Bulgarian migrants were particularly likely to use. Explored through in-depth interviews, financial advisors, or 'accountants' as they were referred to by Bulgarian participants, were identified as conationals who had been in London for a longer period of time and who were able to provide language-specific financial services and advice on a range of issues including tax returns, arranging appointments to apply for National Insurance numbers as well as opening UK bank accounts. Pepa, a Bulgarian woman, confirmed that "all my friends have bank accounts. They used different ways to open accounts. Most often they pay a Bulgarian accountant." Again, while the decision to hire these advisors was based upon language difficulties, and the imperative to open accounts as quickly as possible, it was also attributable to either a lack of recognisable identification documents or, specifically in the case of Bulgarian migrants, because national identification documents, the *lichna karta*, had to be translated from Cyrillic script. Furthermore, there was some appreciation that while friends were willing or able to provide translation services, this had its own costs. Reflecting these various motivations, Anastas, who had some knowledge of the UK's banking system having worked as a seasonal agricultural worker in a previous migration, had decided to hire an accountant to open a bank account. He rationalised his decision to do so on the grounds that having secured a job within two weeks of arrival in London, for which he required an account to receive his wages, he needed to:

> "organise all the needed documents quickly ... [I knew] it was not easy to open bank account, I wanted it done fast, that is why I paid for it. It is more expensive to ask a friend or somebody to help you, than to ask an accountant. One has to calculate the money his friend loses – not to go for work, but to spend the day with you going to various institutions. I think eight out of 10 Bulgarians here in London pay to an accountant, and the other two of 10 for sure have somebody very close – parents or children. If it was now, I would do what I had to do at that time very fast – [in] two days I would have everything [I] needed, but in the beginning it was very difficult, one just does not know where to start from. An accountant recommended by my brother helped me. I paid for that, of course. She took me

to the interview for my National Insurance number, and for a bank account."

In other cases, financial advisors were a last resort whose services were sought after migrants had been unsuccessful in opening accounts by themselves, as in the case of Ralitsa, who had had two previous applications to open an account turned down. Two further points are important here. First, the cost of hiring an accountant varied according to the services offered, ranging quite widely from £25 to £120. Second, the use of accountants or advisors effectively meant that migrant men and women had little choice over which bank they opened accounts in. According to Pepa, who was not entirely sure what accountants did: "I think they work with particular banks and have their own business with those banks." This opinion was corroborated by her compatriot, Kremena, who had paid an accountant £25 to provide proof of address, which in turn had meant that "I had no choice of bank, it was the bank they worked with."

Managing irregularity: erasing irregular identities

"It is a pain to be illegal in a country, I have always been illegal, even in the US. I am tired of it." (Alvaro, Brazilian migrant)

Variously labelled as 'illegal', 'irregular', 'undocumented' and 'unauthorised', the irregular migrant population is highly diverse in the UK, comprising men and women who have been smuggled into the country with or without documentation, those who have breached the terms and conditions of their visas by, for example, overstaying or working more hours than they are entitled to, as well as those who have remained in the UK after their applications for asylum have been rejected (Jordan and Duvall, 2002). As highlighted in the previous chapter, a number of migrant men and women had arrived in London without any documentation or using false passports, others had had applications for asylum turned down, while others still had let their tourist and student visas expire. Furthermore, and illustrating the dynamic nature of irregularity, men and women who had regularised their status by the time of the research, could still recall the destabilising impact that previous irregularity had had on all aspects of their lives. For example, Kat, who had migrated to the UK several times prior to Poland's ascension to the EU in 2004, and had even been refused entry on one occasion, admitted that "it is nice [now] not to hear anything about work permits, about [the] Home Office ... when I think about all these years when I thought about the Home Office and how people were afraid ... I mean now it's funny and we forget that but then it was like crazy, people didn't speak on the phone, didn't go to hospitals" (see also Datta et al, 2009).

Partly reflecting both the increasingly restricted opportunities for non–EU migrants to (legally) enter the UK as well as the imperative for the British government to appear to be in control of especially irregular migration, researchers have noted the intensification of both external and internal controls on migration and migrants through initiatives such as enhanced border control, the use of biometric technologies as well as the closer monitoring of migrants once they have entered the country (Broeders and Engbersen, 2007; Vasta, 2008; Wills et al, 2010). In turn, both external and internal controls are reliant upon the 'paper regimes' prevalent in a number of advanced economies (Vasta, 2008). Consisting of different documents including passports and national identity cards, these 'paper regimes' are critical in the construction of national identity and belonging as well as inculcating a sense of duty and responsibility among citizens. However, they are also crucial in actively marginalising those who are deemed as 'others' or 'aliens', particularly in terms of access to work and welfare. In the face of such exclusions, migrants may develop 'innovative identities and cultures of resistances around papers and documentation' as they seek to escape the power of the 'state's gaze by becoming invisible' (Vasta, 2008: 3).

Within the context of banking inclusion, the management of irregularity was effected through the mobilisation of civic, social and financial assets, resulting in strategies that ranged from the legal to the illegal. Considering these in turn, the strategic accumulation of transnational civic assets was evident in the actions of both Brazilian and Somali participants in relation to claiming European citizenship prior to their arrival in the UK. Commenting upon how migrants can challenge the cohesiveness of nation-states, Fitzgerald (2000: 10) argues that migrants 'often live in a country in which they do not claim citizenship and claim citizenship in a country in which they do not live ... Alternatively, they may claim membership in multiple polities in which they may be residents, part-time residents, or absentees.' This finding is supported by research that documents the growing phenomenon of onward and multiple migrations which challenge, as McIlwaine (forthcoming) argues the 'bifocality' or 'dual frame of reference' which has continued to structure much work on transnational migration (Guarnizo, 1997; Vertovec, 2004; Van Liempt, 2011). Thus, even while transnational linkages are often explored within the context of home and host country contexts, contemporary transnational migration may also involve 'in-between' places which are important in terms of migrants' asset accumulation (McIlwaine, 2010). Within the context of inter-European migration, onward migration flows are increasingly diverse comprising of not only (white) European nationals but also refugees and migrants from the global South whose right to this more cosmopolitan mobility is hard earned often taking a number of years to materialise (Van Liempt, 2011).

The migratory routes of a number of Somali and Brazilian migrants reflected these diverse and multiple movements. While some Somali men and women made their way to London directly from Somalia (42 per cent), others came via refugee camps located in neighbouring African states such as Kenya and Ethiopia (25 per cent), the Middle East or a number of European countries including Turkey, Denmark, Sweden, Italy and France (33 per cent) (see also de Montclos, 2003). Furthermore, like other diasporas produced through conflict and displacement, a number of participants corroborated wider research findings that they had little prior information of their end destination and were primarily guided by a search for security, the availability of entry visas, the destinations offered by smugglers, as well as the financial resources that could be mustered up (Van Hear, 2004; Datta, 2011a).[1] In turn, a number of Brazilian migrants had arrived in London via Portugal, Spain, Italy and Germany (55 per cent in total). Again, this is supported by wider research, which estimates that of the 3 per cent of the Brazilian population living outside their country of birth in the 2000s there are significant concentrations in a number of European nations, including – in addition to the countries already identified above – France, Switzerland and Belgium (Padilla, 2011). Importantly, unlike Somali migrant men and women who had ended up in other European countries almost by default, a number of Brazilian migrants had deliberately migrated to these countries where entry was relatively easy and/or where there were opportunities to secure European citizenship (see also McIlwaine, 2009). It is clear that the Brazilian state has used its status as an emerging power to intervene on behalf of its citizens living abroad. This is evidenced by a number of bilateral and multilateral negotiations, including the 2003 Lula agreement between Brazil and Portugal that has sought to regularise irregular Brazilian migrants living in Portugal, and vice versa (Padilla, 2011). Perhaps unsurprisingly, those migrants who could avail themselves of opportunities to acquire European nationality had done so. These included Jurema and Mario, whose respective grandparents were Italian, and Jacinto, who had a German passport. Indeed, Rita, a Brazilian woman, reflected that "all of the Brazilians I know here have a European passport, except me and another friend. All in my circle have double [dual] nationality. But it is true, it [a Brazilian passport] can make life a little difficult."

The motivations to engage in onward migrations to the UK varied between Somali and Brazilian migrants. Among the former, migration to London was linked to a desire to reunite families (which had been fractured across transnational spaces as different family members had settled in different places), coupled with a higher regard for the British education system, as well as perceptions that London as a multicultural city would be more accepting of Muslim migrants (see also Van Liempt, 2011). This included men like Abdi Khadar, who had left Somalia for Dubai, then moved to Denmark, where he had lived for five years, before migrating to the UK to join his siblings who had previously moved here. His compatriots, Ali Hasan, Abdifateh and Zahara, had followed similar trajectories, although they had come to London via Sweden, France and Italy, respectively. Brazilian migrants rationalised their decisions to migrate to London because of perceptions that employment opportunities were more readily available here, the relative strength of Sterling in relation to other currencies, as well as further education opportunities, with a number of men and women expressing their desire to improve their English language skills (as discussed earlier; see also Margolis, 1998; Evans et al, 2007). Encapsulating some of this, Jacinto had moved to London from Germany because "the Germans are very closed ... even being a direct descendant of Germans. They are closed to foreigners. They treat me like a foreigner, not as a German. I don't know why. Maybe I went to the wrong places."

Importantly, of course, once in possession of European passports, migrants were able to engage in legal onward migrations, thus relieving themselves of the fears and anxieties associated with being irregular. European passports also enabled an invisibility, or what Broeders and Engbersen (2007: 1598) refer to as an 'obliteration of legal identity'. Brazilian migrants in particular reported that their nationality was often linked to irregular migration status by authorities. Wider research confirms the different values attached to different passports and the varying rights and freedoms associated with these (Vasta, 2008). For example, Jacinto reflected that "[my] Brazilian passport does not exist for me here, only when I go back to Brazil. There is not a single rubber stamp on it. If I use the Brazilian passport here they think I am an illegal, so I only use the German passport" (see also Vasta, 2008). In turn, European passports also played a pivotal role in securing access to bank accounts in the UK. Again, these passports were often used in preference to Brazilian passports to open accounts because of migrants' perceptions that bank staff were wary of accepting the latter as proof of identity. Rosana, who held dual nationality, recalled what had happened when she had attempted to use her Brazilian passport to open a bank account:

> "The guy who saw me at the bank, he took all my documents in, had a look, and came back, but then I was not dressed up, I was dressed casual, and he said 'I am very sorry' and that he could not open the account because I did not have proof of address, but I think there was something else too. So, I went back home and returned two days later to this same bank, xxxx [high street retail bank], and took in my Italian passport and saw the same guy. He then said it was OK and that I could open the account, but then I did not want to open it there any more. I simply said that I was the same person who had come in with the Brazilian passport two days earlier. The British do not know about the possibility of one holding dual nationality, so a person can actually have two passports, so I don't know whether he thought the Brazilian one was fake or what and then declined to open the account, but then when he saw the Italian, he said it was OK. But then I did not want the account there. I had already meant to open an account with xxxx [another high street retail bank]."

Ironically, when she subsequently opened a bank account, she "did not bother showing the Brazilian passport. I did not want the hassle of the first experience."

For those who could not mobilise transnational civic assets and acquire European nationality, a second strategy to facilitate banking inclusion was through the sharing of bank accounts. Even while Polish and Bulgarian men and women reported that they had never heard of anyone sharing accounts (and often confused this with joint accounts held with family members), Somali, Turkish and Brazilian migrants all confirmed that they had either heard of this practice or engaged in it themselves. Investigated primarily through in-depth interviews, the need to share accounts arose because of a lack of appropriate documents again, as explained by Jibril Osman: "the Somali community, because we are mostly immigrants, asylum seekers and so on, we do not have all the papers needed, so if you don't know the right channels you have to share an account". This research uncovered both migrants who were depositing their wages in someone else's account as well as migrant account holders who were sharing their own accounts. Indeed, in a limited number of cases, accounts were shared with more than one person. Soraya, a Brazilian woman, reported that she had "lent" her account to three friends because "they don't have the papers, their visa has expired and they can't open a bank account". Furthermore, while the majority of migrants presented this as a temporary arrangement until they had secured the documents necessary to open their own accounts, migrants like Amaldo, a Brazilian man, had used his friend's account for two years before he opened his own account.

Sharing was premised upon the availability of banked family members or friends who were willing to participate in this activity, and was therefore largely dependent upon the social networks or capital at migrants' disposal. Although investigations of social capital have often tended to focus upon families, highlighting the density and strength of familial bonds in comparison with other relationships, more recent research has identified the importance of friends and friendship networks in facilitating migration and settlement in host countries, particularly within the context of what may be termed as elite migrations (Collyer, 2005; Conradson and Latham, 2005; Ryan et al, 2009; Gill and Bialski, 2011). Interestingly, within this study the older, more settled Somali and Turkish communities reflected on the importance of familial bonds, including Ayse, a Turkish woman, who had migrated to London from Turkey. Having initially planned to emigrate to Germany, where many of their family members lived, she and her husband had decided to move to London on the basis of reports of an increasingly hostile German state and society and growing numbers of deportations. Yet, she reflected that "in Germany we have lots of extended family. Here we just have a couple of friends. This saddens me – if I have a problem who do I go to? Friends are friends and family is family. It is two different things. A friend no matter how good cannot take the place of family." Somali migrants also stressed the importance of clan networks, with the majority of the men and women either belonging to the Isaaq or Darod clans (see also de Montclos, 2003; Sporten, et al, 2005). In contrast, newer migrants from Brazil, Bulgaria and Poland emphasised the importance of friends. Investigations of friendship networks reflect a common distinction between 'friends from home' and 'childhood friends' and friendships that are formed in host countries (see below; also Datta et al, 2009; Gill and Bialski, 2011). The latter may assume a more instrumental character, being formed for specific purposes and lacking the strength and durability of older friendships. As described, 'an individual may mobilize resources for particular purposes at one point in time, but as objectives change, the source of help may also change ... Sometimes people mobilize networks to attain a particular objective, but these can assume an ephemeral existence; after having fulfilled their objective, they may disband, and a new network may not have the same composition' (Menjívar, 2000: 115).

The sharing of accounts was usually arranged between family members (as in the case of Adey and Daoud Ahmed, both Somali migrants who were sharing their accounts with a niece and a sister, respectively, who had recently arrived in London and needed accounts to receive their wages) or 'close' friends. The latter arrangement was evident in the case of Maurico, who was sharing an account with a friend:

> "[she is] like a sister to me. In the first place, she is a Brazilian friend, that I've known from Brazil, I approached her and said '[I] will only be paid wages through a bank account, so I need an account', and she said, 'no problem, you can use mine', and I even know her PIN, we are very close friends. She is my best friend. At one stage, because I did not have my own account, I left around £6,000 in her account."

Importantly, and in contrast to other research, which points to the 'renting' of bank accounts, this practice was predominantly presented as a social rather than an economic arrangement (see Vasta, 2008). The use of the term 'sharing' was itself symbolic, highlighting the non-economic basis for this arrangement that was depicted as being embedded within dense social networks, trust and reciprocity. This is perhaps unsurprising in as much as some of the migrants interviewed were sharing their own accounts and were keen to present this as an altruistic practice that was shaped by notions of reciprocity, given that they had themselves used someone else's account when they had first arrived in London. Furthermore, those who were depositing their wages and/or benefits into other people's accounts emphasised that they trusted the account holders implicitly.

The sharing of accounts also led to a sharing – or increasingly erasure – of migrants' identity. Migrants across the five communities concurred that while in the past employers could be persuaded to deposit employees' wages in someone else's account while the former went through the process of opening their own accounts, this was becoming increasingly difficult. As such, migrants had little option but to falsify their identities. An example within this context is the experience of Amaldo, a Brazilian migrant who was depositing his wages in his friend's account:

"[one has to] falsify a bill or bank statement and hand it to your boss. The account is in the name of the person like my friend. All you do is change her name and put in yours and hand that in to your boss and the wages will be paid into that account. [I did this] most of the time I have been here until I opened my own account ... [I did not experience any problems as] the payrolls here are very large and they don't check names."

The third strategy utilised by irregular migrant men and women to facilitate their access to bank accounts required a mobilisation of financial assets to purchase false identification documents and/or accounts. Wider research notes that the progressive criminalisation of migration has been accompanied by a concomitant growth in an associated migrant industry that trades in forged documents (as discussed earlier; see also Spencer, 2011). Achieved through the mediation of 'middlemen' who advertised their services in ethnic media – and who, according to Marcia, "made money out of thin air, it is like selling water in the desert" – such services ranged from the sale of National Insurance numbers and bank accounts as well as bank loans. Importantly, these activities often required some form of collusion between bank staff and middlemen. Rafael from Brazil admitted that he had "got the phone number of a Brazilian guy that sells bank accounts from a [Brazilian] magazine. He charges £150. Even without visa he managed to open an account for me. He paid someone who works at xxxx [high street retail bank]. He opened my account for me in one day." In other cases, these middlemen offered integrated services involving first the purchase of National Insurance numbers and then bank accounts. Describing this process at greater length, Celina recalled that her friend:

"got in touch with a person [who had advertised his services] in xxxx [a Brazilian magazine]. The middlemen did get all these documents for me, and then a few weeks later we met outside Holborn station for him to go to the bank with me, and I realised, from seeing the bank manager, that he was well aware of what was going on. Even without being able to speak much English, I could understand. I remember he asked me, when I showed him the National Insurance number I had bought, he asked whether it was mine, and I said 'Yes', without knowing what I was supposed to say, but then he checked this information on his computer and I could see from his face that he could tell it was not mine, as if he was saying 'Well, it is not yours, were you not aware of that?', so the paper I had on me had my name on it, but the number must belong to somebody else. But he opened the bank account all the same, I paid about £100 to the Brazilian guy who was the middleman. That is what he does for a living, and through him I opened the account, and I thought it great because I had a full current account [not a basic bank account]. And I think they've [the British authorities] lost control over this because the number of Brazilians who have these National Insurance numbers is very high."

As an illustration of the similarities in the ways in which financial advisors, accountants and middlemen worked, the charge for opening accounts varied and generally escalated according to the number of banking services that migrants required (as discussed earlier; see also Broeders and Engbersen, 2007). Thus, as Marcia, a Brazilian woman, explained:

"Today [the cost of opening an account], it is around £200, £250, £150. It depends on the type of account that you want. They will ask you that. Like, 'Do you want an account with [ATM] card?', and cost goes up according to what you want the account to have."

Risky (counter) strategies?

"When I arrived, this colleague in school gave me a lot of information about what was needed to open an account. I had this idea that I did not want much contact with Brazilians here but he warned me that there was no point in trying to get away and that Brazilians here would be both a source of help as well as problems. (Guilherme, Brazilian migrant)

It is important to acknowledge that some of the strategies, and in particular counter strategies, that migrant men and women deployed to engender banking inclusion entailed significant risks. In particular, but not exclusively, these risks related to strategies that verged on or involved illegal activities such as the sharing of accounts, purchase of identification documents or bank accounts.[2] The most commonly identified risks that migrants highlighted in relation to the sharing of accounts was money getting 'stuck' in accounts and/or account holders absconding with the money deposited by migrants. Indeed, even while the majority of men and women who engaged in this practice generally voiced positive experiences (as described earlier), there was widespread awareness of such incidents, as confirmed by Celina, a Brazilian migrant, who said that "we know that this happens a lot here. I have friends who have been swindled in all possible ways." Similar stories were also told by Somali migrants like Daoud Ahmed, who recalled that when he had experienced difficulties in opening an account that he needed to secure a job he had been advised by co-nationals to share an account, and he had "ended up using this guy that I met, his account to get my wages". Although this arrangement had worked well in the beginning, he then encountered significant problems when the account holder refused to hand over his savings to him:

> "Yes, I could not find my money. He [the account holder] would not give me my money. I only used to take out what I used and leave the rest in there as savings each month. When I finally asked for my money, the man dragged his feet and would not give me my money. For months I kept asking him. I had to slowly get it from him. He would say 'I only have £100' one month, then next month I come back and I say, 'Look, I need you to give me something.' I did this for years. After when there was about £500 left, it was getting really bad, and I had to just leave it. There is nothing you can do really. I just left it."

In more extreme cases, account holders absconded with all the savings that migrants had deposited in their accounts with no prior warning. This was evidenced by the experience of Joel, an irregular migrant from Brazil. He had been sharing an account with his flat-mate, Arturo, into which he deposited the wages that he earned from working two jobs as an office cleaner during the week and cleaning Wembley Stadium on the weekends. Returning from his shift at Wembley Stadium one day, he found that Arturo had left the flat without giving notice to anyone, taking £1,700 of Joel's savings with him.

In turn, purchasing documents or bank accounts also entailed risks, with migrants reporting instances where friends had either been swindled by the middlemen that they had employed to facilitate banking access, or had had bank accounts shut down by bank staff.

In either case again the chances of recovering the money that had been spent on these services and/or accumulated in bank accounts were slim. Marila, a Brazilian woman, recalled that her friend had paid a man £100 to help her open an account but when she turned up on the appointed day to do this, she was informed: "'Gee, sorry, it did not work out because there is a document missing', and that is it. He [the middleman] just pocket[ed] the money." Reflecting the risks that bank staff who opened accounts on the basis of false or missing documentation faced, it was also reported that these accounts could be shut subsequently with any money accumulated in them frozen. For example, Soraya, a Brazilian woman, argued that "all the documents used were false, and the person in the bank who opened the account knows that [when he opens the account] and so decides to remove the risk by shutting the account".

Migrant men and women put forward a range of explanations to try and make sense of these experiences. For some, the main issue was that migrants who were swindled had not shared accounts with 'close friends' who could be trusted or had used unknown middlemen whose services had not been recommended by family and/or friends. Marcia commented:

> "It happens a lot, a lot, with naive Brazilians, simple people. They are always being caught in these scams ... And those ads in magazines, they are worth nothing. If you really need to do it, you need to go round asking people. Best to have it recommended by someone than use an advert."

This said, it was also recognised that while co-nationals and migrant communities at large could be a source of help, this was not always or necessarily the case. Corroborated by wider research that notes the fissures existing within migrant communities, commentators have highlighted the contradictory notion of 'mistrustful solidarity' that operates within migrant communities (Levitt, 2001; see also Broeders and Engbersen, 2007; McIlwaine, 2009). In this research, a number of men and women commented upon the internal heterogeneity of their communities. For example, Alvaro, a Brazilian man, represented his own community as "a bit of bedlam, so many Brazilians from all backgrounds", noting that he would not have had much to do with "such people" in his everyday life in Brazil. Echoing wider findings, there was some appreciation that irregular migrants were particularly marginalised and exploited by their co-nationals. This said, there were important differences between communities, in that Somali migrants argued that even in cases where trust was occasionally misplaced, the importance of maintaining a good reputation within the community meant that disputes, such as those that arose around shared accounts, could potentially be resolved. Thus, Jibril Osman argued that: "Somalis have a lot of trust placed in each other and whatever difference occurs, it would always be settled within the circle and you will get your money regardless of whether you are on good terms or not."

More broadly, the risks which migrants' strategies entailed highlight the clear limitations of the agency that men and women are able to exercise, which is undermined by a range of interrelated socioeconomic exclusions as well as their immigration status (Wills et al, 2010). Broeders and Engbersen (2007) argue that counterstrategies such as the adoption of false identities, obliteration of legal identities as well as concealment of irregular status amount to everyday forms of resistance that can be characterised as 'weapons of the weak" and that are only marginally significant in terms of challenging state policies (Scott, 1985). Nonetheless, it could be argued that they are still significant in terms of affording migrants some space to manoeuvre.

Conclusion

Utilising frameworks that have sought to theorise how households have coped with significant and multifaceted socioeconomic and political exclusions, this chapter has highlighted the diverse strategies that migrants devise in order to engender their access to banking services in London. These strategies are underpinned by the capitals that migrant men and women both bring with them and also accumulate in London, ranging from financial, civic, human to social assets. Mobilised both locally and transnationally, social capital in particular was highly significant in terms of not only speeding up the process of banking inclusion through the provision of information and translation services but also the identification of 'migrant-friendly' bank branches or tellers. In turn, for those whose primary obstacle to accessing banking services related to their immigration status, 'counter strategies' often revolved around the management or erasure of identities by drawing upon civic assets that were accessed transnationally, or by sharing accounts or purchasing identification documents and/or accounts. It is apparent that the growth of a super-diverse migrant population in London has been matched by a concomitant expansion of a migrant industry that caters for various socioeconomic, immigration and increasingly financial needs of migrant men and women and that provides both legal and illegal services.

This said, the strategies that some migrant men and women devised were not without attendant risks. In particular, the purchase of bank accounts, as well as the sharing of accounts. sometimes resulted in the erosion of assets. For example, bank accounts that had been opened were subsequently closed or migrants experienced difficulties in accessing the money that they had deposited in the accounts of 'friends'. While these experiences were attributed to a number of factors, they also illustrated the fragility of the strategies that migrant men and women devised and the internal cleavages which divided migrant communities. Having considered how migrant men and women strategise for their inclusion into formal financial circuits, the next chapter moves on to consider how they coped with their exclusion, particularly in relation to savings and credit facilities.

Note

[1] Moreover, if asylum seekers are caught en route to their destinations, they then they have to ask for asylum under the Dublin Convention (Van Liempt, 2011).

FIVE

Coping with savings and credit exclusion: alternative practices of reciprocity and trust

"We Somalis have a culture, that if someone is facing problems or needs help then people who are in a better situation or able to help will help them and it is not a loan. If they need help and you are able to help them then you are expected to contribute and would do so." (Abtee, Somali man)

There is growing academic consensus that financially excluded households engage in diverse money management practices, thus contradicting a perception that they do not or cannot save or draw credit, and that they progress from informal to formal financial practices (Leyshon and Thrift, 1995; Matin et al 2002; Collins, 2005). Detailed investigations of household economies reveal the management of money outside or alongside formal banking systems through the development of 'mix and match' financial practices (Rutherford, 2002). These 'diverse', 'informal' and 'alternative' practices, as they are variously labelled, entail saving and borrowing from a range of sources and are premised upon the development of relationships with individuals, groups and institutions and a reliance upon both market and non-market financial services that are offered by regulated and unregulated providers (Rutherford, 1999; Ruthven, 2002; Kempson and Finney, 2006; UN, 2006; Bryne et al, 2007; Stenning et al, 2010a). Shaped simultaneously by exclusion from formal financial organisations as well as by the availability of alternative financial instruments and services that enable poor households to capitalise themselves, these practices are mediated by households' socioeconomic status, their agency and the assets at their disposal, financial knowledge and geographies, which collectively result in the creation of distinctive 'financial ecologies' (Ford and Rowlingson, 1996; Stenning et al, 2010a).

While preceding chapters have focused upon the formal financial lives of migrants and predominantly focused upon banking, this chapter details their more diverse savings and credit-related practices, which rely upon unregulated market and non-market services. These practices are particularly significant in facilitating migrants' access to financial resources, given that even while the majority of men and women are banked, their access to formal credit, and to a lesser extent, savings instruments is far less secure (see Chapter Three). Organised in two parts, the chapter begins by considering informal savings and credit-related practices, which are undertaken on an individual and one-to-one basis and range from saving cash at home, the conversion of cash savings into gold, reciprocal borrowing and lending, as well as the (limited) interactions of migrant men and women with unregulated credit providers including moneylenders and pawn brokers. It then moves on to consider group-based financial practices focusing particularly upon the Somali and Turkish communities, where membership of Rotating Savings and Credit Clubs (ROSCAs) was noted. In so doing, the chapter investigates the dynamics of trust and reciprocity that these informal engagements entail, drawing particular attention to the nature and scale of these practices. It also debates the extent to which these informal practices can potentially serve as alternative spaces and institutions of accumulation that can capitalise migrant men and women.

Migrants' money management beyond the formal

Researchers have long noted the ability of financially excluded people to manage their money outside of formal banking systems, particularly within the context of research undertaken in the global South (Rutherford, 1999, 2002; Collins et al, 2009). This research notes the various ways in which households manipulate or manage their cash flows through saving and borrowing, utilising a variety of devices and institutions (Rutherford, 2002). Importantly, such money management practices highlight the nexus between credit, savings and insurance even while the focus of much research has been on the availability of credit. The operation of a 'mini-economy' in poor communities, where production, consumption, trade, exchange, saving, borrowing and income earning all occur in small amounts with regular discrepancies between income and consumption, leads to high levels of insecurity and risk. These are addressed via consumption-smoothing strategies that involve the depletion and accumulation of financial resources via borrowing (where people 'save down', acquiring a lump sum now in exchange for savings made in the future via repayment installments) and saving (where people save up for a lump sum), with both substituting as a form of informal insurance (Rutherford, 1999; Matin et al, 2002).[1] Furthermore, and within the context of transitional and advanced economies, it is recognised that the economic restructuring associated with neoliberal transition has led to the development of diverse economic practices whereby 'households manage their precarious budgets [by] engaging in a multiplicity of lending and borrowing and credit and debt that combine the old and the new, the formal and the informal, the global and the local' (Stenning et al, 2010a: 119). Remarkably diverse in nature, informal saving and borrowing practices are undertaken on an individual basis (including saving cash at home, buying saving stamps, over-paying fuel prepayment meters), on a one-to-one basis (reciprocal interest-free lending and borrowing, interest-bearing loans acquired from moneylenders, pawning of assets, handing savings over to money managers for safe keeping) and on a mutual basis in group-based informal savings clubs, including burial clubs, Christmas clubs as well as Rotating Savings and Credit Clubs (ROSCAs) (Kempson 1998; Matin et al, 2002; Rutherford, 2002; Kempson and Finney, 2009).

These 'informal' or 'alternative' financial practices are played out in different financial spaces and organised through a number of financial organisations. Leyshon and Thrift's (1995) typology of retail financial services developed within the context of advanced economies distinguishes between regulated and non-regulated and market and non-market services (see Table 5.1). In turn, informal financial services are provided by both unregulated market providers (moneylenders, loan sharks, pawn brokers) as well as unregulated non-market providers (through family and friend networks), such that these arrangements and instruments reflect different types of relations with family, kin and community and varying levels of reciprocity, trust and duty (Leyshon and Thrift, 1995; Ruthven, 2002).

Table 5.1: An expanded typology of retail financial services

	Regulated	**Unregulated**
Market	**(a) Regulated market services** Banks, insurance companies, building societies	**(b) Unregulated market services** Moneylenders, pawn brokers, loan sharking
Non-market	**(c) Regulated non-market services** Social funds, credit unions, community development banks, *micro-finance organisations*	**(d) Unregulated non-market services** Family/friendship networks, *informal savings clubs (burial societies, Christmas savings clubs)*, ROSCAs

Note: Italics indicate author's additions to original table.

Source: Adapted from Leyshon and Thrift, 1995: 321

While research has commonly focused upon in situ populations or urban migrants, a small body of research also documents how transnational migrants and diasporic communities carry these practices with them (Khatib-Chahidi, 1995; Srinivasan, 1995; Summerfield, 1995; Kempson, 1998; Atkinson, 2006; Ardener, 2010). Within the context of this study, a holistic perspective of migrants' saving, borrowing and lending practices reflected their engagement with a number of regulated and unregulated, market and non-market services. Importantly, a distinction could be drawn between savings and credit-related practices, in that while the former predominantly involved depositing savings in bank accounts held in the UK or home countries, the latter largely occurred within the unregulated non-market sector (see Chapter Three). These diverse financial instruments had varying time horizons: some, such as borrowing and lending between family and friends, were open and shut within days, whereas others, including, for example, group-based lending and borrowing. survived for longer periods of time (Collins, 2005). Given that migrants' formal financial practices have been considered in previous chapters, the focus here is explicitly on informal savings and credit practices, with individual and group based savings and credit practices considered in turn.

Individual and one-to-one borrowing and lending among migrants: the importance of 'safe haven assets'?

> "Somalis get killed and robbed because they always have to carry their cash with them, so whenever a robber comes they go for Somalis. We are called ATMs – whenever you want money, you go to [rob] a Somali." (Dirive Adnan, Somali man)

The propensity to save in cash is documented in both rich and poor countries, and is especially prevalent among financially excluded low-income groups, who are described as storing savings as change in jars, piggy banks or mud banks, in different envelopes each earmarked for specific expenses or sewn into petticoats (Rutherford, 2002; Matin et al, 2002; Collard et al, 2003; Kempson and Finney, 2009). While a minority of all migrant savers – 15 per cent – held their savings in cash (see Table 5.2), this rose significantly in the Turkish community, where 62 per cent of men and women reported on this practice, followed by just under a quarter of Somali (24 per cent) and 16 per cent of Polish men and women. Investigated predominantly through in-depth interviews, this practice was attributed to a number of interrelated factors. For some, like Awale, it reflected the continuation of transnational saving practices and keeping their "old culture [alive] ... [Somalis] never used banks and used to keep the money in their houses"; others explained it in relation to receiving cash wages that were held at home, low levels of savings that rendered trips to banks or post offices redundant, being unbanked, and irregular immigration status. Furthermore, other migrants like Ali, a Turkish man, highlighted the ease of accumulating savings at home. Having only started to save after his wife and daughters joined him in London in 2003, he argued that since their savings were so small, it was easy to "keep them safe – a house is a big place and there are lots of places to hide money".

Table 5.2: Migrants' formal and informal credit and saving practices

	Numbers	**%**
Source of loans:		
Family and friends in UK	53	35
Family and friends in home country	40	26
Family and friends in UK and home country	12	8
UK bank	29	19
Bank in home country	8	5
Moneylender	2	1
Combination of above	7	5
Saving practices:		
UK bank account*	126	60
Bank account in home country	9	4
Cash	32	15
ROSCAs	16	8
Combination of above	27	13

Note: * This included current and savings accounts, and savings held in individual, joint and shared accounts.

Source: Questionnaire surveys

While money saved in cash is primarily used to meet regular anticipated and short-term expenses, it can also be converted into other assets depending on the levels of savings accumulated (Kempson, 1998; Whyley et al, 2000). As detailed in Chapter Three, the majority of migrant men and women saved small amounts as and when they could, and therefore fell in the category of 'instrumental savers'. As such, their expenses associated with raising families in London often consumed their meagre cash savings. This said, in cases where migrants were able to accumulate more substantial amounts – often over an extended period of time – there was some evidence of cash savings being converted into other assets. Particularly applicable to Turkish migrants in this study, just under a third of men and women interviewed from this community (31 per cent) invested their savings in gold (see also Kempson, 1998; Whyley et al, 2000). Elaborating upon this practice, Ebher, who worked as a butcher in a Turkish supermarket, reported earning a weekly cash wage of £250, which was supplemented by jobseeker's allowance. Wary of paying his wages into the same account in which his benefit payments were deposited because "the government might get suspicious if I put too much money into my current account", like many of his compatriots he stored his wages in cash at home. Furthermore, when his wife and he had saved up £400–£500, they purchased gold jewellery, which his wife wore. Importantly, the holding of savings in this manner not only reflected the cultural and symbolic value attached to gold, but also past experiences of financial crisis associated with the steep depreciation of the Turkish lira and volatile exchange rates (to be discussed later; see also Khatib-Chahidi, 1995; Ruthven, 2002 for similar practices in India). Within such a context, gold was undoubtedly viewed as a 'safe haven' asset. Its wider cultural significance was highlighted by women like Ayse, who recalled that: "I had some gold from what family and friends had put on me when Ismail and I got married. These are things that I saved for a rainy day – I still have two of the bracelets for sentimental reasons. They mean a lot to me." This storing of savings in kind also meant that it could be sold during times of economic need to release capital (Datta, 2007a; see also Vonderlack and Schreiner, 2001).

Cash savings were also remitted to home countries as and when sufficient money had been saved and/or foreign exchange rates were favourable. As discussed in greater length in the next chapter, nearly a third (29 per cent) of migrants who sent money home reported that their remittances were explicitly funded via both banked and unbanked savings. It is important to note here that a proportion of savings that were held in cash in London were subsequently deposited in bank accounts in home countries, thus demonstrating the connections between informal and formal financial systems (see also Chapter Six). The remitting of cash savings was particularly explained in relation to immigration status, whereby irregular migrants who were fearful of being apprehended and deported chose to send money home at frequent intervals. For example, Celina, a Brazilian woman, recalled that when her visa had expired, "for quite a long time, my wages would clear into my account and I would withdraw it, because there was a time that I was here illegally, and then because of the way I opened my bank account [she had purchased her account] I [was] always worried to death that the manager might discover and freeze my account, so I kept the money at home for a time and then remitted it back home."

However, commentators note that informal savings stored at home lose their value because of inflation, do not accrue interest which may be negligible in any case if small amounts are saved, and may be stolen or more easily spent (Rutherford, 1999). All these factors were acknowledged by migrants in this study. Reflecting their living arrangements, men and women particularly highlighted the risk of theft, given that many shared their homes with a number of other people (see Chapter Three). Kat, a Polish woman who had been unbanked for a number of years, recalled that "I really can't imagine how I did it [kept my savings at home]! It was crazy. I had to keep an eye on my luggage [where she stored her savings] at home all the time, not trusting anyone in the flat." Faced with this, an alternative although nonetheless equally risky strategy adopted by a select number of migrants was to carry – or attach – savings on their person (see also Vonderlack and Schreiner, 2001). Amaldo, a Brazilian man, who had amassed a considerable sum of £3,800 argued that:

> "I thought it was better to have it on me than to leave it under the mattress, or anywhere else. So I thought, 'If anything happened, it would be near me. It would not happen because someone could not take it without my seeing it.' [I did this] for more or less four months, and I would go to night clubs, and drink a lot, but nothing ever happened. Because I thought, 'When the money is on me, the risk is on me too.' I ended up sending it to Brazil because people would keep telling me it was not safe."

It is important to acknowledge that the migrant men and women who deployed these savings mechanisms often presented these as positive choices, partly related to the fact that these were tried and tested practices that had been honed in home countries, with saving in cash particularly enabling greater control over household budgets and economies. Perhaps most importantly, these saving practices were also used by some in preference to depositing savings in banks with formal savings products deemed as being unduly complicated and prohibiting easy access to savings (see Chapter Three; see also Datta, 2007a). Indeed, given that this research coincided with the economic downturn and the near collapse of some UK high street banks, migrant men and women commented that while savings held in cash could be stolen, putting savings in banks was not an altogether safe practice either.

Reciprocal borrowing and lending

Moving on from financial practices undertaken on an individual or household basis, informal financial practices also entailed one-to-one borrowing and lending, which comprised the bulk of the credit-related transactions undertaken by migrant men and women in this study. This finding is corroborated by wider research, which notes that the incidence of these transactions is in fact likely to be under-reported both because they are part of the 'norm' (and hence invisible ways) of covering deficits and bridging cash flows, and because of the small sums of money involved (Dreze et al, 1997; Matin and Sinha, 1998; Rutherford, 1999; Ruthven, 2002; Collins, 2005). Noted among both poor financially excluded households as well as in non-poor communities, 69 per cent of the men and women who had acquired a loan in the year preceding the interviews had borrowed money from family and friends located in the UK, in home countries or both (Matin and Sinha, 1998; Rutherford, 1999; Lacoste, 2001). This ranged from all of the Turkish migrants, 95 per cent of Somali, 80 per cent of Bulgarian, 64 per cent of Brazilian and 14 per cent of Polish migrants (see Table 5.2). While the prevalence of these practices was undoubtedly shaped by migrants' exclusion from formal credit markets (for reasons that have been elaborated upon in Chapter Three), they also derived from broader motivations and were embedded within wider social relations and the mobilisation of multilayered networks that connected migrants to family, clan members, friends, co-nationals and wider migrant communities located in London, their home countries and across diasporic spaces (Nee and Sanders, 2001; Ruthven, 2002; Muzvidziwa, 2010).

Research investigating the dynamics and nature of borrowing and lending between family and friends is limited, and even more so in relation to migrant men and women (although see Dreze et al, 1997). Sometimes referred to as 'network finance', commentators emphasise that while these financial practices are shaped by reciprocity and trust, they are also structured by other factors common to all credit transactions, which relate to interest, repayment schedules, requirement for collateral and treatment of default (Dreze et al, 1997; Ruthven, 2002; Stenning et al, 2010a). Indeed, Ruthven (2002) argues that informal borrowing and lending may assume standardised forms in certain situations, whereby the terms of repayment, in particular, are carefully specified. Looking at these dynamics in turn, the reciprocity associated with one-to-one borrowing is itself structured by the motivations underlying these practices. These are identified as 'social obligation', understood as operating between close family members, and 'balanced reciprocity', whereby there is a recognition that participants are both borrowers and lenders, with resources circulating between friends, relatives and neighbours who are deferring current consumption to lend to others (Dreze et al, 1997; Matin et al, 2002). Within the specific context of migrants' financial practices, reciprocity was structured by the nature of the relationship between borrowers and lenders with a clear distinction being made between loans acquired from parents, from other family members and from friends and co-nationals. As such, while the latter were often presented as reciprocal, loans acquired from family members and particularly from parents in the form of an inter-generational transfer of resources were usually perceived as 'gifts' to which migrant men and women were entitled (see also Stenning et al, 2010a). Highlighting these sentiments, Marila, a Brazilian woman, argued that "what is my family's is mine, it is not really borrowing", while her compatriot Mauricio, who had borrowed money from his mother on numerous occasions, identified the social obligation underwriting such loans:

> "Well, like, this week I will need a 'loan'. I am going to call home and ask my mum for £300. She will send [it to] me. And it has been over six months since I last asked her for money. It is a like a present. Well, it is not a present. She'll send it because, well, she'll feel she has to. I have never paid her back. It was actually 'given' to me."

Somewhat in contrast to this, borrowing and lending between friends and co-nationals was identified as a balanced and reciprocal practice (see also Matin et al, 2002). For example, Rafael, a Brazilian migrant, spoke about the "mutual agreements" that he had with his friend whereby "we lend money to each other when we need it but we don't charge interest".

Moving on to consider the wider 'conditions' attached to these borrowing and lending practices, while such loans are usually interest free, there are instances in which they may include concessionary interest rates or interest being charged on part of the sum borrowed (Dreze et al, 1997; Ruthven, 2002). In general, migrant men and women stressed that the loans that they had acquired and gave to family and friends were interest free. Svetla, a Bulgarian woman, who had taken a loan of £600 from her friends when she first arrived in London, said: "There was no interest charged – we are friends! I returned money within the two first months [but] even if I couldn't do it in two months they would not charge me for an additional month of delay, I am sure." In only a handful of cases did migrant men and women repay money with interest, sometimes voluntarily to show appreciation for these loans. Furthermore, the majority also stressed the flexibility of repayment terms of these informal loans in contrast to bank credit. This was expressed most succinctly by Jibril Osman, a Somali man, who had borrowed £2,500 from a number of family members and friends during a protracted period of unemployment:

> "I would ... borrow from family and friends. For me, it is the only place I would go. They can relate to me, I can be very informal and tell them about my situation, whereas the banks would not care or understand my situation. I can tell a friend I have this and that to do this month and I would give you your money next month and he can relate to me. Whereas if I rang a bank and said I can't pay this month, they will say 'We don't care what you are going through, you need to pay up.' The terms [of loans acquired from family and friends] are pay whenever you can, however you can. There is no 'in-your-face, pay it back right now or we are going to take you to court' attitude. It is like a helping hand. If you borrow you have to pay it back, but the difference is how long it takes you, and that is the biggest difference between borrowing from a friend and bank ... No matter how long it takes me to repay a loan, no interest is charged."

Importantly, however, pressures to repay loans were heightened when the financial situation of the borrower was perceived as having changed for the better. For example, Jibril went on to say that "all the people I borrowed from know my situation, and if it changed, then they will bring it up and say 'Hey, I know that you are well off now and your job pays you well, so can you pay us back, but not yet'." Indeed, even while loans from parents were often presented as gifts, it was not always the case that parents did not expect to be paid back. Although parents contributed towards the migration costs incurred by their sons and daughters, and in some cases even sent reverse remittances when jobs failed to materialise, there was some expectation that these exchanges would mature into reciprocal support when their children had established themselves in London (see Chapter Three). As such, it could be argued that loans were offset against future remittances sent back to family members including parents (see Chapter Six). Where loans had been acquired from a variety of family members and/or friends, migrants often assessed which loan to repay first in relation to the financial needs of their creditors, as highlighted by Jibril, who argued that "I would pay back according to whoever is in a worse situation and needs the money back … I am conscious of who needs their money and when and that is how I pay it back."

Moving on to examine the scale at which one-to-one borrowing practices functioned, it is clear that these relationships drew in family and friends located in home countries and in the UK as well as relatives and friends who were living elsewhere in advanced economies (see also Ryan et al, 2009). In particular, and perhaps unsurprisingly, family (usually parents but also siblings and extended family) and friends had been particularly important sources of finance prior to emigration, with family members bringing together the resources needed to fund migration (see also Chapter Three). Aziza's migration to the UK from Somalia had been funded by "friends, family, neighbours who did a collection for me to help me, I think it came up to a couple of thousand [US] dollars. They were people who were just helping us out, it is not a loan. Maybe I would be able to help them one day." In turn, relatives who had already emigrated and were part of a wider diaspora were also crucial in funding these migrations. Again, this was particularly evident in the case of Somali migrants, who reflected that husbands, parents, siblings and extended family who were already resident in the UK, in other European countries, as well as in the US had helped put together the sums of money required to leave Somalia. While Oraji's husband paid for her and her children to come to the UK, Abtee's sister who was living in America financed his migration to the UK, which he summed up in terms of "help. It is Somali culture. When someone is leaving the country, he asks his family for help."

Even while a number of migrant men and women continued to turn to their families at times of crisis, usually associated with periods of unemployment, problems associated with receiving money from home countries as well as the strength of British Sterling, meant that other relationships assumed greater importance over a period of time. As such, family and friends in the UK as well as those who had migrated elsewhere were relied upon with increasing regularity. Josana, from Brazil, speculated that while she could always call upon her mother if she was in trouble, she preferred to rely upon friends in London who had already helped her by lending her money to renew her visa. As she reflected, "there are friends here who I could count on … It is easier to borrow from here, because borrowing from Brazil you may lose track of the exchange rate." This said, family members or friends who had migrated elsewhere in the global North were also crucial sources of support, especially in instances where they were perceived as being in a position to extend financial help. Marilena, a Brazilian woman, argued that while the exchange rate made it difficult for her family in Brazil to help her, she relied upon her father-in-law who was in the US: "he has helped us to put the deposit on our flat here and he gave us a car as present." Yet, of course, despite this neat categorisation, it was evident that credit-related practices were also based upon combinations of people who could be approached. To this end, Lucila, who was married to a German national, had borrowed money from a number of family and friends, including an uncle who lived in Brazil (from whom she had borrowed £1,000), her sister-in-law who lived in London (from whom she had borrowed £500) and her brother-in-law who lived in Germany (a further £600).

Notwithstanding the generally positive accounts of these informal credit-related practices, migrants did identify some limitations associated with borrowing from friends and family. For a start, the availability of informal loans depended on the social networks at the disposal of migrant men and women, and especially access to family members or friends who could afford to lend money. Partly reflecting the limited means of their contacts, the majority of men and women concurred that this type of borrowing afforded access to relatively small sums of money – typically ranging from as little as £10 to £300. As such, these loans were largely suitable for meeting everyday shortfalls in income rather than the accumulation of assets in either London or in home countries. As articulated by Anastas, a Bulgarian man, "if I need money – not a vast amount of course – I would first ask family and friends. But if it is for a bigger sum, I would go to a bank." This said, there were instances when more considerable amounts of money were being borrowed or lent, although these were largely evident among Brazilian migrants, where both employment and wage levels were higher (see Chapter Three). Thus, for example, Rosana had borrowed £2,000 from her friend in order to pay for her father's medical treatment in Brazil, while her co-national Guilherme reported that it was possible to borrow up to £2,000–£3,000 from friends.

In turn, the consequences of failing to repay loans by a given date or time, while largely non-economic, were nonetheless significant (see also Ruthven, 2002). Dreze et al (1997) argue that while poor financially excluded households are often perceived as acquiring the cheapest loans that are available to them, this has to be measured against the important social costs that the failure to repay loans acquired from family or friends entail, including a loss of face and prestige in the community as well as strained social relations. For this reason, not all participants were equally enthusiastic about borrowing from family and friends. Angelina, a Bulgarian woman, felt that "when a person has a financial relationship with friends [it] is very bad for the friendship. The rules of the banks are clear, it is not always the case with the friends. It is easier to cope with being dependent from a bank than from a person." The use of social sanctions and peer pressure in order to ensure timely repayment of loans was particularly problematic for those migrants who had low incomes, were benefit dependent and/or had dependants to take care of in London, as was the case of women like Asha. Her migration to London from Somalia had been funded by a maternal aunt, who had sold her property to raise US$5,000, which was needed to purchase false documents and meet other migration-related expenses. Asha's subsequent inability to repay even part of this loan had resulted in considerable pressure from her family, leaving her fearful of the social stigma that this potentially entailed. She complained that:

> "It was a lot of money, particularly at that time, but it was expected if you go outside of Somalia that it would be easy to pay that money back ... I have not paid anything back yet. They [her relatives] ask me and remind me, 'When are you going to send my money?' I mean, she [her aunt] is not here. I avoid her calls now because I hate telling her that after all these years I still don't have her money. She does not know what kind of life style I have. It really bugs me that I owe someone money and they keep reminding me like I forgot. It is really bad, because they are family, they know your parents and your family, and they will send you people [from the community to enquire about the repayment of the loan]. People will talk; it is shameful. They could even ask the elders to go and get their money for them since I am not giving it to them, and that would be really bad. It will really mess up the family relations. But it has not reached that far now. *Alhumdulilah,* I hope to pay it off before then."

Given the crucial importance of family, friends and co-nationals in negotiating everyday life in London, and the diverse roles that they played in providing information, emotional support as well as financial resources, the threat of being socially ostracised was very significant for many migrants (see also Chapter Four).

Borrowing from informal moneylenders

As highlighted in previous chapters, individuals and households excluded from regulated market credit providers because of poor credit histories, bad debts or low incomes are often regarded as being 'expelled' to the unregulated credit market, where they are served by 'unscrupulous' credit providers (Leyshon and Thrift, 1995; Ford and Rawlingson, 1996). Indeed, the growing number of people who are credit excluded has been matched by the growth of what Stookey (2006: 12) refers to as a 'poverty industry' or a highly diverse subprime credit market, which in the UK includes both regulated and unregulated credit providers (see Chapter Two; also Leyshon and Thrift, 1995; Collard and Kempson, 2005; Carbo et al, 2007; Cox et al, 2011). Although research has documented the exploitative terms and conditions of the subprime credit industry at large, more nuanced investigations have also drawn attention to the wider dynamics of such borrowing. Highlighting how low-income groups counter their exclusion from formal credit markets by acquiring credit from a range of different sources, the use of unregulated credit providers is attributed to a number of other factors including the inter-generational transfer of financial traditions and knowledge, speedy disbursement which is of vital importance in emergency situations, and easy access, with doorstep delivery offered by some credit providers such as moneylenders (Sinha and Matin, 1998; Leyshon et al, 2004; Leyshon et al, 2006; Byrne et al, 2007). The fact that these loans are issued without any moral judgement or 'lecture' on financial mismanagement or lack of financial knowledge and awareness may be an added attraction (Byrne et al, 2007). Importantly, these credit relationships may mimic some of the attributes of other informal borrowing practices noted earlier, whereby close relationships are forged between borrowers and credit lenders even while these are clearly based upon manipulation and encouragement of further borrowing (Gloukoviezoff, 2006). Engagements with subprime credit providers, and in particular moneylenders, may also emerge in situations where individuals or households do not want to incur the wider social obligations or strain these important relationships via engagement in reciprocal lending and borrowing practices (as discussed previously; see also Rutherford, 2002).

This said, migrant men and women across all of the five communities included in this research reported a very low incidence of borrowing from unregulated credit providers (see Table 5.2). It is important to highlight the particular silence in migrants' narratives on the use of subprime credit, which is perhaps attributable to a perception that this reflected poor financial judgement and management on their part. Given the exclusion of some migrant communities from formal credit as well as the professed need for credit (see Chapter Three), the incidence of these practices is almost certainly underestimated in this study. Notwithstanding this, migrant men and women's opinions of moneylenders and other informal credit providers were overwhelmingly negative, with pejorative terms such as 'dangerous' and 'criminal' often used to describe these individuals and their financial products. These attitudes were sometimes shaped by transnational experiences in home countries, with Jurema, a Brazilian woman, reflecting that failure to repay a moneylender could result in "murder, especially in Brazil. I don't know here, but generally in Brazil, if you don't pay, you die! They'll take every penny from you and their interest rates are high." Furthermore, a Polish man, Andrez, argued that taking a loan from a moneylender would be "suicidal ... from a Pole [moneylender], I can't expect too much ... Poles are pretty nasty ... not only do they [moneylenders] rip people off, they may even send a Gypsy mafia on you so you don't get noisy about it ... I would never think of taking a loan from these guys." While only applying to a handful of cases, it is important to point out that for some the desire to avoid informal moneylenders actually translated into a lack of access to even this form of credit. Although there was some confusion of the distinction between regulated and unregulated credit providers, and secured and unsecured loans, at least among some migrants like Amina and Asha Sureiya, both from Somalia, a lack of assets that could be used as collateral led to inaccessibility to these loans. In another isolated case, the research uncovered a male migrant, Amaldo, who appeared to be a moneylender himself, having lent money to his relatives in Brazil as well as friends and a former flat-mate in London. Even while he claimed that loans to the former were interest free, he was charging interest on the £3,000 he had loaned to his former flat-mate, although he would not be drawn upon the rate of interest or the broader terms and conditions of this loan.

Having identified the key informal financial practices undertaken by migrant men and women on an individual and one-to-one basis, and explored the key dynamics of these relationships, the next section focuses more explicitly upon group-based saving and credit practices.

Hagbads and altin günü: ROSCAs as alternative institutions of accumulation?

"Many of us want to live here, buy a house or plan for the future, but everything is tied to interest, so we don't trust

the whole system, particularly with recent economic events,
which illustrate the reason why interest rates are not good
and can lead to your downfall when they go up or change."
(Hamda, Somali woman)

Originally conceptualised as intermediate organisations located
between traditional forms of cooperation and formal financial
institutions that would fade away with time, group-based savings and
credit organisations, or ROSCAs, are celebrated both by advocates
of financial development as well as those who prioritise the social
development associated with informal finance (Geertz, 1962; Ardener
and Burman, 1995; Copestake, 1996). Indeed, even while ROSCAs
are seen as a 'poor' substitute for formal financial organisations, it is
recognised that they play a vital role in facilitating access to financial
resources especially during periods of economic downturn when
formal credit markets shrink (Muzvidziwa, 2010). Furthermore, they
are also identified as providing important and diverse non-economic
functions including the nurturing of interpersonal relationships via
initiatives such as group-based lending mechanisms, where social
collateral forms the basis for financial relationships (UN, 2006). More
broadly, ROSCAs are acknowledged as being informal precursors to
the microfinance industry[2] or 'revolution', which, while originating
in poorer parts of the world, has since migrated to richer countries.
Attributed with capitalising poor households within the overall
context of poverty elimination and economic growth, the creation
and mobilisation of social capital that underlies microfinance is also
seen as being vital in addressing social exclusion in more advanced
economies (Johnson and Rogaly, 1997; Mosley and Steel, 2004; UN,
2006).[3] Collectively, ROSCAs, microfinance and other 'alternative'
initiatives are acknowledged as being part of 'more socially responsive
economics' (Affleck and Mellor, 2006: 304).[4] Commentators note
that within the context of informal financial mechanisms, ROSCAs
afford some form of financial intermediation that is absent from
other types of informal practices (Matin et al, 2002). Furthermore,
while the predominant focus is on the credit-related activities that
ROSCAs (and indeed microfinance initiatives) perform, they are also
crucial in affording financially excluded individuals the opportunity
to accumulate additive savings that inculcate saving habits while being
characterised by an absence of formality (Matin et al, 2002).

ROSCAs are broadly defined as 'associations [which are] formed
upon a core of participants who make regular contributions to a fund
which is given, in whole or in part, to each contributor in rotation'

(Ardener, 2010: 11). Although they are particularly prevalent in the global South, researchers have also noted the reproduction of ROSCAs in migrant and diasporic populations in advanced economies. Within the specific context of the UK, these include *pardners* in the African Caribbean, *kommittis* in the Pakistani, *tontines* in the Cameroonian and *hagbads* in the Somali populations in London (Summerfield, 1995; Atkinson, 2006; Datta, 2007a, 2011a; Aznar, forthcoming). The preference for 'alternative' forms of saving and drawing credit among migrant households has been explained in relation to the fact that these are culturally embedded, tried and tested methods of accessing financial resources (Anderloni et al, 2008; Kempson and Finney, 2009; Ardener, 2010). As such, it is important to acknowledge that even while ROSCAs may be positioned as an 'alternative' to the formal, for the people who participate in them, they may be very much part of the mainstream (see also Pollard and Samers, 2007; Aitken, 2010).

Within the five communities included in this research, participation in ROSCAs was evidenced in the Turkish community, with migrants participating in *altin günü* (gold days), and among Somali migrants who were part of *hagbads*. Details of the operation and management of these groups reflected key differences between these two organisations. Beginning with Turkish *altin günü*, wider research identifies these as one of three dominant types of *günü* prevalent in Turkish communities: namely *şeker günü* (sugar day), *altin günü* (gold day) and *dolar günü* (dollar day) (Khatib-Chihida, 1995; Eroǔlu, 2010). Operating along similar lines as other ROSCAs, these are all based upon a verbal contract, do not have named managers, membership is fixed at the start of a 'round' and the order of rotations is determined by drawing lots. Importantly, and reflecting the extent to which informal savings and credit-related practices are shaped by broader financial conditions and (in)stability, the contributions and lump sum paid out in all three types of groups are clearly linked to specific commodities and/or currency whose value is protected against inflation during the life of the *gün*. Eroǔlu (2010) notes that contributions from individual members are highest in *dolar günü* and lowest in *şeker günü*. In turn, Turkish migrants in London reported participating in 'gold days' or *altin günü* that were based upon the contribution of quarter gold coins and/or the equivalent value in cash. Ayse, a Turkish woman, detailed her involvement in one such group in London:

> "I told a friend at my daughter's school and she told me of her gold day. I know of gold days but I don't have enough close friends to invite. Bless her, she said she would invite

her friends from her own group. And that is what we did. Some people brought large gold pieces and others brought £100. At the end of the day I got just under £1,500. I will have to sell the gold and when I do so the gold will lose some of its value. Over the next two or three years, the women will arrange gold days and they will invite me to their houses and I will do what they have done and so give them a large piece of gold or £100. I do not have to pay interest or anything [on the loan] so that is nice."

Operating somewhat differently, Somali *hagbads* were led by (usually) older women who managed groups ranging in size from 10 to 25 members. In contrast to *altin günü*, members of *hagbads* were either related to each other and/or connected via clan affiliations, although in some cases members only knew the manager of the group (to be discussed later; see also Summerfield, 1995; Ardener, 2010). Given this, *hagbad* managers performed a very active and vital role in terms of screening potential group members so as to exclude those who were deemed as being unable to maintain regular contributions, assuming primary responsibility for collecting and storing members' contributions on a weekly or monthly basis and then paying these out as agreed by the group. Asha Abdillahi, a Somali woman, described her group as follows:

"I don't know how many people [are in the *hagbad*] because this other lady is in charge. It is for six months and I pay £25 every two weeks. It is the Somali community and I know the lady in charge, so it is safe. I don't know everyone participating, but I know the lady [the manager]. There are no problems. It is only Somali ladies in the community. Before the *hagbad* starts, it is the person in charge's responsibility to only allow people who they know is good to pay [to join the group]."

As group-based financial mechanisms, a great deal of attention has focused upon the social and moral dimensions of ROSCAs, which are premised upon solidarity and mutual aid obligations and credited for re-inscribing the social back into financial relations (Ardener, 1995, 2010). Engendering what has been termed as 'trust-based lending', they are important in both building/bolstering social capital as well as putting trust back into financial systems (Johnson, 1998; Phillips, 2010). Furthermore, while in some cases trust pre-exists the formation of ROSCAs as a result of broader economic and social connections between individuals, in other cases it is created through action. Rutherford (1999: xxvi) observes that 'perfect strangers, coming together for the limited aim of running a ROSCA, can sometimes construct and practise trust more easily than people with histories of complex relationships with each other.' Furthermore, the longer a ROSCA cycle, the greater the level of trust involved, with members building reputations for prudence and reliability through their successful participation in these groups (Ardener, 2010). Applying these broad findings to the two ROSCAs identified in this research, while members knew each other in advance of the creation of *altin günü* groups, trust was also clearly created through regular meetings held over a period of time. In contrast, in *hagbads*, trust primarily resided in group leaders or managers who, as highlighted above, were often elders who commanded respect in the community and could – because of their knowledge and oversight of local communities – be relied upon to reduce the risks associated with the premature exit of members who received their lump sum early in the group's cycle or with failure to meet regular contributions (Khatib-Chihida, 1995; Summerfield, 1995; Ardener, 2010; Eroŭlu, 2010). The fact that *hagbads* did not serve the same social function associated with *altin günü*, where (women) members came together regularly, can also be explained in relation to the fact that poorer households may lack the actual resources to host what can be quite large, and in some cases very elaborate, social functions in which hosts seek to outdo each other in terms of the food that they lay out and the hospitality that they provide (see also Khatib-Chihida, 1995; Eroŭlu, 2010).

In turn, and echoing the social sanctions associated with reciprocal borrowing and lending, the social sanctions associated with non-payment often acted as a deterrent to participation in these ROSCAs. Asha Sureiye, a Somali woman, said that while she wanted to join a *hagbad*, "I can't afford it at the moment". Other women, like Fardiuso, while being well aware of the multiple advantages of joining such groups, argued that:

> "It works for some people, but it requires commitment for a period of time, and a certain amount each month. Everyone must stay till the end. There could be various events that could happen that you can't account for. For example, I might get ill, no longer get any money or be able to afford it. Some other problems could face me, so it is risky."

In relation to their ability to capitalise poor households, pay-outs from ROSCAs are predominantly associated with meeting everyday consumption needs, although there is evidence that in some cases these may be more substantial and related to the acquisition of assets including property (Nelson, 1995). While the latter are clearly associated with more affluent and middle-class members who are able to afford larger regular individual contributions, in this research the loans acquired through participation in these informal clubs were almost always used for everyday expenses including the payment of bills, but also for emergencies. While Ahmed Ahmed from Somalia used his ROSCA loan to fund holidays to visit relatives in Canada and the US, Ayse (mentioned previously) had joined an *altin günü* because her sister was ill:

> "I had to raise £1,500 to send her for hospital costs. In Turkey it is not like here, where the government pays for hospital fees and medicine costs. It is very hard for people there. You have to come up with the money or you get no treatment. I don't have that much money. My husband doesn't even work!"

Even while ROSCAs may not necessarily emerge as alternative institutions of accumulation, it is important to recognise other elements of alterity that they encompass. For a start, group-based saving and credit practices are widely associated as gendered, with broader research noting the participation of women in ROSCAs as well as microfinance schemes, where nearly three quarters (74 per cent) of participants are women.[5] In part the suitability of these interventions for women is predicated upon their lack of access to formal financial markets shaped by a broader unequal access to physical and economic assets. This said, although wider research notes the prevalence of women-only ROSCAs, there is evidence to suggest that men also come together to save and rotate credit in both single-sex and mixed-sex groups. However, important distinctions exist between male and female groups in relation to the size of the fund that rotates, the importance placed on the social aspect of ROSCAs and the implications of non-payment or early exit from a group (Ardener and Burman, 1995; Johnson 2004). In particular, male ROSCAs are associated with higher failure rates so that they are more risky propositions for men. In contrast, gender norms potentially mean that women place a great deal of value on the social networking and solidarity inherent in such group participation. Women often prefer to belong to single-sex groups, which, although smaller in size and involving smaller contributions, enable them to engage in savings that may be kept secret from their husbands and families. The sanctions associated with non-payment in women's groups are likely to be perceived as being stronger, such that female members are more likely to highlight the shame and disgrace associated with non-payment and more likely to borrow from friends to pay into ROSCAs. In fact, the success of women's groups may lead to men joining these groups via female relatives (Johnson, 2004).

Predominantly explored within the context of Somali *hagbads,* which have traditionally been identified as being the domain of women, this research uncovered the participation of a small number of men in these group-saving practices, thus reflecting the extent to which gendered norms and conventions are rewritten and renegotiated upon migration (Datta et al, 2009; see also Summerfield, 1995). Gutaale observed that even while some people in his community thought that *hagbads* were "women's affairs", he did not think male involvement in these savings groups was "shameful [because] it helps people who can afford it to save money." In turn, these men all reported being part of male-only groups. Reflecting the findings of broader research, a key difference between male and female *hagbads* was the level of contributions, which were higher among the former. Perhaps unsurprisingly, male ROSCAs are associated with larger contributions and funds sometimes utilised for asset accumulation. In the opinion of one male participant, Ahmed Ahmed, while the savings pot of women's *hagbads* amounted to £100, among men this could go up to £1,000, which he attributed interrelatedly to higher levels of employment and savings among men in his community as well as the incidence of fewer dependants in their households. His compatriot, Abdi Khadar, was participating in a group that had 24 members and was "running a course of two years", managed by one of his family members. He contributed £250 a month and viewed this as a safe way of accumulating savings. Reflecting on his own motivations for joining this group, he observed that "I am in the *hagbad* because my family is in the *hagbad*, otherwise I would not have been involved. Pretty much everyone in the cycle is family [clan wise rather than immediate], so it is pretty safe." This said, other men were quite disdainful of what they regarded as women's affairs and also the risk associated with *hagbads.* Awale, for example, argued that, in his opinion:

> "It is better to use banks, because *hagbad* is kept at someone's house and sometimes it could be as much as £10,000. It is dangerous. They could get robbed. Anything could happen, and it is because they don't know how banks work, that's

why they keep the money at home. It is mainly women, older ones. Therefore they need to understand and tell them how banks work and how to use it. Teach them the process [of using banks]."

Conclusion

This chapter has documented the diverse savings and credit-related practices of migrant men and women that are the outcome both of an exclusion from formally provided services and of the availability of alternative financial instruments and services that enable these individuals and households to capitalise themselves (Ford and Rowlingson, 1996). An examination of these practices reveals a range of activities that are undertaken on an individual, one-to-one and group basis, albeit with some important variations between and within the five migrant communities included in this research. Unsurprisingly, these more diverse practices were particularly evident among Brazilian, Somali and Turkish migrants, who faced significant obstacles in accessing saving, and particularly credit services. Furthermore, and particularly in relation to group-based financial practices evidenced through participation in ROSCAs, these alternative financial practices are influenced by transnational practices that are re-created in London. The chapter has further investigated how these alternative financial practices are underwritten by more socially inscribed ways of doing finance that rely upon relationships with family members, friends and co-nationals who are both resident in London but also in home countries. The following chapter focuses upon transnational financial practices more specifically through an investigation of migrant men and women's remittance practices.

Notes

[1] The nexus between savings and credit is also recognised in the microfinance industry, whereby an initial focus on credit has been replaced by the provision of a range of financial services to financially excluded populations. This also reflects a consensus that while not all people are credit-worthy or want debt, most people are deposit-worthy and want assets (Kabeer, 2001). It is particularly argued that savings may be more appropriate for poor women than borrowing, which is regarded as being more risky, and savings are voluntary, while repayment of loans is mandatory (Vonderlack and Schreiner, 2001).

[2] It is argued that the emergence of microfinance as a credible alternative to the informal sector has led to an erroneous assumption that dependence on the latter has declined (Sinha and Matin, 1998).

[3] Mosley and Steel (2004) argue that expansion of microfinance initiatives in advanced economies has been modest and largely geared towards niche markets. In their opinion, the upscaling of microfinance here is dependent upon better targeted state support, attention to the pricing of loans as well as offering a wider range of loan products.

[4] This said, others have argued that the microfinance and other alternative initiatives have increasingly become another mechanism for expanding the reach of the formal financial sector by capitalising financially excluded households sufficiently so as to engender their inclusion into formal financial sectors as well as identifying the 'bankable unbanked', comprising individuals who can potentially afford credit, insurance and a range of other financial products. This trend is further illustrated by the recent shift in public policy focus from microfinance to inclusive finance, which sees a continuum between informal, semi-formal and formal financial institutions. Perhaps unsurprisingly, this agenda is linked to the provision of a range of financial services to poor households that would enable them to 'increase their incomes, acquire capital, manage risk and work their way out of poverty' (UN, 2006).

[5] While the focus of microfinance programmes on women has often been interpreted as illustrating their capacity to promote gender equality and women's empowerment, it is important not to conflate the two (Johnson, 2004). Even while microfinance programmes explicitly target women, they do so for a variety of reasons reflecting quite diverse understandings of gender and resulting in a variety of gender outcomes, including potentially the disempowerment of women (Kabeer, 2001; Mayoux, 2005; Datta, 2007b). In particular, commentators dispute the benefits of extending loans to women over which they may have little subsequent control (Goetz and Gupta, 1996). As such, it is evident that many aspects of gender relations, both within households and the wider community, come into play and mediate the impact of loans given to women (Mayoux, 1999).

SIX

Transnational money: the formalisation of migrant remittances

"Well, I have the house in Brazil, and a few studio flats, five actually, that is a family property, my mum's really, which are managed by an estate agent. And besides that, I have money invested in shares, in Brazil, I have around R$40,000 (about £11,000) invested in Banco do Brasil, Petrobrás, Vale do Rio Doce [major steel producer], and other riskier investments. My brother-in-law works at the Banco do Brasil and he is looking after the investments for me. He keeps an eye on the market 24 hours." (Amaldo, Brazilian migrant)

One aspect of migrants' financial lives that has captured a great deal of academic and public policy attention is remittances – or more specifically financial remittances[1] – which migrant men and women send to their home countries. Importantly, for a number of migrants these transfers represent a first personal interaction with the global economy as they engage with financial services that offer international payments (Toxopeus and Lensink, 2007). Once viewed as a graphic indicator of the failure of development, migration is now conceptualised as being a potential contributor, or indeed, panacea for development, with labour emerging as the most valuable export commodity in a number of countries in the global South (Piper, 2009; Phillips, 2009). Much of this euphoria rests upon remittances, which, within a dominant migration–development discourse, are viewed as being critical in unlocking the developmental potential of migration and beneficial for both the global South and North. In the former they are deemed as having a positive impact upon poverty alleviation and economic growth on a range of scales extending from the household to the nation state. In the latter, where remittances have been viewed as an indication of migrants' lack of integration in host societies and a loss of resources, they are now recognised as being vital for the development of migrants' home countries, thus reducing pressures to migrate and so relieving the pressures caused by migration in host countries like the UK (Datta et al, 2007b; Migration Watch, 2009; Van Hear et al, 2009).

Within this context there has been a growing interest in the ways in which money travels back to home countries, with a particular drive to promote the use of formal remittance channels (Ameudo-Dorantes and Pozo, 2005). This imperative arises from a number of interrelated priorities based primarily on a consensus that remittances can be leveraged to promote financial inclusion as migrants and their families are drawn into formal financial circuits and afforded the opportunity to access a range of financial services (Hernández-Coss and Bun, 2007; Yujuico, 2009). The resultant expansion and development of the formal financial sector – particularly in migrants' home countries – is seen as being intimately related to economic growth (Levine, 1997). Proponents argue that formally remitted monies are more likely to be invested in productive activities in home countries, facilitating individual and familial asset accumulation as well as broader economic development. Although remittances have been embraced enthusiastically in some quarters, others have been more critical of what they interpret as a financialisation of remittances, whereby what are essentially intra-household transfers of money are being incorporated into global financial architecture (Datta et al, 2007b; Hudson, 2007; Datta, 2009a). As Silvey (2008: 15) argues, international development agencies, and one might add both host and home states, have 'aggressively promoted economistic and neoliberal approaches to the circulation, investment and productive use of migrants' earnings', which is attributed by some to a crisis in both development and capitalism (see also Hudson, 2008).

This chapter traces the formalisation of remittances in London. The argument is developed in three stages. First, the chapter details how and why remittances have emerged as highly significant financial flows in the contemporary world. Second, it explores how remittances are being 'tamed' through processes of formalisation and financialisation by identifying how national and global institutions propose to integrate these flows into formal financial circuits. In so doing it draws particular attention to the 'nuts and bolts' of the remittance industry and the diverse ways in which money travels back from migrants to their home villages, towns and countries. Third, the chapter highlights how these aspirations are somewhat at odds with migrants' remittance-sending practices with respect to motivations for sending remittances, the sacrifices that this entails, as well as the ways in which they remit. It could be argued that remittance sending can exacerbate the financial marginalisation of migrants who, if they are working at all, are located in the lower echelons of London's labour market. Furthermore, an over-zealous formalisation of remittance sending poses significant challenges for some migrants. In concluding, the chapter considers how current policy debates run the risk of transforming flows of finance that are potentially structured around an alternative economy organised around altruism and reciprocity to one governed by economic rationality (Faist, 2004; Hudson, 2007).

From altruism to the new development finance?

Simultaneously positioned as an 'ideal neoliberal currency', 'the new development finance', 'bottom-up finance' as well as 'third-way finance', remittances have captured the attention of global institutions and national governments as well as non-governmental organisations. This said, it is apparent that understandings and interpretations of remittances differ significantly, such that they appeal to both neoliberal economists as well as grass-roots communitarians (Kapur, 2003; Ratha, 2003; Wimaladharma et al, 2004; Adams and Page, 2005; Hernandez and Coutin, 2006; Datta, 2009a). The interest in remittances rests upon a number of key factors. For a start, global remittances are on an upward trajectory increasing from US$2 billion in 1970 to US$ 31.1 billion in 1990; and from US$131.5 billion in 2000 to US$416 billion in 2009 (Ratha et al, 2008; Ratha and Mohapatra, 2009; World Bank, 2011).[2] Outward-bound remittances from the UK were estimated at US$3.6 billion in 2009, and were sent to more than 50 countries located in the global South, and East and Central Europe (Isaacs, 2008; Vargas-Silva, 2011; World Bank, 2011). Furthermore, London is a particular focal point for remittance sending because of the large and diverse migrant population found there, such that the city is the epicentre of a significant number of remittance corridors[3] that link it to towns and cities across the globe (Wills et al, 2010). Located within these networks of transnational connections are the places from which the migrant communities included in this research originated (see Table 6.1).

The lack of remittance data relating to Somalia is attributable to the difficulties in enumerating transfers from refugee diasporas, where a significant proportion of remittances may be sent to families displaced outside of their country of origin. Notwithstanding this, Somalia is identified as one of the most remittance-dependent countries in the world, with inward receipts estimated at between US$500 million and US$1 billion by the 2000s (Van Hear, 2004; Carling et al, 2007; Lindley, 2010). Composed of small but regular transfers, these remittances are all the more remarkable given the precarious legal and economic statuses of many Somali migrants (see Chapter Three; see also De Montclos, 2003).

Table 6.1: Inward-bound remittances to migrants' country of origin

	Stock of emigrants as % of population, 2010	Remittances, 2009 (US$ million)	Top 10 destination countries for migrants, 2010
Brazil	0.7%	4,234	US, Japan, Spain, Paraguay, Portugal, UK, Italy, Germany, Argentina, France
Bulgaria	16%	1,558	Turkey, Spain, Germany, Greece, Italy, Moldova, UK, US, Romania, Canada
Poland	8.2%	8,816	Germany, UK, US, Belarus, Canada, France, Italy, Israel, Ireland, Spain
Somalia	8.7%	No data available	Ethiopia, UK, US, Yemen, Djibouti, Kenya, Egypt, Saudi Arabia, Canada, Sweden
Turkey	5.6%	970	Germany, France, Netherlands, Austria, US, Belarus, Belgium, Saudi Arabia, UK, Switzerland

Source: World Bank (2011)

In turn, the identification of remittances as the 'new development finance' arises from an insufficient if varied flow of finance to the global South, trends that have worsened since the 2008–10 economic downturn (to be discussed later; see also Hudson, 2008; IDS, 2009). Hernandez and Coutin (2006) argue that while the immediate post-war period witnessed the evolution and expansion of Overseas Development Assistance (ODA), the oil and debt crisis of the 1970s and 1980s, and the ensuing 'lost decade of development', led to a growing neoliberal faith in Foreign Direct Investment (FDI), promoted through Structural Adjustment Programmes (SAPs) (see also Chapter One). In turn, the currency and foreign exchange crisis precipitated by these neoliberal policies gave a new visibility and importance to remittances such that 'neo-liberal economic policies focused new attention on the possibility that remittances might play a significant role in national development, or at least national solvency' (Hernandez and Coutin, 2006:188). Remittances have since overtaken or come a close second to ODA, FDI and earnings from export. Indeed, in some poor countries they are the *primary* financial flow, outstripping ODA by some 20 per cent and double FDI (Black and King, 2004).[4] Again this can be illustrated by looking at the situation in Somalia, where, in the early 2000s, aid inflows were between US$115 and US$170 million and export income between US$125 and US$265 million, thus falling well short of estimated remittances (Van Hear, 2004). More broadly, it is not uncommon for remittances to constitute between 5 and 10 per cent of total GDP in (small) developing countries (World Bank, 2005). Furthermore, as Yujuico (2009) argues, unlike other financial flows such as debt securities or equity stakes, which incur interest or dividend payments respectively, remittances do not entail any future outflows of finance from home countries.

Crucially, remittances are also resilient (de Haas, 2005; Orozco and Ferro, 2007; World Bank, 2008; Datta, 2009a). Migrants continue, and indeed may even intensify, remittance sending at times of political, economic and/or environmental crisis, such that remittances can function as a critical source of informal insurance against risks (Mazzucato, 2006).[5] As an example, while remittances did decline during the economic downturn – and particularly sharply in specific remittance corridors – this decrease has to be measured against the fact that private capital flows to poorer countries were slashed by half while most donor countries also reneged on promises to expand their development aid budgets (*The Economist*, 2009; IDS, 2009; Ratha and Mohapatra, 2009; Sward with Skeldon, 2009; World Bank, 2011). As such, remittances are less volatile and reversible in comparison with other capital flows to poorer countries (Bugamelli and Paternò, 2006).

Given these attributes, it is not surprising that remittances lie at the heart of a conviction that migration can serve as a catalyst for development (Nyberg-Sørensen et al, 2002a, 2002b). Much attention has focused upon the impact of money transfers upon poverty alleviation and economic growth, with remittances commonly classified as being used either for subsistence or investment purposes. While the former are sometimes rather spuriously represented as leading to excessive consumption, it is now recognised that subsistence remittances are often spent on the purchase of food, health and education, which are arguably critical for the wellbeing and welfare of households and families, and cognisant with both sustainable livelihood and capabilities perspectives on development (Chappell and Sriskandarajah, 2007). Indeed, as Connell and Conway (2000) point out, higher levels of consumption are an indication of major welfare gains and improvements in basic needs (Van Hear and Sørensen, 2003; Carling, 2004; De Haas, 2005). Presenting evidence from a World Bank study of 71 developing countries, Adams and Page (2005) report that remittances reduce both the level and depth of poverty. Thus, a 10 per cent increase in remittances from each migrant potentially leads to a 3.5 per cent decline in the share of people living in poverty as well as reducing income inequality.[6] As intra-household transfers that are directly targeted at migrants' families, remittances therefore have multiple beneficial impacts while also functioning as safety/welfare nets, which cash-strapped national governments have been incapable of providing in the aftermath of neoliberal structural adjustment (Orozco, 2006). Importantly, there is also a potential continuum between subsistence and productive remittances that are invested in the purchase of land, housing and service sector-based businesses (Connell and Conway, 2000; Ballard, 2003; Carling, 2004; De Haas, 2006). As such, remittances can have important multiplier effects on local economies (Carling et al, 2007). Within this context, it may be more useful to consider them within the assets-based framework set out in Chapter Four. As Orozco (2010: 12) argues, 'finance and access to financial resources are cornerstones components of material asset accumulation', and, as financial assets, remittances can be used to purchase both non-material *and* material resources. In turn, research documents that households that receive remittances are much more likely to accumulate assets than non-remittance recipient households (see Chapter Three; see also Orozco, 2010).

Yet, notwithstanding the link between subsistence and investment, and non-material and material assets, in reality a significant proportion of remittances are devoted to meeting the subsistence needs of migrants' families, with only 10 per cent being invested in entrepreneurial activities (Orozco and Fedewa, 2005). In fact, the majority of migrants and their families typically only accumulate two or less assets. This failure to capitalise on remittances arises from a range of factors including the inability of economic and social structures in home regions to absorb and transform remittances into assets, as well as the nature of migration (Orozco, 2010). Where migration is undocumented and/or where migrants are located in low-paid precarious employment, they are unlikely to accumulate transnational assets. As such, policy makers at both ends of the remittance chain are exhorted to get their policy frameworks right in relation to labour markets, immigration policies and – especially important in this context – financial conditions.

The 'taming' of remittances: processes of formalisation and financialisation

Creating the 'right' *financial* conditions in order to leverage the development potential of remittances is increasingly seen as being dependent upon two key and interrelated processes: first, the formalisation of these financial flows and, second, the expansion of the financial outreach of formal financial institutions to peoples and places that have hitherto been excluded (Hudson, 2008). Furthermore, both global and national initiatives to achieve these twin ambitions are clearly evident. Before considering these in greater detail, it is important to recognise that ambitions to formalise remittance flows are driven by a number of broader imperatives. For a start, the actual volume of remittances is predicted as being anywhere between two to 10 times greater than already identified because of the significance of informally sent remittances, which are especially prevalent in certain corridors. For example, it is estimated that informal inflows comprise between 45 and 65 per cent of formal inflows in sub-Saharan Africa in comparison with 5–20 per cent for Latin America, while one-third of UK remittances leave the country via informal channels (Blackwell and Seddon, 2004; Freud and Spatafora, 2005; Pieke et al, 2007). The economic downturn of 2008–10 is also associated with an increase in informal remittance sending, particularly by migrants who have lost their jobs in the formal sector and want to keep transaction costs to a minimum, as well as the continued difficulty faced by those who do not have the prerequisite identification documents to send money home via formal channels (Ratha et al, 2009). Furthermore, the securitisation of migration in the post 9/11 world and the growing tendency to conflate the informal with the criminal and corrupt has led to greater public policy interest in the identities of both remittance senders and recipients as well as the purposes to which remittances are put (Faist, 2004; Yujuico, 2009). Proposals to 'follow the money', as it were, have been fostered by a particular suspicion and surveillance of informal remittances, which by their very nature leave little or no paper trail, and which have been linked not only to money laundering and tax evasion but also (erroneously) to terrorist financing (De Goede, 2003; Horst, 2004; Atia, 2007; Pieke et al, 2007; De Goede, 2008). Thus, as Lindley (2009) and others argue, notwithstanding broader tendencies towards the deregulation of the financial sector, the drive for powerful states to regulate certain global financial flows after 9/11 – including informal remittances (which are depicted as something of a 'loose cannon') – has been substantially reinvigorated on the grounds that these may undermine the stability of global financial, economic and political systems (Robinson, 2004: 5).

Follow the money: the formalisation of remittance flows

A multi-billion dollar remittance industry or 'marketplace' has emerged in response to the global demand for remittance services (Maimbo, 2004; Orozco, 2004, 2005; Pieke et al, 2005; Lindley, 2009). Defined as 'encompassing various actors, institutions and procedures through which money is transferred from migrants to their families' (Pieke et al, 2005: 14), this sector is highly diverse and complex, comprising a number of actors subject to varying degrees of local, national and global regulation (Orozco, 2004, 2005; Carling et al, 2007). The distinction between formally and informally sent remittances rests upon several markers (Carling et al, 2007). Remittance transfer systems typically include both a mechanism by which money is sent and the service providers used to do so. Collectively these determine how funds are made available, sent and accessed. The key actors in a remittance chain are remitters (migrants), recipients and remittance service providers (RSPs) (and/or their agents) in host and home countries, with both information and money being relayed across the remittance chain (see Carling et al, 2007 and Orozco, 2005 for further details). The mechanisms used to send remittances range from cash to cash, cash to account, account to cash, account to account, card to card, mobile transfers and internet-based transfers (Carling et al, 2007; Isaacs, 2008). Cash-to-cash transfer mechanisms dominate the global remittance market, whereby remittances are sent and received in cash, with services differentiated by the speed with which a transaction is completed. Account-to-account transfers depend upon both remitters and recipients being banked, and while this money can be tracked across transnational space, these transactions are often more expensive and limited in use because of banking exclusion in both host and especially poorer home countries, where an average of 5 per cent of the population have bank accounts (Isaacs, 2008). Cash to account and account to cash are variants of the above. The use of prepaid cards, mobile-based and web transfers are all recent innovations that have benefited from the rapid spread and take-up of ICT, and particularly mobile telephony, in parts of the global South (Yujuico, 2009; see also Photo 6.1).

The RSPs or financial intermediaries involved in the remittance marketplace range from formal to semi-formal and informal providers. At the formal end of the spectrum, these include banks, post offices and credit unions and non-bank financial intermediaries (NBFIs) of which money transfer organisations (MTOs) are the most important. The latter can be subdivided into large global enterprises such as Western Union and MoneyGram[7], which offers its services via the Post Office network in the UK (see Photo 6.2), and 'specialist', 'niche', or 'ethnic' MTOs, which concentrate on specific remittance corridors and which, in certain contexts, may be more usefully identified as semi-formal RSPs. The UK is rather unique in Europe in terms of the size and diversity of

Photo 6.1: Cheap phone calls: the glue of transnationalism

its MTO sector, with approximately 3,750 registered businesses in mid-2009 operating through some 30,000 outlets, in contrast to 60 MTOs in Spain, 30 in Germany and three in France (Financial World, 2008; Vargas-Silva, 2011). This can be partly attributed to a highly diverse migrant population as well as the hitherto 'soft' approach to regulating these enterprises (as discussed further below; see also DFID, 2005; Financial World, 2008; Wills et al, 2010). Despite the difference in size (including turnover) between large and small operators, niche MTOs can emerge as significant competitors in specific corridors because of their ability to offer faster, cheaper and, crucially, more user-friendly services (Blackwell and Seddon, 2004; Pieke et al, 2005; Orozco, 2005; Datta, 2007a, 2011a). For example, Lindley (2009) documents that the MTO, Dahabshiil, which accounts for 60 per cent of all remittance transactions in the Somali diaspora, has 24,000 agents and branches; operates in 144 countries; employs 2,000 people worldwide and has regional offices in London and Dubai. Furthermore, its services are used by Care International, Save the Children and Oxfam to operate their development programmes in Somalia (www.dahabshiil.com) (see also Table 6.2). Moving to more informal providers, RSPs may also assume the form of businesses that offer money transfer services in addition to other services, as well as hand delivery/couriers (Pieke et al, 2005). Hand carrying of remittances – by migrants, their family and friends, bus and taxi drivers, cross-border traders – accounts for

40 per cent of all informal transactions in certain African corridors because of poor financial development and banking infrastructure (Blackwell and Seddon, 2004; Horst, 2004; Pieke et al, 2007). Yet, it is *hawaala*, an informal value transfer system, that has generated the most public policy interest and anxiety in relation to informal remittances (for further details see De Geode, 2003; Farrant et al, 2006; Fugfugosh, 2006; Atia, 2007; Lindley, 2009).

Photo 6.2: The partnership between the Post Office and MoneyGram in the UK

Importantly, while the distinction between formal and informal remittances often rests upon the mechanisms and particularly the service providers used to remit, the demarcation between the two is blurred because of a number of reasons (Pieke et al, 2005, 2007; see also Blackwell and Seddon, 2004; Maimbo, 2004). First, formal/informal boundaries shift over space and time as money transfer transactions cross jurisdictions (Lindley, 2009). As such, what starts off as an informal transaction may become formal in later stages as funds are deposited in banking systems. RSPs may themselves have a diverse status. For example, while Dahabshiil dominates the Somali remittance market in the UK, it has been refused a licence to operate in Norway (Carling et al, 2007). Second, remittance systems evolve over time, in that first cohorts of migrants may utilise formal providers because of an absence of alternatives, which emerge as their numbers grow. Informal remittance systems are themselves adaptive, with informal RSPs transforming into registered companies that 'aspire to become multi-functional financial institutions' (Maimbo 2004: 16).Third, diverse and partially overlapping criteria are used to distinguish between formal and informal remittance transfers including regulation, registration, licensing, supervision, law enforcement, and requirements to keep records and report transactions.

Expanding financial outreach: including people and places

Notwithstanding the difficulties in distinguishing informal from formal remittance sending, the channelling of remittances through formal channels ticks a number of public policy priorities that rest upon a consensus that the functioning and development of financial systems is critically linked to economic growth (Levine, 1997).What is certainly evident is that formalisation processes potentially entail the expansion of the financial sector through the remittance market as well as the leveraging of remittances to generate more capital through securitisation: processes that, in turn, point to the financialisation of remittances (Hernández-Coss and Bun, 2007; Hudson, 2008).

The formalisation of remittances potentially initiates the process of financial inclusion not only of migrants in host countries, but also of their families in home countries.This is arguably one of the reasons why remittances have become particularly important for financial inclusion advocates. Research conducted predominantly in the US suggests that banked migrants are able to save more, acquire assets, build up a credit history and invest their remittances in productive enterprises (Ameudo-Dorantes and Bansak, 2006). In contrast, in situations where appropriate and accessible financial products and services are absent, it becomes difficult for recipients to accumulate savings, with a higher proportion of transfers subsequently spent on more 'unproductive' items (Connell and Conway, 2000). Such tendencies may be further exacerbated by the absence of adequate information about investment opportunities leading to an over-investment in service-based micro-enterprises that are at best 'marginally productive' (Potter and Phillips, 2006: 587).

The financial inclusion of migrants can also engender the financial incorporation of their family members if remittances travel back and/or are paid out via banks and if these banks then provide supplementary financial services (Ballard, 2003; Farrant et al, 2006; Toxopeus and Lensink, 2007).Thus, promoting financial awareness among remitters can serve as a driving force for increased financial inclusion and literacy among remittance recipients by fostering relationship building between banks, remitters and recipients, which is itself facilitated by the informational and direct value attached to remittances (Toxopeus and Lensink, 2007). For instance, remittance receipts give banks an opportunity to accumulate information about new clients, who are thus able to build up a financial history. Based on this history, and checked against present and future remittance receipts, banks may be encouraged to cross-sell financial products such as savings accounts and loans to these low-income households. The risk of default on loans is lowered as remittances serve as a form of (informal) insurance. Remittances also flow as direct value to banks enabling low-income households to move into higher-income brackets, which are more appealing to financial institutions. Importantly, formally accumulated remittances potentially promote entrepreneurship, with both present and future remittances acting as collateral for loans, thus enabling a transnational accumulation of assets.

There is some evidence that the banking sector is showing greater interest in remittances in both sending and receiving countries, spurred on no doubt by the size of these financial flows, even while their penetration in this market remains fairly modest[8] (Toxopeus and Lensink, 2007). Milligan (2009) documents the activities of Banco Solidario, a microfinance institution in Ecuador, which has formed partnerships with Spanish banks in an attempt to encourage migrants to remit using their products. Such initiatives are part of a strategy to foster broader financial relationships with migrants, who are also offered short-term credit to meet their financial needs in Spain as well as savings, insurance and mortgage products in Ecuador. Other banks, such as the Indian ICICI, Andhra Bank and State Bank of India, all provide free money transfers if minimum balance requirements are met. Meanwhile in migrant host countries like the US, Wells Fargo have pioneered the financial inclusion of Mexican migrants by accepting Mexican identification documents, the *Matricula Consular*, in order to open accounts. Once banked, migrants are offered remittance products through the bank's ExpressSend service, which waives service fees in conjunction with other financial services. Yujuico (2009) argues that even while the remittance services offered by banks are 'loss leaders', the ambition is that they will drive up the usage of other financial services through strategies of 'cross-selling' (selling financial products which complement remittance sending) and 'up-selling' (providing more sophisticated financial services), which will enable banks to expand their financial reach and market share (Yujuico, 2009).

Formal remittance receipts also promote broader financial depth and development in home countries through the accumulation of foreign exchange reserves, enlargement of tax bases and improved national credit rating via securitisation. As the 2009 UNDP Human Development Report points out, transnational migration itself involves significant costs made up of official fees charged for issuing documents such as passports, clearances including visas, and costs related to travel expenses, including departure taxes. While some of these revenues may disappear into the pockets of officials as bribes, a proportion do potentially contribute to national coffers. There is also a link between remittances and improved national credit rating arising from the securitisation of money transfers (Hudson, 2007). Traditionally focused upon the conversion of mortgages, loans and credit card receipts, the securitisation market has diversified considerably and now extends to the securitisation of future flows of remittances as an income stream. The advantages of this become apparent where they achieve high credit ratings, enabling poorer governments to secure low-cost but long-term credit, which is often in short supply, particularly in periods of economic downturn. Thus, financial flows that start off as intra-household transfers can potentially emerge as a new development finance.

UK initiatives to formalise remittance sending within a global context

The global initiative to formalise remittance sending has been spearheaded by organisations such as the World Bank. Working with a special task force on retail payment systems, the Committee on Payment and Settlement Systems, it has identified five key principles that the international remittance service edifice should rest upon.[9] Collectively these seek to render the formal remittance industry more competitive, transparent and accessible so that it emerges as a viable option for a greater number of migrants across different remittance corridors. Endorsed by the G8, the G20 and the Financial Stability Forum, these principles have since been adopted and implemented through a series of public–private partnerships. The World Bank has itself created an institutional apparatus that focuses on research and forecasting of global remittances (via the Migration and Remittances team), advice on financial regulation as it relates to global payment systems (via the Financial Integrity Group), as well as the explicit connection of remittances to microfinance initiatives (via the Consultative Group to Assist the Poor – CGAP). In addition it operates a Remittance Price Database, set up in 2008, and designed to enable migrants to compare remittance costs in numerous remittance corridors.

Public policy interest in formalising remittance flows in the UK can be traced back to the publication of a joint report produced by the

Department for International Development (DFID) and Banking Codes Standard Body (BCSB), which sought to detail available remittance products (DFID, 2005). This coincided with the establishment of the UK Remittance Group within DFID as well as the development of a website, Send Money Home, a remittance price comparison website available to UK-based migrants (www.sendmoneyhome.org).[10] In addition, the UK Remittance Group produced a Remittance Charter, which aimed to spread best practice among RSPs (Datta, 2009a). In more recent years, attention has particularly been afforded to addressing weaknesses in the UK regulatory framework as it relates to the Payment Services industry (Orozco, 2005, 2010). This framework defines and structures the ways in which money transfers take place, the institutions authorised to engage in international payments and the conditions under which foreign currency transfers are allowed. Key areas of concern include anti-money laundering requirements, 'know-your-customer' (KYC) requirements, level of enforcement and compliance types and remittance transfer processing. In turn, the agency charged with tightening up regulations is the Financial Action Task Force (FATF).[11] This intergovernmental taskforce set up by the G8 countries has sought to address variance across the EU in terms of the treatment of remittance service providers, ranging from a simple registration of money transmitters (so-called 'soft' regulation identified in the UK) to the same level of licensing and supervision applied to retail banking (the 'hard' regulation evident in a number of European nations such as Germany) (Pieke et al, 2005; Vleck, 2006; Carling et al, 2007). In a bid to get its house in order and following the introduction of the Payment Services Directive in 2009, the UK's Financial Services Authority (FSA) took over as regulator of remittance financial intermediaries from Her Majesty's Revenue and Customs Department and phased in a twin system of registration (applicable to smaller NBFIs) and authorisation, with the critical distinction being that the latter requires a safeguarding of clients money as well as FSA checks on all associated agents. The clear intention is that all financial intermediaries will acquire an authorised status over a period of time.

It is important to acknowledge that the move to formalise remittance systems has been welcomed by some on the grounds that remittances are quite complex financial products that entail service fees, foreign exchange conversions and identification requirements and often operate in a sphere where clients lack access to redress (Isaacs, 2008). As such, some level of formal intervention and competition is deemed as being in the interests of migrants, in light of the periodic collapse of MTOs, which potentially leave migrants bearing significant remittance losses (Saini, 2007). It is also recognised that pressures to formalise have necessitated greater professionalisation among RSPs, who are increasingly expected to provide a better and more secure service to their clients (Lindley, 2009).[12] Notwithstanding this, the benefits accruing to migrant men and women from the formalisation of remittance transfers are more debateable and are considered in further detail later.

Migrants' remittance-sending practices in London

The preceding discussion has highlighted the drive to formalise remittance flows on the grounds that these can engender financial inclusion, promote financial depth and development in both home and host countries and thus contribute to broader economic development as well as asset accumulation among migrants and their families. In this section, the remittance-sending practices of the migrant men and women are considered to highlight some of the inconsistencies in these arguments. It focuses specifically on the reasons why migrants remit and the personal sacrifices that remittance sending involves, as well as the ways in which remittances travel back to migrants' home towns and countries.

Motivations for sending remittances

> "I live in a country that is free and peaceful and I work, but they [his family] are in a civil war, without a state, and they cannot work, so I don't mind sending them money. Sometimes I might make sacrifices, but their living standard is low, so sometimes I have to put them first." (Awale, Somali man)

The remittance-sending practices of migrant men and women in this study reflected considerable variety, which is perhaps most graphically illustrated in the extracts taken from interviews with Amaldo and Awale, in turn. Overall, 67 per cent of migrants remitted, ranging from 76 per cent of Somalis, 75 per cent of Polish, 71 per cent of Brazilian, 63 per cent of Turkish to 43 per cent of Bulgarian migrant men and women. The frequency with which money was sent back home also varied, with just over half (53 per cent) of remitters sending money home regularly once a month, 6 per cent remitting more frequently, between two and three times a month, and 17 per cent sending money home occasionally, usually once or twice a year. Importantly, the narratives of migrant men and women also revealed that there were diverse motivations for remitting, which did not always or simply revolve around asset accumulation. This finding is echoed in the broader literature, which highlights the complex macro and micro level factors that shape remittance sending (Datta et al, 2007b). A framework that has sought to explicate this places the factors that shape remittance behaviour on a broad continuum ranging from 'altruism' at one extreme to 'self-interest' at the other, with positions of 'enlightened self interest/ tempered altruism' in between (Lukas and Stark, 1985; see also Brown, 2006; Datta et al, 2007b). In turn, insurance – either individual or family-based co-insurance – shapes these, enabling migrants to shore up their positions in their households and communities (Carling, 2008). This framework further suggests that while remittances sent for altruistic reasons are often used for consumption/subsistence purposes by recipients, those guided by self-interest are likely to be invested in physical asset accumulation (such as land and housing) and/or financial assets (in savings accounts, pensions and so on). In reality, of course, people send money for both sets of reasons depending on their own and their family's circumstances, their position in the life course, the nature of their obligations back home, and their financial situation in London. However, this distinction is still a useful heuristic device in understanding the uses and motives for sending remittances (Datta et al, 2007b).

Within the context of this research, migrants often attributed remittance sending to altruism, justifying it by drawing attention to their families' situation in their home countries. Somali men and women in particular predominantly focused upon the moral obligation to remit, which was necessitated by the ongoing conflict and instability in Somalia that had destroyed local livelihoods and led to widespread displacement (see also Lindley, 2010). As such, women like Zahra argued that even while she could only send £50 every month or two, this money was vital "for the homeland to be peaceful, and it's important to help the people left behind. The international community does not give them anything. People in Somalia have nothing, they cannot work, there are so many problems and [they are] needy people, nor can we support them. But they need help." Some of Zahra's compatriots, like Amina, expressed this obligation even more strongly, speaking about her mother's entitlement to a share of her income – in her words "the money has to stretch". As McKenzie and Menjívar (2011) argue, the emotional meanings and importance attached to these material transfers, however small and irregular they may be, should not be overlooked as they serve as a mechanism by which relatives are reassured that their transnational family units will remain intact and survive migration. Poverty in home countries, and particularly of families left behind, also motivated altruistic remittance sending across the five communities, although this varied according to the class position of migrant men and women. For example, Pepa, a Bulgarian migrant, reported that she was sending "money from my savings. My father is ill, everybody (my mother, my father, my brother, his wife and his child) live in the same house and only my brother works. There is no work in Ivailovgrad."

It is important to acknowledge that even while migrants' narratives may be framed around a discourse of altruism, part of the obligation to remit arises from the fact that many of the relatives who were receiving remittances had helped migrants to fund their move to London in the first place. As highlighted in Chapter Three, while the costs of migration varied according to geographical distance, right to enter the UK and routes into the country, a number of men and women incurred significant expenses, which they raised through a mixture of income, savings and loans, often acquired from family members (Datta, 2007a). Reflecting on the subsequent obligation this support engendered, Turkish migrants like Ali, whose father-in-law had encouraged him to move to London and then also allowed Ali's wife and children to move into his own house so that they could begin to save to migrate themselves, argued that subsequent demands for financial help could not be ignored: "my father-in-law and other family ask for money at times and we can't say no. At the end of the day they are family, so we send when we can and when they ask" (see also McKenzie and Menjívar, 2011).

In turn, altruistic remittances predominantly contributed to the daily subsistence requirements of various family members, accounting for 98 per cent of Somali, 65 per cent of Bulgarian and 17 per cent of Brazilian remittances. These sums of money enabled family members to pay for food, basic utility bills and school fees, as well as medical bills. Within the Somali community, the experience of men like Faisal was fairly typical: "I support 15 individuals – all my immediate [family], mother, brothers, sisters. I don't have any control over what they do with the money, but they use it for consumption, clothes, food and use it all by the end of the month." Other migrants highlighted that they were paying towards the education costs of children. For example, Svetla, from Bulgaria, was sending money home every month to support her ill and unemployed husband, pay for her son's school fees and support her daughter, who was employed in a low-wage job. As such, her remittances were "not a matter of investment, it is a matter of survival".

Moving on to focus on self-interest, it was apparent that some migrants were sending money back home to cement their financial position through the accumulation of financial and physical assets as well as the disposal of financial liabilities including debt. As highlighted above, asset accumulation among migrants and/or their families depends on both the economic position of migrants as well as financial and investment conditions in their home countries. Perhaps unsurprisingly, remittance sending that was shaped by self-interest was more evident among those migrants who originated from middle-income countries including Brazil. In this community, 45 per cent of migrant men and women were remitting to pay bills in their home country, which included not only utility payments and outstanding credit card bills but also mortgage payments and pension contributions, while a further 12 per cent were investing in land, housing or businesses. Fleshing this out further and highlighting intra-community differences, Rita, a Brazilian woman, reported that her remittances were contributing to mortgage payments for a flat she was buying and added:

> "If there is a need, I may send to relatives, but everybody in Brazil is doing fine, they don't need it ... I am tight-fisted anyway! And as I said before, our profile [class position] is slightly different from that of the majority of Brazilians here."

Her co-national, Jacinto, remitted £300 to his Brazilian bank account to pay his mortgage, credit cards bills, life insurance and membership fee of his football club, while another, Guilherme, sent £200 a month to pay into a pension plan he held in Brazil (see also Chapter Three). Viewed from the opposite end of the spectrum, in part at least, Somali migrants' remittances were overwhelmingly used for subsistence purposes both because the sums remitted were insufficient to fund investment, as well as the fact that opportunities to invest these were few and far between. As such, women like Asha, who sent money to her sister's children for their daily subsistence needs, argued that she would need to send at least "US$2,000" in order to set up a business for her relatives, which was beyond her means given that she herself was dependent on benefit income. In turn, the dearth of investment opportunities in home villages and towns also prohibited investment-related remittances. Asha's compatriot, Ahmed Ahmed, who sent money to his wife, argued that "she can't invest, because she lives in a small village. You open a shop, there is no one but her family, so there is no point in her investing."

Remittance sending and financial precarity

"Well, I help my parents with all my heart, but my mum sometimes says, 'You have to think about your own future, you are not married, you are 35, soon we won't be here.' But I think like this: I am healthy, I am 35 but I don't feel it, I have no children, I have no debts, and I am adaptable. So, I am in good health, so I can work. This money which I give to them now, it is like, how much did they spend on raising me and giving me an education? So, I don't think like 'I am foregoing this or that.' But, sometimes, this issue of the debt sometimes weighs me down, and the money I've already sent, well, I don't regret it, but then I could already have bought my own place, so this weighs on me. It is the wrinkles I have on my face, of having to get up very early in the morning and go to bed at 3 am. Sometimes I go to work in a bad mood ... then my sisters get talking. Only two of my brothers help my parents, not my sisters. My family is complicated." (Marcia, Brazilian woman).

Far from engendering the financial inclusion of migrant men and women, it can be argued that remittance sending can in fact contribute to financial precarity among migrants. Often treated as 'products of love rather than labour', there has been no thorough investigation of whether remittances are funded from wages, savings, debt or a combination of these (Hernandez and Coutin, 2006: 190; see also Amuedo-Dorantes and Bansak, 2006; Datta et al, 2007a). In turn, interviews with migrant men and women revealed that remittances were funded through a mixture of wages, savings, loans and even benefits (see Figure 6.1). Although income and savings emerged as significant, it is important to contextualise this within the low incomes that many migrant men and women earned as well as the high cost of living in London, which made it difficult for many to save without considerable sacrifices (see Chapter Three).

Given that 17 per cent of remitters were unemployed, remittances from these households were funded through benefit payments, or, where one member of the household was employed, through a combination of benefit payments and income. This was particularly apparent in Somali and Turkish households, where 26 per cent of remittances in each community were funded through benefit payments, with a further 8 per cent in the Somali and 74 per cent in the Turkish community based upon benefits and income. In these households, London–based family units were often rendered financially vulnerable until subsequent benefit payments were received. Fardiuso, a Somali woman, commented that at times she had to halve her benefit income, spending her share on her children's basic needs in London and sending the rest to her parents in Somalia, who were ill. It is important to recognise that unanticipated expenses in home countries – particularly those related to medical emergencies but also the payment of pressing debts – pressurised migrants even further. Often involving larger sums of money than normally sent, these demands were met by acquiring loans, usually from family and friends in order to remit (see Chapter Five).[13] For example, Rosana had to acquire a loan of £1,000 from a friend in order to send money home to her mother in Brazil, while Lulu, whose uncle had arranged for her and her children to come to London from Somalia, reported that "when I borrowed the £300, it was partly because he was ill and in hospital. I can't ignore him and stay silent."

Figure 6.1: Sources of funding for remittances

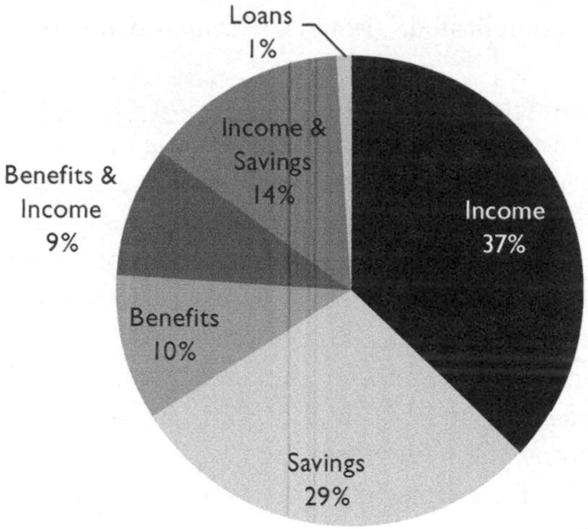

Source: Questionnaire survey (n=215)

Given the economic marginalisation of many migrants, it is not surprising that migrants agreed that remittance sending entailed sacrifices that ranged from cutting back on basic necessities to forgoing what some termed as luxuries. Thus, migrants spoke about not being able to take advantage of further education and training activities, being unable to travel or top up mobile phones. An assessment of these sacrifices often led to more nuanced discussions of the tension between voluntary remittance sending and the expectation or obligation to remit. In a focus group discussion held with Brazilian men and women there was a sense that migrants had to work much harder in London than they had in their home countries, a fact that relatives in home countries did not necessarily recognise or appreciate. Furthermore, it was reported that family members often had unrealistic expectations, in that a "consequence [of remitting] is that people [back home] think that you got rich. The investments that you make there give this impression that you got rich." This in turn could lead to inter-family tension and in extreme cases could lead to disengagement with family members. This was perhaps best exemplified in the case of Ali Hassan, a Somali man, who explicitly attributed his decision not to continue with remitting to the demands made by a large family, who not only expected him to remit but would also call him to ask "where *their* money was" if remittances were late.

RSPs used to send money home

Given that migrants display different motivations for remitting and often endure significant hardship in so doing, it is not surprising that they exhibit considerable financial savvy in selecting remittance-sending mechanisms that best suit their interests. The remittance marketplace in London reflects a wide array of institutions that have responded to the demand for remittance-sending services and that involve formal as well as semi-formal and informal actors (see Table 6.2).

Within this research the banks' share of the remittance market was low, at 5 per cent: none of the Polish and Somali communities used banks, and only 2 per cent and 11 per cent of the Brazilian and Turkish communities, respectively, used them. Migrants like Marcin, from Poland, argued that:

> "These transfers are shit. They are expensive ... look all this talk about the European Union and you cannot transfer money from one bank to another just because it is in another country ... I think some is blocking the money so it will not fly from this country ... I think they do not want the outflow of cash from Britain to be too large ... because then it would be big scale, with all this thousands of Poles they would have everything out."

The highest usage of bank facilities was recorded in the Bulgarian community, where 30 per cent of migrant men and women reported

Table 6.2: Mechanisms for sending money home, by percentage

	Brazilian (n=85)	Bulgarian (n=23)	Polish (n=27)	Somali (n=61)	Turkish (n=19)	TOTAL (n=215)
Banks/ Post Office	2% (Banco de Brasil; Post Office)	30% (NatWest)	0%	0%	11% (Turkiye is Bankasi)	5%
Large MTOs	4% (Western Union)	22% (Western Union; MoneyGram)	11% (Western Union)	2% (Western Union and Dahabshiil)	0%	6%
Smaller niche MTOs	94% (LCC; Intertransfer; Speedfast; Moneyone Express; Money transfer; Safe Transfer; Easy Transfer; Transfast; Other*)	0%	74% (Sami Swoi; LCC; Gosia Travel; Hascobar; Cheque-point)	98% (Dhabshiil; IFTIN; Qaran Express; Mustaqbal; Amal; Somalia hawaala)	0%	74%
Hand carry	0%	48% (themselves and/or friends)	15% (themselves and/or friends)	0%	89% (family and friends)	15%

Note: * Including a hair salon and travel company

Source: Questionnaire surveys

using banks, and specifically NatWest, in order to remit. The reasons for this became evident in in-depth interviews when a number of migrants, like Anastas and Ivana, identified NatWest's 140 account,[14] which enabled them to open current accounts in the UK with an attached money transfer account (see also Chapters Two and Three). Wages received in current accounts could subsequently be transferred into the Money Transfer Account, with migrants nominating (a) named remittance recipient(s) in home countries who were issued a card and pin number enabling them to make withdrawals as and when necessary. The cost of this service is fairly high, with migrants charged £2 per month for these accounts, a further £4 for each transaction between their current and money transfer account, as well as an additional foreign exchange fee of 2.5 per cent per withdrawal (www.natwest.com). Despite these charges, for migrants like Anastas the availability of this facility was useful; he reported that: "when my mother needs money, she could use the card and there is no need to send money." This said, similar initiatives were not evident in the other migrant communities included in this research, with the handful of other migrants utilising bank remittance services often using the national banks of their own countries: Banco de Brasil and Turkiye is Bankasi, respectively.

In contrast, the majority of migrant men and women used MTOs to remit money, with 80 per cent of remittance sending routed through these organisations. A distinction could be made between the usage of the large MTOs, including Western Union and MoneyGram, and niche agencies. Again there were national differences in that while 22 per cent of the Bulgarian migrants used Western Union and MoneyGram, only 2 per cent of Somali respondents reported having used Western Union and/or MoneyGram, and then only in conjunction with Dahabshiil to send money to family members living in a refugee camp in Kenya. For the migrants who did use either of these two providers, the main reasons given were a faith in a global brand and the fact that remittances always got to their destination even while transaction costs were not always necessarily competitive. In the opinion of Andrez, a Polish man, who used Western Union:

> "It's OK, I think … [the money] goes quick … it's expensive maybe … I send via Western Union and they are expensive … yes, but they are reliable and I [have] never heard of anyone being cheated … some smaller companies can be dodgy… you know, bank accounts that do not exist, weeks delays while they use your money, so I prefer to send via [Western Union]. They are reliable."

This said, niche remittance service providers emerged as being particularly significant, with just under three quarters of the whole sample reporting that they used these agencies to remit money home, rising to 98 per cent of Somali and 94 per cent of Brazilian migrants. As evident in Table 6.2, migrants in both of these communities could identify a number of specialist agencies, a finding corroborated by London-based Brazilian magazines and newspapers, which indicate around a dozen or so operational money transfer agencies. Given the fierce competition both within this sector as well as with the larger MTOs, it is not surprising that many niche MTOs offer a number of incentives to attract customers. These include the introduction of loyalty cards, such as the 'Dahabcard' by Dahabshiil, whereby customers are able to collect points that they can redeem against lower transaction costs in the future, and the partial or complete waiving of the transfer fee. For example, a number of Brazilian migrants reported that they used the MTO, Intertransfer, as it did not charge a transfer fee, while Marcin from Poland reported that LCC had various deals whereby the first transfer was free, the second priced at £3 with every fifth transaction also being free. Other specialist services were identified by a Polish respondent; he had tried the LCC and Western Union, but reported that "Sami Swoi are the best – the best exchange rate, they text the family that money has been sent, the service is really very helpful."

While there is some debate on whether niche MTOs can be classified as formal or informal, with some arguing that (at least some of) these are perhaps best identified as semi-formal organisations, there were more informal remittance services subsumed within this sector, including those which operated out of other businesses and *doleiros* services in the Brazilian community. Taking these in turn, migrants across the five communities were able to identify businesses which offered remittance services in combination with other business services. This was highlighted in particular by a Brazilian migrant, Jacinto, who argued that many remittance agencies in London were in fact a "facade" and that there were "many dodgy agencies" around:

> "When I arrived here, there was this one called VIP ... When you actually went in, you were entering a mobile phone shop, and at the back they had the agency, a till, for making remittances, but I would not know about their legitimacy. I went there on a Friday to make my first remittance, but I did not like the look of the agency much, so I went to LCC. On the Monday VIP had closed down, with a debt of about £500,000."

Brazilian migrants also identified the operation of *doleiros*, defined as 'black' market currency dealers and/or people who own unlicensed and illegal money transmitting businesses in Brazil. Commonly associated with money laundering, these businesses offer both outward- and inward-bound currency transaction services (Dwyer, 2006). Within the context of remittances, migrants approached *doleiros* agents operating in London, providing them with the names and bank account details of recipients. This information was then passed on to collaborators in Brazil, with remittances being deposited in cash either at a bank till or via ATM. In this way a transnational remittance transaction was effectively registered as a domestic transaction. It is important to recognise that *doleiros* are able to make use of the banking infrastructure, given the relatively high levels of banking penetration at least in urban areas of Brazil, where 40 per cent of the population is banked. The agents then settle the transaction, often by means of the UK agent depositing the money in an offshore bank account. In the opinion of one Brazilian woman, Marcia:

> "You know that this issue of sending money home, it is illegal. These money transfer agencies are illegal. If the police descend on them, they can close them down, because it is money laundering here. When you send money from here, your money does not go straightaway. It goes to the account of a person who then will withdraw it and pay into your account, in cash. If you ask for someone to check it and look at their bank account to see how the money was received they will see an entry 'cash paid in', or still 'online payment into account', where 'online' means an internal process, a transfer made within your country."

Furthermore, Valério, also from Brazil, argued that "we know that it [remittance system] is run by the 'dollar men' there [money launderers]. They go and pay money into the accounts of those here who made the remittance. And we don't even know how their money gets in [Brazil]. It must be this transit of people who come and go."

Hand carrying was the final informal remittance mechanism identified and was important among migrants who came from countries that were geographically proximate to the UK and where remittances could be carried by migrants, family or friends travelling back to home villages, towns and cities. While the highest proportion of hand carrying was recorded among Turkish respondents (89 per cent), it was also significant in the Polish and Bulgarian communities, where cheaper travel opportunities meant that migrants were able to travel and hand carry money home frequently. As expressed by Andrez, a Polish man, who also used Western Union to remit: "of course the best way is to give to your family in person or to give to someone to hand over ... my brother-in-law took some cash some time ago and this is a safe way. You know one must trust the family." In an in-depth interview, a Turkish woman, Ayse, highlighted the advantages of hand carrying:

> "When I can I send money to my family by hand with friends that I have here, my family just go to the place where my friend lives and collects the money. It's not like with the banks and other organisations like MoneyGram, where you have to pay money to send money and where

at the receiving end the other person has to also pay some money. I just ask the friends if they are willing to [carry] some money and if they say yes, that is that – very simple and safe."

Clearly, trust played a key role in such informal mechanisms with all the migrants who sent remittances through family and friends highlighting that the money always got to its destination. Indeed, hand carrying also potentially enables migrants to balance demands for remittances on the grounds that if no one is travelling back to home countries then money cannot be sent.

Factors accounting for choice of RSPs

Broader research assumes that the key factor determining migrants' choice of RSPs is the cost of remitting, which consists of three elements: namely a transaction fee, foreign exchange spread and profit margins. To date, fee structures have often been opaque, with hidden charges and poor foreign exchange rates that penalise migrants, especially those sending small remittances, which comprise a large share of the remittance market. Given the significance of remittances in the contemporary global economy, even a small decrease in transaction costs can translate into noteworthy increases in remittance receipts (Carling et al, 2007). With the World Bank spearheading efforts to reduce the transaction costs of formal remittance services, the global average transaction cost has declined from 9.8 per cent to 8.72 per cent of the principal value in recent years (Hugo, 2010). Yet, despite this, the services offered by formal RSPs such as banks are still more expensive in comparison with semi-formal and informal RSPs. Within the UK, while the cost charged by SWIFT for account-to-account transfers is low, banks charge a flat fee to cover their administrative charges, which starts at £20 (Isaacs, 2008). In comparison, informal channels as a whole have an average cost of between 3 and 5 per cent of the principal value, while the cost of *hawaala* sending is less than 2 per cent and remittances sent by hand are often free (Sander, 2003; Hugo, 2010). Differences between official and 'black' market foreign exchange currency rates can also contribute to flourishing informal remittance markets.

In turn, the importance of cost in shaping migrant choice was evident in this research. This was perhaps best expressed by Jacinto, a Brazilian migrant, who argued that migrants who worked in the low-wage economy had to "sweat a lot to earn money here and send it over to

Brazil" and were therefore very mindful of the "tips" or transaction costs associated with remittance sending. Furthermore, formal RSPs, including banks, often came off worst in price comparisons not only because of high transaction costs but also because of poor exchange rate spread. The latter was evidenced in a focus group held with Brazilian migrants in which all the participants agreed that the exchange rate offered by the Brazilian state bank, Banco de Brasil, was "not so good, the exchange rate of remittance agencies is much better." Importantly, formally sent remittances also ran the risk of being picked up by tax authorities in home countries. Jacinto reflected that a number of his compatriots avoided using Banco do Brasil in case the Inland Revenue in Brazil taxed these. In his words, one did not want to "work hard here to pay the layabouts over there."

Yet, it was not only cost that drove migrant choice of RSPs. Although only a handful of migrants reported that their remittance transfers had failed to arrive at their destination in the year preceding the interview, 'trust' or 'security' featured prominently in migrants' narratives on why they had chosen specific RSPs and/or mechanisms to remit money. Thus, a number of migrant men and women argued that while cost was important, this had to be balanced against security. In the same focus group discussion identified above, the participants agreed that while niche MTOs offered more competitive prices: "it is dangerous [to use these], like with Banco do Brasil it is all above board, so you send your money and you know it will arrive, but the exchange rate is no good, whereas with the agencies it is dangerous but their exchange rate is much better. You really risk [losing your money] in the remittance agencies." In all cases, migrants ensured that remittances had reached their destination by either phoning or emailing relatives, or vice versa. Within this context, the instant messaging services offered by some MTOs like Sami Swoi (already identified) were highly valued.

In turn, irregular migrants were at a particular disadvantage in cases where remittances failed to arrive in home countries, again reflecting the matrix of vulnerability that they were exposed to. Marina, from Brazil, who had experienced significant delays in one of her remittance transactions, recounted how when she complained to her remittance provider that she would go to the police, she was asked to produce her passport:

> "And immediately I realised that what he wanted to see was my visa, to check whether I was here illegally. So he must have thought, 'If she is illegal, she won't go to the police.' He thought I was bluffing and that I could just kiss

the money goodbye. So I showed him my Italian passport, and then he said, 'OK, we'll sort this out by tomorrow, no need to go to the police.' So, it all calmed down."

Given her dual nationality (see also Chapter Four), Marina was able to confront staff employed at this RSP. In her opinion, however, others were not so fortunate, as she went on to ruminate:

"So, imagine someone who sends all their savings. He works a whole year and sends it all in one go, say £5,000. How is he going to complain [if it goes missing] if he is an illegal, how is he going to deal with the police? So, it is difficult … I still use this same money transfer [organisation], and it is tricky, really, when you're dealing with money."

The increased demand for identification documents by some RSPs also has an important bearing upon migrants' remittance-sending practices. As highlighted in Chapters Two and Three, banks in the UK are obliged to comply with a range of anti-money laundering regulations, a number of which relate to the production and verification of identity documents. Furthermore, following the introduction of the Payment Services Directive in the UK, more pressure might potentially be brought to bear upon other RSPs regarding 'KYC' requirements. To date, NBFIs – and especially niche MTOs – have been much more flexible than banks, with the majority not requiring any identification for transactions below £600 as well as for repeat transaction customers (Isaacs, 2008). Furthermore, informal discussions with several representatives from the MTO sector revealed the incidence of what may be termed 'front of shop' and 'back of shop' services, whereby the latter could be used to remit larger sums of money without having to produce the prerequisite identification documents. This was explained in terms of the intense competition endemic in this sector and the consequent importance of retaining clients.

Again, 'KYC' requirements pose particular challenges to irregular migrants. A Polish migrant, Marcin, commented that prior to his country's ascension to the EU, when Polish migration to the UK was much more constrained, it was common practice to send money back home in letters or parcels even though these were at risk of being stolen because "I am sure in Poland whenever someone saw a stamp from that town [in Scotland, where he worked at that time] the envelope or the parcel [would] disappear." Yet, it was not only irregular migrant status that led to a distrust of KYC requirements. Within the Somali community, suspicion about the collection of personal information, as well as a general fear of surveillance, meant that where large sums of money were being sent back home, the identification requirement was circumvented by multiple trips to a remittance agency over a period of time or by organising a number of family members to each remit smaller amounts of money. Crucially, even while formal mechanisms may replicate some of the strengths of informal remittance systems such as transaction costs, longer operating hours, remote service provision and language provision, they cannot address the requirement for anonymity (Hudson, 2007).

Finally, customer service also featured prominently among the reasons identified for the use of specific RSPs. At least part of the attraction of (especially niche) MTOs is undoubtedly related to the fact that they are tailored to a migrant client base. The physical presence of niche MTOs in the communities in which migrant communities dominate as well as longer opening hours are particularly suited to migrants' working patterns (see Chapter Three). Furthermore, many provide language-specific services to their clients, are familiar with the places and the people that have been left behind and have a wider presence in their communities. Banks would be hard pressed to compete with the services that MTOs offer. Indeed, even while remittance agencies are often seen as 'transaction based' businesses as opposed to 'relationship based' banks, it could be argued that these agencies are more in the business of building relationships with migrant communities by re-inscribing social relations into financial transactions. Yet, many of these operators are themselves identified as 'high risk' businesses and face considerable hurdles in opening business bank accounts in high street retail banks.

Conclusion

This chapter has identified the growing importance of remittances, which are increasingly positioned as the 'new development finance' in the contemporary global economy. Based upon an emerging consensus among both global and national policy makers of the interconnections between economic and financial development, these flows of finance are being linked to broader ambitions of financial inclusion and the notion of 'financial democracy' (Hudson, 2008). The key to unlocking the development potential of migration has been increasingly interpreted as resting upon the formalisation and, some would argue, financialisation of remittance flows and the inclusion of greater numbers of people in formal financial circuits. Yet, an investigation of migrant men and women's remittance-sending practices revealed considerable diversity in motivations to remit and the funding of remittances as well as the ways in which money travels back to home countries. Clearly evident from what are complex financial practices is the fact that remittance sending cannot simply be understood within the context of asset accumulation. Given the diverse national backgrounds of the migrant communities included in this research, the money that migrants send home continues to function as a crucial safety net for impoverished families. In turn, it is also clear that remittance sending can heighten the vulnerability of migrant households, who are either surviving on low incomes and/or benefits and/or supporting young children and families in a very expensive city. In this context the obligation to remit weighs heavily on some.

The mechanisms through which money is remitted back to home countries also vary both across and within migrant communities. Even while the broader ambition may be to channel a higher proportion of remittances through formal financial organisations including banks, the findings here suggest that semi-formal and informal mechanisms, including a vibrant niche MTO sector, play a highly significant role in channelling the remittance traffic between London and the villages, towns and countries where remittances are sent. Furthermore, although there is evidence of some malpractice within the informal sector, in that initiatives related to making the remittance marketplace more transparent and competitive are in the interests of migrants, offering them some level of protection and redress, it is also clear that migrants balance different and often competing priorities when deciding how to remit money back home. These choices relate not only to economic imperatives such as keeping transaction costs low, but to a wide range of factors including security, trust and a quest for anonymity. It is often the most vulnerable migrants – asylum seekers, refugees and undocumented – who are more likely to use informal remittance systems, which are attractive for precisely the reasons why governments and global institutions are wary of them: there is no paper trail (Al-Rodhan, 2006). Implicit in policies to improve transparency and reduce costs is also an attempt to cajole, if not force, remittance recipients to save more and consume less, which is not necessarily best for their welfare (Hudson 2008). The challenge then is to find a balance between the formal and the informal, and to do so in the interests of migrants and their families.

Notes

[1] Financial remittances are part of broader social, political and cultural connections between migrants and their home countries (Levitt, 1998; Faist, 2008; Datta, 2009a; Levitt and Lamba-Nieves, 2011). In turn, financial links are themselves diverse, including not only remittances but also philanthropic giving and capital investment (Orozco, 2007).

[2] Developing countries' share of these global flows amounted to US$81.3 billion in 2000 and US$307.1 billion in 2009 (World Bank, 2011).

[3] Remittance corridors link remitters in home countries to recipients in host countries. Very geographically specific, it is estimated that in 2005 there were 15,000 active remittance corridors operating across the globe (Orozco, 2005).

[4] Typically remittance inflows surpass ODA in middle-income countries and FDI in low-income countries (Toxopeus and Lensink, 2007).

[5] The *Financial Times* reported that while the main banks immediately closed their vaults in the aftermath of the earthquake in Haiti in 2010, the 42 offices of a microfinance agency that transferred remittances from the US, Fonkoze, remained open.

[6] Carling et al (2007) point out that the impact of remittances upon income inequality depends upon the class position of migrants and their families. If migrants come from the poorer strata of society, remittances may reduce income inequalities. However, the sending of remittances by middle-income migrants is likely to exacerbate income inequalities in poor communities.

[7] Both of these MTOs have extensive geographic coverage: Western Union has 470,000 agent locations across 200 countries while MoneyGram has 233,000 agents working in 191 countries (www.westernunion.com). The large market share of these MTOs in certain 'light traffic' remittance corridors gives them near monopoly status, which can result in higher transaction fees (Yujuico, 2009).

[8] Banks only serve 5 per cent of the remittance market in the US, with the main hurdle being limited banking penetration in home countries through which remittances could potentially be paid out (Yujuico, 2009).

[9] These principles include transparency and consumer protection, improvement of payment system infrastructure, sound and proportionate legal and regulatory environment, competitive market conditions, and appropriate governance and risk management practices (Committee on Payment and Settlement Systems and World Bank, 2006).

[10] Similar services are offered in Spain via the www.remesas.org website, the Netherlands (www.geldnaarhius.nl) and Norway (www.sendepenger.no) (Carling et al, 2007). In turn, the need for such services is evidenced by mystery shopping exercises that reveal a wide variation in remittance fees. For example, Isaacs (2008) reports that the fees charged for a £100 remittance from the UK to Nigeria ranged from £3 to £21.

[11] Although it is widely recognised that FATF recommendations are essentially 'soft law', it is also the case that these recommendations carry considerable weight because of the political and economic pressures that can be exerted on non-compliant sectors and countries (Vleck, 2006; Lindley, 2009).

[12] This said, regulation may result in higher morbidity rates among smaller MTOs whose operating costs will increase (Lindley, 2009).

[13] The use of loans to underwrite remittances was more evident in in-depth interviews and was under-reported in the questionnaire surveys.

[14] The HSBC passport account (discussed in Chapters Two and Three) also provides access to a Western Union Gold Plus Card, which enables migrants to make savings on remittance transaction costs.

SEVEN

Looking forward: from exclusion to inclusion and back?

In bringing the book to a close, this concluding chapter summarises the main findings of the research underpinning *Migrants and their money* before considering its wider implications. Thus far, the book has detailed the dominance of finance in the UK, which is the outcome of extensive neoliberal restructuring of the British economy and state. These processes of financialisation have been accompanied by ,and shaped the nature and scope of, financial exclusion, as particular peoples and places have been pushed to the fringes of financial circuits because of a complex intersection of marginality. Furthermore, given the penetration of finance into all reaches of economic and social life, the consequences of financial exclusion have been shown to be not only severe and multifaceted, but also reinforcing of broader processes of socioeconomic and political marginalisation thus potentially eroding the range of rights and entitlements afforded to excluded groups.

This book has demonstrated how migrant men and women, originating from five diverse countries in the global South, and East and Central Europe and confronted by the sophisticated financial landscape of London, negotiate their access to a range of banking, savings, credit and remittance services. Undoubtedly, the key financial resource for migrant men and women was banking, primarily because of the role that it played in structuring access to London's labour market and the welfare state. As demonstrated in Chapter Three, almost irrespective of the reasons why migrants had migrated to London, work – and in particular formal sector employment – assumed a special importance for many, which in turn necessitated banking access because of the declining incidence of cash wages. For those unable to work, access to welfare payments was also dependent upon having a bank account. Importantly, and reflecting the value attached to financial access in a financialised economy, a number of migrant men and women also raised the significance of banking in terms of demonstrating the legitimacy of their presence in the city as well as augmenting their social standing within their own and wider communities. Yet, this said, the fact that bank accounts predominantly served as vehicles for the receipt of wages and/or benefits was highlighted by migrants' banking practices, on the basis of which the majority could, in fact, be categorised as 'marginally banked'. A more nuanced investigation of the types of bank accounts that were held, the ways in which these were used and their everyday financial practices highlighted, with some exceptions, a continued preference for the management of household economies in cash and a fairly limited use of wider banking services.

Demonstrating the significance of banking in facilitating broader socioeconomic access, high levels of banking inclusion across the five communities were largely attributable to the persistence of migrant men and women. As discussed in Chapter Four, despite policy interventions designed to address some of the particular constraints that excluded groups face when opening accounts, high street retail banks continue to implement varied and unduly complicated procedures that block entry for those who are not part of the mainstream. Utilising theoretical frameworks to understand how migrants strategise to cope with wider exclusions in host countries, this book has highlighted the diverse legal and illegal strategies deployed by migrants to engender banking inclusion, which were shaped by the nature of the obstacles that they encountered. While for some migrants the key imperative was to 'speed up' the process of opening accounts, for others the obstacles were more significant and related to the management of irregularity. Premised upon both local and transnational financial, civic, human and social assets, these financial strategies then assumed diverse forms. These included the utilisation of social networks consisting of immediate and extended family and friends as well as wider migrant communities. These were deployed to access financial information, with local contacts providing financial advice, acting as interpreters and directing migrants to particular bank branches and even tellers willing to accept the identification documents migrants had at their disposal. For others, these strategies focused upon an elision of an irregular identity, achieved through the acquisition of dual nationality, purchase of identification documents and/or bank accounts as well as sharing of accounts. Perhaps unsurprisingly, these strategies carried significant risks for migrants, reflecting the inherent fragility of their inclusion strategies.

Away from banking, the savings, credit and remittance-sending practices developed by migrant men and women displayed far more variety. Taking these in turn, as demonstrated in Chapter Three, despite being concentrated in low-wage work or dependent upon benefits, migrant men and women displayed a significant propensity to save, although this varied across the five communities. Identifiable as 'rainy day', 'instrumental' and 'non-savers', the motivations for saving were diverse, reflecting both short-term and long-term financial priorities from meeting everyday expenses, saving for children as well as investment in either the UK or home countries. Correspondingly, while many were only able to save small amounts, in a number of cases migrant men and women were putting aside a significant proportion of their weekly wage packet. Given the low wages earned by those located at the bottom end of London's labour market, these kinds of savings were only possible through both the intensification of work, by having two or more jobs, working long hours, combining formal and informal work, as well as cutting back on everyday expenses by living in multi-let accommodation and shopping around for the best deals in relation to food and clothing. The ability to do this was, in turn, shaped by household structure in London, with those with young children less able to pursue these strategies. Differences between the numbers of savers and levels of savings in the five communities can also be traced to other factors including unemployment, benefit dependency as well as poverty. Importantly, a significant proportion of migrants' savings were deposited in bank accounts although much of this accumulated in current accounts as opposed to savings accounts or other savings products. The decision on whether to accumulate savings in the UK or in home countries was explained in relation to migration plans as well as immigration status. Unsurprisingly, many irregular migrants viewed their stay in London as temporary, while fears of being apprehended and deported meant that savings were sent back home at regular intervals.

In turn, attitudes towards credit and debt were ambivalent, with many migrants reflecting a desire to avoid debt largely due to a realistic assessment of their (in)ability to pay back these loans. Others argued that access to formal credit was desirable for a range of purposes including bridging cash-flow gaps relating to everyday expenses incurred in London; the re-payment of loans from family and friends; overdrafts and credit card bills accumulated in home countries, often in relation to funding migration; as well as the acquisition of assets. While there was a demand for formal credit in the form of overdrafts, credit cards and personal loans, the experiences of a number of migrants reflected how access to such credit was varied. Some migrants had attempted to access bank credit and been refused, while others had not tried to access formal credit at all. Importantly, while both the Polish and Bulgarian migrant communities commented upon the availability of credit in London, Brazilian migrants in particular complained that credit was often withheld from their community because of perceptions of fraud, illegality and risk. In turn, Somali and Turkish migrants often made little attempt to even attempt to access formal credit because of an appreciation that they would be unlikely to receive these loans given their informal and irregular employment, low incomes and lack of credit history with banks.

While the significance of banking to migrant men and women's lives has been engineered by changes in the ways in which payments are made in the UK, migrants were able to exercise more choice in the ways in which they saved and, in particular, in the ways in which they drew credit. It is important to acknowledge here that these financial practices are both shaped by exclusion but also by a preference for more informal ways of 'doing finance'. An examination of savings and credit-related financial practices highlighted a range of activities undertaken on an individual, one-to-one and group basis, albeit with some important variations between and within the communities covered by this research. In particular, the research uncovered the importance of reciprocal borrowing and lending practices that occurred between family members and friends as well as group-based lending and saving clubs in the Somali and Turkish communities. The persistence and resilience of these savings and credit practices that have been transported and then re-created over transnational space is significant. Furthermore, these practices are underwritten by trust, which manifests itself in myriad ways as reciprocal relationships draw in family and friends located in both local and transnational spaces.

Remittance sending was a dominant practice in all five of the migrant communities. Motives for sending remittances could be divided into three interrelated categories: altruism and obligations to family members left behind; payment of debts, often incurred by migrants and/or their families to finance migration; and investment purposes. Reflecting the political and economic reality of their families and home countries, the majority of Somali and Turkish participants remitted money to meet the subsistence needs of their relatives, with both men and women articulating a moral obligation to remit. The high incidence of remittance sending in these two communities is all the more remarkable because of low wages, unemployment and benefit dependency. Among other migrant men and women, remittance sending could be linked to asset accumulation both in the form of savings held in bank accounts or investments in property and businesses. This research uncovered the use of wages, savings, loans and even benefits, to fund remittances. Reflecting the diversity of London's migrant community, migrant men and women identified a range of remittance service providers from the formal to the informal. These included banks, large Money Transfer Organisations (MTOs), smaller specialist MTOs as well as hand carrying. Migrants illustrated a high level of financial capability when it came to remitting, with the choice of remittance service provider premised not only on cost (itself shaped by transaction fees and foreign exchange rates) but wider factors including trust, security and language. For many migrants these more complex considerations resulted in the use of informal or semi-formal remittance service providers.

Building upon these findings, it is possible to extrapolate broader insights as to the factors which shape migrant men and women's financial practices in London. Particularly significant is the fact that experiences of financial exclusion are by no means homogenous among and within migrant communities. As noted in Chapter One, London's migrant communities reflect significant intra- and inter-community diversities, whether this is measured in terms of their national origins, labour market position, immigration status, duration of migration, language competencies, gender, ethnic and class compositions. In turn, these diversities crucially shape migrants' access to, and usage of, a range of financial services, the strategies that they devise in order to engender inclusion as well as those that enable them to cope with exclusion. This suggests the critical importance of understanding the financial needs, practices and priorities of specific migrant communities when devising local financial inclusion policy and development.

Immigration status warrants special attention when considering migrant communities' access to and usage of financial services, a finding highlighted by the focus of this research on very diverse communities that included asylum seekers, refugees and economic migrants whose migration status ranged from the regular to the irregular. Arguably, irregular migrants, asylum seekers and refugees are subject to a matrix of vulnerabilities that are shaped by their immigration status, labour market position and financial exclusion. Broader research suggests that the immediate needs of migrants upon arrival in a new country arc jobs, housing and, increasingly, in the context of the financialisation of advanced economies, a bank account. Even while regular migrants may face delays in accessing one or all of these, irregular migrants are likely to be particularly marginalised. As such, immigration status drives the 'choices' that migrant men and women make, with irregularity making illegal financial arrangements much more likely. Within this context, there is a clear need for initiatives that address the conundrum faced by irregular migrants whereby irregularity prohibits the legal management of money, thus further heightening vulnerability.

Transnationality also structures migrants' financial lives. As highlighted in Chapter One, the 'daily rhythms' of migrants lives are played out across transnational spaces and governed by multiple sets of laws and institutions (Levitt and Glick-Schiller, 2004). As such, the financial practices that migrants pursue in host countries are crucially shaped by their transnational assets and liabilities, the particular sets of financial knowledge that they bring with them, the financial habits that they have developed in other places, the transnational obligations that they bear, *as well as* the financial landscapes that they encounter in host countries and cities like London (Datta, 2011a).

In sum, it is clear that a focus on what may be termed as a 'practices' approach to financial exclusion and inclusion, which considers migrants' financial lives in the round, is warranted. The adoption of such a holistic approach demonstrates how the repertoires of financial practices that migrant men and women develop are shaped by processes of exclusion *and* inclusion, mediated by migrants' agency and the mobilisation of local and transnational assets, and draw upon both formal and informal or alternative financial spheres. Remarkably diverse and extending far beyond remittances, which have been the usual focus of attention, these practices are crucial in ensuring their wellbeing and myriad integrations into financialised societies.

Looking ahead: finance, migration and in/exclusion

The research underpinning *Migrants and their money* coincided with a deeply damaging and prolonged economic downturn, the impacts of which continue to reverberate across multiple domains. In late 2011, the Governor of the Bank of England, Sir Mervyn King, admitted that the UK was in the 'most serious financial crisis, at least since the 1930s, if not ever' (Kirkup, 2011). This influenced his decision to inject a further £75 billion into the British economy as part of a wider 'quantitative easing' package in an attempt to support economic recovery, despite fears of the potentially adverse impact of this upon rising inflation rates (Elliott and Allen, 2011). The Eurozone debt crisis poses the most recent challenge to a fragile recovery, which is already predicted as being 'anaemic' and protracted (Fix et al, 2009; ONS, 2010; Sumption, 2010). Perhaps unsurprisingly, this period of economic turmoil has been accompanied by significant political change as the New Labour government, in power for 13 years, was replaced by a Coalition government formed by the Conservative and Liberal Democratic parties in May 2010.

In turn, these events have undoubtedly had, and will continue to have, profound implications on academic and policy debates relating to finance, migration and exclusion for some time to come. As discussed at the start of this book, the economic downturn did challenge the unquestioning dominance of finance in the UK. There is a clear public appetite for the reformation of the financial sector and institutions, particularly banks, both in the UK and beyond. Illustrating the erosion of public confidence and trust in banks, a survey conducted by the UK *Which?* magazine in 2011 revealed that 43 per cent of consumers believed that banks would not be sympathetic if they got into financial difficulty while over a third, 37 per cent, did not trust financial institutions to act in the best interests of the British economy. Coalescing around anti-capitalism demonstrations, diverse groups have demanded a reformation of national and global financial industries in the UK, across Europe and in the US. Despite this, the political response in the UK has been to tread carefully amidst unconfirmed fears that too much intervention will lead to financial firms abandoning the country.[1]

Within the specific context of financial inclusion, it is important to acknowledge that criticisms of the New Labour governments' programmes were growing even prior to its departure from office. These were articulated around concerns that initiatives introduced to facilitate access to a range of financial services including banking, savings and credit had predominantly focused upon expanding inclusion into mainstream financial markets rather than facilitating broader choice and innovation (see Chapter Two; see also Runnymede Trust, 2009). Thus, critics argued that even while '[the UK] needs a revolution in financial service provision, not some token reform of the current regime', government-led programmes were largely driven by a 'market-based agenda' that prioritised the demands and needs of the financial services industry as opposed to a rights-based approach that would have emanated from the perspective of people located at the margins of financial circuits (Hannam, 2009; Khan, 2009). As detailed in Chapter Two, even while a number of financial products and services have been developed over the last decade or so, these have largely been shaped by the interests of a neoliberalised economy, reformed welfare state and a powerful financial services industry, all of which are collectively dependent upon a financially included *and* literate citizenry.

While the incoming government was largely silent on financial inclusion, with scant attention having been paid to these issues in the election campaigns of both the Liberal Democrat and Conservative political parties, once in office the Coalition terminated a number of financial inclusion programmes on fiscal grounds (see Chapter Two). Furthermore, its emerging agenda reveals a continued emphasis upon *personal* responsibility as evidenced in a speech made by the Financial Secretary to the Treasury, Mike Hoban, in 2010, in which he argued that 'families themselves need to take responsibility for providing for their future, especially as the cost of doing so is rising inexorably' (www. hm-treasury.gov.uk). In turn, the Coalition has three broad ambitions in relation to financial inclusion that are not substantively different from those of its predecessor: to build a stable and responsive financial system, to enable customers to take a responsible approach to personal finance, and to make provisions for vulnerable customers by supporting their access to essential financial services (www.hm-treasury.gov.uk). These ambitions are to be realised through the establishment of a new regulatory body, the Financial Conduct Authority (FCA), which will oversee the financial services industry; the Money Advice Service, which will provide financial advice; the development of a 'new suite of simple products' (as yet largely unspecified), aiding consumers to save and plan for their retirement (which has been postponed to 67 years of age); and an examination of issues relating to lending (www. hm-treasury.gov.uk).

Even while the details of the Coalition government's vision on financial in/exclusion are emerging, some tentative conclusions can be drawn here. For a start, it is clear that the priority that financial inclusion was once afforded in public policy agendas, detailed in Chapter Two, is much less evident as politicians are more focused upon shoring up the financial sector in general rather than addressing issues related to exclusion per se. The appetite for creating niche products and services that would serve the needs of marginalised groups, including migrants, is certainly not evident. Nascent policies continue to be shaped by 'supply side' or 'market demand', with little innovation apparent in terms of widening choice for individuals and households and supporting viable alternative financial institutions that can capitalise people who are on the margins of formal financial circuits such as migrants (see Chapter Two). It is perhaps ironic that in a context in which access to financial resources such as credit is becoming increasingly restricted, and savings are being eroded, it is individuals and households who will continue to bear responsibility for engendering their inclusion into financial circuits, as well as suffer the consequences of being unable to do so.

Turning to consider the implications of these broader changes on migrants and migration, as discussed in Chapter One, the economic downturn coincided with high levels of immigration to the UK (Papademetriou and Terrazas, 2009; Rogers et al, 2009; Sumption, 2010; Datta, 2011b). As recognised in wider research, economic downturns do not affect all groups equally, such that even within disadvantaged groups some are more affected than others (Hudson et al, 2007; Khan, 2009). Public hostility against migrants and migration was evident even in the early days of the downturn. An opinion poll conducted in February

2008 in the UK reported that more than 40 per cent of the British electorate rated race relations and immigration as their most pressing concern (Ipsos MORI, 2008). Such concerns subsequently manifested themselves in the Lindsey Oil Refinery strikes, which articulated a particular vision of economic nationalism and the need to protect 'British jobs for British workers', as well as a sustained campaign of racist intimidation against Romanian immigrants in Northern Ireland, leading many to temporarily or permanently abandon their homes.

It can be argued that two sets of policies have developed in relation to migration in the UK: those which seek to control the entry of people into the country as well as those related to the integration into British society of those already in the country. Despite the fact that the underlying drivers for migration to the UK remain in place – including a demand for migrant labour in both top- and bottom-end jobs due to the continued shift to a service-based economy, the role that skilled migrants in particular could play in regaining a competitive edge in a global recession as well as the demographic challenges posed by an ageing population – the Coalition government has sought to intensify immigration controls (Dobson et al, 2009; Somerville and Sumption, 2009; UNDP, 2009). Seizing on the anti-immigration sentiment evident during the 2010 national election, the Conservative party's election manifesto pledged to 'take net migration back to the levels of the 1990s – tens of thousands a year, not hundreds of thousands', with the UK Prime Minister, David Cameron, undertaking to pursue 'good immigration, not mass immigration' (BBC, 2011). Furthermore, the Liberal Democrats' campaign pledge to grant an amnesty to irregular migrants who were already in the UK did not survive the negotiations that preceded the formation of the Coalition government. Within this context, the public policy focus has been on particularly curtailing non-EU migration, even while partial restrictions relating to A8 and A2 migrants have also been renewed (see Chapter One). As a result, the avenues for legal migration into the UK are being eroded and/ or restricted, particularly for those coming from poorer parts of the world. Immigration status in turn, is clearly significant in determining access to a range of socioeconomic, political and financial rights and entitlements.

Inter-relatedly, migrant exclusion from labour markets is also recognised as escalating during times of economic contraction (Datta, 2011b). Broader research suggests that at times of downturn jobs may be reserved for native workers: migrant workers who are the 'last hired' are also the 'first fired' and face higher than average unemployment, partly due to their concentration in those sectors of the economy that are particularly exposed to downturn, including construction, manufacturing and retail (Rogers et al, 2009; Datta et al, 2011b). While UK unemployment in the third quarter of 2008 was 6 per cent, it was 20 per cent higher among migrant workers and 40 per cent higher for non-OECD migrants (Somerville and Sumption, 2009). Thus, migrants – and particularly those coming from poorer parts of the world – are likely to fare the worst, potentially becoming detached from the labour market for significant periods, thereby damaging their subsequent chances of finding employment (Somerville and Sumption, 2009). Furthermore, given the concentration of migrants in low-paid, low-skilled jobs, those who are in employment have had to put up with eroding or stagnating wage levels, and worsening working conditions (Fix et al, 2009; Rogers et al, 2009; Somerville and Sumption, 2009). Given that migrants' access to welfare and benefits is restricted, periods of unemployment not only exacerbate their financial and economic vulnerability but also push them into taking on any job, rendering them further vulnerable to an erosion of working standards during economic downturns (Fix et al, 2009; Somerville and Sumption, 2009). Competition between both migrant and British-born workers, and between migrant communities themselves, have also been shown to have intensified (Glossop and Shaheen, 2009; Rogers et al, 2009). Beyond the labour market, migrants' demands for public services such as education, housing and transportation have been an area of concern for some time now, which may be exacerbated as 'the new fiscal austerity' begins to bite (Sumption, 2010). While the assumption that migrants may return home at a time of financial crisis is supported by some data, this does not apply across the board to all migrants, particularly those who have come from further afield and whose routes into the UK are being systematically eroded. Indeed, even European migrants, who are often portrayed as 'regional free movers' who come and go as economic circumstances dictate, may choose to stay, particularly if they have been joined by partners and children (Favell, 2008: 203).

As this book has detailed, these multiple and potentially intensifying social and economic exclusions clearly interplay with financial exclusion. As such, the current shifts towards economic austerity as well as highly restrictive immigration legislation may potentially threaten future generations of migrants arriving in London and elsewhere in the UK to engender their access to financial services so as to secure their integration into British society.

Note

[1] This said, the government has convened an Independent Commission on Banking to investigate the structure and competition of UK banks, introduced a bank levy, required banks to sign up to a Code of Practice on taxation and made some attempt to clamp down on banks' 'bonus culture' by linking these to evidence of greater lending to small and medium-sized businesses, which are seen as being critical to economic recovery (www.hm-treasury.gov.uk).

Methodological note

The research material presented in this book was generated as part of the 'Migrants and their Money' research project based at Queen Mary, University of London between 2007 and 2009. A mixed methods methodological framework combining quantitative and qualitative methods was deployed in the research, which involved the use of a range of research tools including two questionnaire surveys, in-depth interviews and focus group discussions. The project focused primarily upon Brazilian, Bulgarian, Polish, Turkish and Somali migrants in London. The decision to focus on these five migrant communities in London was shaped predominantly by the fact that this would enable an investigation into various dynamics that are known to have an important bearing upon migrant experiences of financial in/exclusion including labour market position, immigration status, transnational financial practices, diverse gender- and class-based positions and ideologies, language competencies, as well as length of stay in the UK. The 2001 National Census reported total UK-based populations of 8,000 Brazilians, 5,350 Bulgarians, 44,000 Somali, 52,893 Turkish and 60,711 Polish migrants. More recent studies estimated that the size of these communities vary between 60,000 and 100,000 Somalis, approximately 200,000 Brazilians, between 515,000 and a million Polish, and 40,000 and 170,000 Bulgarians (Olden, 1999; Ahmed, 2000; Sporten et al, 2006; Duvall 2007; Evans et al, 2007; Council of Ministers 2008; Home Office 2010; Hopkins, 2010). Furthermore, while Brazilian, Somali and Turkish populations are particularly concentrated in London (ranging from between 65 and 80 per cent, between 55 and 68 per cent and 74 per cent, respectively), Polish and Bulgarian populations are more geographically dispersed, partly as a result of their routes into the UK (Olden, 1999; Ahmed, 2000; Sporten et al, 2006; Erdemir and Vasta, 2007; Evans et al, 2007). Just under a quarter of Polish migrants are found in the capital (Duvall, 2007; Council of Ministers, 2008; Home Office, 2010; ONS, 2011). As highlighted in the book, inter- and intra-community differences in immigration status (ranging from asylum seekers, refugees, irregular migrants, those who had entered the UK as tourists and students to A2 and A8 migrants), labour market participation (including those who were unemployed, working informally and in the formal sector), as well transnational financial practices and awareness were crucial in understanding migrant experiences of financial in/exclusion.

Undertaken in two stages, the first questionnaire survey was conducted in partnership with London Citizens in 2007, and involved the design of a survey for the use of five interns. The questionnaire sought to capture baseline information on migrants' socioeconomic characteristics including; their household composition; migration and labour market histories; access to, and use of, financial services, including banking, savings, credit and remittance transaction agencies; barriers to utilising financial services; and financial practices in relation to savings, debt and remittances. Combining both closed and open-ended questions, a total of 188 questionnaires were completed in the first stage, with migrants drawn from 11 different nationalities including Brazilian, Somali, Turkish and Polish (see Datta, 2007a). In the second stage of the research, the same questionnaire was used to interview Bulgarian, Somali and Brazilian migrants, and at this stage of the research a further 166 questionnaire interviews were completed. The book draws upon a total of 319 questionnaires.[1] See Table App.1.

Table App.1: Gender and nationality profile of questionnaire respondents

Country of origin	Number of male participants (n=167)	Number of female participants (n=152)	Total number of participants (n=319)
Brazil	61	58	119
Bulgaria	24	30	54
Poland	22	14	36
Somalia	45	35	80
Turkey	15	15	30

Source: Questionnaire surveys

In addition to the questionnaire survey, 89 in-depth interviews were conducted, 41 with male participants and 46 with female participants. The key issues explored in the in-depth interviews included participants' pre-migration financial practices; their migration history, with a particular focus on the motivations guiding migration, their migratory pathways, as well as the funding of migration; their financial lives in London in relation to banking, savings, accessing credit and managing debt; their remittance-sending practices; and the strategies adopted to access financial services as well as cope with financial exclusion. Migrants were also asked their opinions on how financial services could be improved to meet the needs of their respective communities. Some of the participants were identified in the first phase of the questionnaire survey. In-depth interviews proved to be an extremely useful tool in accessing more detailed and nuanced information regarding financial practices and experiences.

Three focus group discussions were arranged at the end of the research involving migrants drawn from the Brazilian, Bulgarian, and Somali communities. These included eight participants in the Brazilian community (three men and five women), nine respondents in the Bulgarian community (three men and six women), and seven respondents in the Somali community (two men and five women). The focus groups were held in various locations including St Anne's Catholic Church in Whitechapel, and the homes of migrants in South Ealing and Tower Hamlets. Techniques such as participatory diagramming were used to explore how migrants managed their financial resources, their awareness of financial products to save, access credit and send remittances, the potential take-up of new financial products and how financial exclusion could be addressed by community-based organisations and financial institutions. Furthermore, given that this research coincided with the economic downturn, the focus groups also provided an opportunity to discuss at length the impact of the recession on migrant workers (see Datta, 2011b).

Overall, two strategies were adopted to access migrant workers, who often represent a 'hard to reach' population, including a combination of 'cold calling' and snowballing. Multiple entry points were utilised in all communities so as to avoid bias. London Citizens networks were used to facilitate access in the first stage of the research. Advertisements were placed in a range of relevant London-based migrant media including the Bulgarian Newspaper, *BG BEN*, as well as a weekly Brazilian newspaper. Community organisations were particularly utilised in the Somali and Brazilian communities, particularly, in the case of the latter, the Brazilian Association in the UK. Furthermore, the inclusion of community researchers[2] enabled a targeting of specific areas in London where these five communities were known to be concentrated, including places of worship and work. Once initial interviews had been conducted, snowballing was utilised to identify and recruit further participants. Interviews were subsequently carried out across London in a range of locations varying from churches, restaurants, language schools, community centres, public libraries, hair salons, as well as the homes of the research participants. All the interviews were conducted face-to-face in the languages spoken by migrant men and women, which ranged between Portuguese, Spanish, Turkish, Polish, Somali, and French. The research data was analysed using computer software. The quantitative data derived from the two questionnaire surveys was entered into SPSS for analysis while the in-depth interviews were digitally recorded and subsequently translated into English. The names of all the research participants as well as banks in specific contexts have been anonymised to protect their identities. The project was approved by the Queen Mary, University of London Ethics Committee.

Notes

[1] While a total of 354 questionnaires were completed, this book draws specifically upon the 319 interviews conducted with Brazilian, Bulgarian, Polish, Somali and Turkish migrants.

[2] I am particularly indebted to the five interns who participated in this project via the London Citizens Summer Academy in 2007, they are Nil Tuptuk, Olivia Sheringham, Ana-Carla Reis França, Awale Elmi and Michal Garapich. I am further indebted to Zahra Gibril, Yara Evans and Irinia Changerova for their contribution to the second phase of this research.

References

Adams, R. and Page, J. (2005) 'Do international migration and remittances reduce poverty in developing countries?', *World Development*, vol 33, pp 1645-69.

Affleck, A. and Mellor, M. (2006) 'Community Development Finance: a neo-market solution to social exclusion', *Journal of Social Policy*, vol 35, no 2, 303-319.

Aglietta, M. (2000) 'Shareholder value and corporate governance: some tricky questions', *Economy and Society*, vol 29, no 1, pp 146–59.

Ahmed, I. (2000) 'Remittances and their impact in postwar Somaliland', *Disasters*, vol 24, no 2, pp 380-9.

Aitken, R. (2010) 'Ambiguous incorporations: microfinance and global governmentality', *Global Networks*, vol 10, no 2, pp 223-43.

Allen, J. (2010) 'The City and finance: changing landscapes of power', in N. Coe and A. Jones (eds) *The economic geography of the UK*, London: Sage Publishing.

Al-Rodhan, N.R.F. (2006) 'Editorial: Informal remittance flows and their implications for global security', *Geneva Centre for Security Policy (GCSP) Policy Series Brief 11*, Geneva.

Al-Sharmani, M. (2010) 'Transnational family networks in the Somali diaspora in Egypt: women's roles and differentiated experiences', *Gender, Place and Culture*, vol 17, no 4, pp 499-518.

Ameudo-Dorantes, C. and Pozo, S. (2005) 'On the use of differing money transmission methods by Mexican immigrants', *International Migration Review*, vol 39, no 3, pp 554-76.

Ameudo-Dorantes, C. and Bansak, C. (2006) 'Money transfers among banked and unbanked Mexican immigrants', *Southern Economic Journal*, vol 73, no 2, pp 374-401.

Anderloni, L. and Vandone, D. (2006) *New market segments: migrants and financial innovation*, Finance, Business and Marketing Working Paper 2, Milan: Universitá degli Studi di Milano.

Anderloni, L., Bayot, B., Bledowski, P., Iwanicz-Drozdowska, M. and Kempson, E. (2008) *Financial services provision and prevention of financial exclusion*, Report prepared for the European Commission Directorate General for Employment, Social Affairs and Equal Opportunities. Available at: www.fininc.eu (accessed 15 August 2008).

Anderson, B., Ruhs, R., Rogaly, B. and Spencer, S. (2006) *Fair enough? Central and East European migrants in low wage employment in the UK*, Report written for the Joseph Rowntree Foundation, published as a COMPAS Report.

Andreotti, A. (2006) 'Coping strategies in a wealthy city in northern Italy', *International Journal of Urban and Regional Research,* vol 30, no 2, pp 328–45.

Angelov, G. and Vankova, Z. (2011) *Bulgarian labour migration: Do restrictions make sense?,* Policy Brief, Sofia: Open Society Institute.

Appleseed and Community Resource Group (2004) *Meeting the financial service needs of Mexican immigrants: a survey of Texas financial institutions,* Austin, Texas.

Appleyard, L. (2011), 'Community Development Finance Institutions (CDFIs): geographies of financial inclusion in the US and the UK', *Geoforum,* vol 42, no 2, pp 250-58.

Ardener, S. (2010) 'Microcredit, money transfers, women and the Cameroonian diaspora', *Afrika Focus,* vol 23, no 2, pp 11-24.

Ardener, S. and Burman, S. (eds.) (1995) *Money-go-rounds: the importance of rotating savings and credit associations for women,* Oxford and Washington DC: Berg.

Atia, M. (2007) 'In whose interest? Financial surveillance and the circuits of exception in the war on terror', *Environment and Planning D,* vol 25, pp 447-75.

Atkinson, A. (2006) *Migrants and financial services: a review of the situation in the UK.* Bristol: Personal Finance Research Centre, University of Bristol.

Aznar, C. (forthcoming) 'To bank or not to bank: Risk, financial exclusion and migrant workers in London', PhD dissertation, School of Geography, Queen Mary, University of London.

Baker, P. and Mohieldeen, Y. (2000) 'The language of London's school children', in P. Baker and J. Eversley (eds) *Multilingual capital,* London: Battlebridge, pp 5-60.

Ballard, R. (2003) *Remittances and economic development,* London: House of Commons Select Committee for Migration and Development.

BBC (2011) 'David Cameron rejects Cable immigration criticism', 14 April, available at http://www.bbc.co.uk/news/uk-politics-13072509.

Beaverstock, J. (2002) 'Transnational elites in global cities: British expatriates in Singapore's financial district', *Geoforum,* vol 33, no 4, pp 525-38.

Beaverstock, J. (2010) 'Immigration and the UK labour market in financial services: a commentary', in M. Ruhs and B. Anderson (eds) *Who needs migrant workers? Shortages, immigration and public policy,* Oxford: Oxford University Press, pp 290-4.

Beaverstock, J. and Smith, J. (1996) 'Lending jobs to global cities, skilled international labour migration, investment banking and the City of London', *Urban Studies,* vol 33, no 8, pp 1377-94.

Beazley, H. and Desai, V. (2008) 'Gender and globalisation', in V. Desai and R.B. Potter (eds) *The companion to Development Studies*, London: Hodder Education, pp 359-64.

Bebbington, A.J. (1999) 'Capitals and capabilities: a framework for analyzing peasant viability, rural livelihoods and poverty', *World Development*, vol 27, no 12, pp 2021-44.

Beck, T., Demirgüç-Kunt, A. and Martinez Peria, M.S. (2007) 'Reaching out: access to and use of banking services across countries', *Journal of Financial Economics*, vol 85, no 1, pp 234-66.

Becker, K.F. (2004) *The informal economy*, Department for Infrastructure and Economic Cooperation, SIDA.

Ben-Galim, D. (2011) *Asset stripping: Child Trust Funds and the demise of the assets agenda*, London: Institute of Public Policy Research.

Berthoud, R. and Kempson, E. (1992) *Credit and debt: the PSI Report*, London: Policy Studies Institute.

Black, R. and King, R. (2004) 'Editorial Introduction: Migration, Return and Development in West Africa', *Population, Place and Space*, vol 10, no 2, pp 75-83.

Black, R. and Sward, J. (2009) *Migration, poverty reduction strategies and human development*, Human Development Research Paper 2009/38, UNDP.

Blackwell, M. and Seddon, D. (2004) *Informal remittances from the UK: values, flows and mechanisms*, Report for the Department for International Development, Norwich: Overseas Development Group.

Blair, T. (1997) 'Bringing Britain together', Speech made at the launch of the Social Exclusion Unit, London, 8 December 1997.

Blake, S. and de Jong, E. (2008) *Short changed? Financial exclusion – a guide to donors and funders*, London: New Philanthropy Capital.

Bloch, A., Sigona, N. and Zetter, R. (2009) *No right to dream: the social and economic lives of young undocumented migrants*, London: Paul Hamlyn Foundation.

Bloch, A., Sigona, N. and Zetter, R. (2011) 'Migration routes and strategies of young undocumented migrants in England: a qualitative perspective', *Ethnic and Racial Studies*, pp 1-17.

Bourdieu, P. (1983) 'Forms of capital', in J.G. Richardson (ed) *Handbook of theory and research for the sociology of education*, New York: Greenwood, pp 241-58.

Boyer, R. (2000) 'Is a finance-led growth regime a viable alternative to Fordism? A preliminary analysis,' *Economy and Society*, vol 29, no 1, pp 111–45.

Broeders, D. and Engbersen, G. (2007) 'The fight against illegal migration: identification policies and immigrants' counterstrategies', *American Behavioral Scientist,* vol 50, no 12, pp 1592-1609.

Brown, S.S. (2006) 'Can remittances spur development? A critical survey,' *International Studies Review,* vol 8, pp 55-75.

Brown, M., Conaty, P. and Mayo, E. (2003) *Life saving: Community Development Credit Unions,* London: NACUW and the New Economics Foundation.

Bugamelli, M. and Paternò, F. (2006) 'Do workers' remittances reduce the probability of current account reversals?', CEP Discussion Paper, London:Centre for Economic Performance, London School of Economics.

Byrne, N., McCarthy, O. and Ward, M. (2007) 'Money-lending and financial exclusion', *Public Policy and Management,* vol 27, no 1, pp 45-52.

Carbo, S., Gardener, E. and Molyneux, P. (2007) 'Financial exclusion in Europe', *Public Money and Management,* vol 27, no 1, pp 21-7.

Carling, J. (2004) *Policy options for increasing the benefits of remittances,* Working Paper 8, Oxford: COMPAS.

Carling, J. (2008) 'The determinants of migrant remittances', *Oxford Review of Economic Policy,* vol 24, no 3, pp 582-99.

Carling, J., Erdal, M.B., Horst, C. and Wallacher, H. (2007) *Legal, rapid and reasonably priced? A survey of remittance services in Norway,* PRIO Report 2007/3, Oslo: International Peace Research Institute.

Carney, D. (1998) 'Sustainable rural livelihoods: what contributions can we make?', Paper presented at the Department for International Development's Natural Resources Advisors Conference, DFID, London.

Castles, S. (2005) 'Hierarchical citizenship in a world of unequal nation-states', *Political Science and Politics,* vol 38, no 4, pp 689-693.

Castles, S. and Miller, M.J. (2003) *The age of migration,* Basingstoke: Macmillan.

Cavanaugh, M. (2010) 'Numbers matter', in T. Finch and D. Goodhart (eds) *Immigration under Labour,* London: Institute of Public Policy Research, pp 30-3.

CGAP (2009) *Financial Access 2009: Measuring access to financial services around the world,* Washington D.C.: World Bank.

Chambers, R. (1995) 'Poverty and livelihoods: whose reality counts?', *IDS Discussion Papers,* no 347, Brighton: Institute of Development Studies.

Chambers, R. and Conway, G.R. (1992) 'Sustainable rural livelihoods: practical concepts for the 21st century', IDS Discussion Papers, no 296, Brighton: Institute of Development Studies.

Chant, S. (1996) 'Gender and tourism employment in Mexico and the Philippines', in S.M. Thea, (ed) *Gender, work and tourism*, London: Routledge, pp 120-79.

Chappell, L. and Sriskandarajah, D. (2007) *Mapping the development impacts of migration: development on the move*, Working Paper 1, London: IPPR.

Charsley, K. (2007) 'Risk, trust, gender and transnational cousin marriage among British Pakistanis, *Ethnic and Racial Studies*, vol 30, no 6, pp 1117-31.

Citizens Advice Belfast (2010) *Financial Inclusion Project 2010,* Belfast: Citizens Advice.

Citizens Advice Bureau (2001) *Summing up: bridging the financial literacy divide*, London: National Association of Citizens Advice Bureaux.

Clark, S. (2002) *Making ends meet in contemporary Russia: secondary employment, subsidiary agriculture and social networks*, Cheltenham: Edward Elgar.

Clark, A., Forter, A. and Reynolds, F. (2005) *Banking the unbanked: a snapshot*, London: Toynbee Hall, SAFE.

Coleman, J.S. (1988) 'Social capital in the creation of human capital', *American Journal of Sociology*, vol 94, pp S95-S120.

Coleman, J.S. (1990) *Foundations of social theory*, Cambridge, MA: Harvard University Press.

Collard, S. (2007) 'Towards financial inclusion in the UK: progress and challenges', *Public Money and Management,* vol 27, no 1, pp 13-20.

Collard, S. and McKay, S. (2006) 'Closing the savings gap: the role of the Savings Gateway', *Local Economy,* vol 21, pp 25-35.

Collard, S. and Kempson, E. (2005) *Affordable credit: the way forward,* Bristol: The Policy Press.

Collard, S., Kempson, E. and Dominy, N. (2003) *Promoting financial inclusion: an assessment of initiatives using a community select committee approach,* Bristol: The Policy Press.

Collard, S., Kempson, E. and Whyley, C. (2001) *Tackling financial exclusion: an area-based approach,* Bristol, The Policy Press.

Collins, D. (2005) 'Financial instruments for the poor: initial findings from the South African financial diaries study', *Development Southern Africa*, vol 22, no 5, pp 717-28.

Collins, D., Morduch, J., Rutherford, S. and Ruthven, O. (2009) *Portfolios of the poor: how the world's poor live on $2 a day*, Princeton: Princeton University Press.

Collyer, M. (2005) 'When do social networks fail to explain migration? Accounting for the movement of Algerian asylum-seekers to the UK', *Journal of Ethnic and Migration Studies*, vol 31, no 4, pp 699-718.

Committee on Payment and Settlement Systems and World Bank (2006) *General principles for international remittance services: consultative report*, Basel: Bank for International Settlement.

Connell, J. and Conway, D. (2000) 'Migration and remittances in island microstates: a comparative perspective on the South Pacific and the Caribbean', *International Journal of Urban and Regional Research*, vol 24, no 1, pp 52-78.

Conradson, D. and Latham, A. (2005) 'Friendship, networks and transnationality in a world city: antipodean transmigrants in London, *Journal of Ethnic and Migration Studies*, vol 31, no 2, pp 287-305.

Copestake, J.G. (1996) 'NGO-donor collaboration and the new policy agenda: the case of subsidised credit', *Public Administration and Development*, vol 16, pp 855-66.

Copestake, J. (2007) 'Mainstreaming microfinance: social performance management or mission drift', *World Development*, vol 35, no 10, pp 1721-38.

Corbridge, S. (1988) 'The debt crisis and the crisis of global regulation', *Geoforum*, vol 19, no 1, pp 109-30.

Corbridge, S. (1992) 'Discipline and punish: the new right and the policing of the international debt crisis', *Geoforum*, vol 23, no 3, pp 285-301.

Corbridge, S. (2008) 'Third world debt', in V. Desai and R.B. Potter (eds) *The companion to development studies*, London: Hodder Education, pp 508-11.

Council of Ministers (2008) *National strategy on migration and integration in Bulgaria. 2008–2015*, Sofia, Republic of Bulgaria.

Cox, R. (2005) *The servant problem: domestic employment in a global economy*, London: IB Tauris.

Cox, J., Gulliver, R. and Morris, J.C. (2011) *On the margins: debt, financial exclusion and low income households*, London: Compass – Direction for the Democratic Left Ltd, Southbank House.

Datta, K. (2007a) *Money matters: exploring financial exclusion among low paid migrant workers in London*, London: Department of Geography, Queen Mary, University of London.

Datta, K. (2007b) 'Gender and micro-finance', *Habitat Debate*, Special issue on Financing for the Urban Poor, vol 13, no 1, p 8.

Datta, K. (2009a) 'Transforming south–north relations? International migration and development', *Geography Compass*, vol 3, no 1, pp 108–34.

Datta, K. (2009b) 'Risky migrants? Low paid migrants coping with financial exclusion in London', *European Urban and Regional Studies,* vol 16, no 4, pp 331-44.

Datta, K. (2011a) *New migrant communities and financial services: keeping themselves to themselves?,* London: Friends Provident Foundation.

Datta, K. (2011b) 'Last hired, first fired? The impact of the economic downturn on low paid Bulgarian migrant workers in London', *Journal of International Development,* doi: 10.1002/jid.

Datta K., McIlwaine C.J., Evans Y., Herbert J., May J., Wills J. (2007a) 'From coping strategies to tactics: London's low-pay economy and migrant labour', *British Journal of Industrial Relations,* vol 45, no 2, pp 409–38.

Datta, K., McIlwaine, C.J., Wills, J., Evans, Y., Herbert, J. and May, J. (2007b) 'The new development finance or exploiting migrant labour? Remittance sending among low-paid migrant workers in London', *International Development Planning Review,* vol 29, no 1, pp 43-67.

Datta, K., McIlwaine, C.J., May, J., Herbert, J., Evans, Y. and Wills, J. (2009) 'Men on the move: narratives of migration and work among low paid migrant workers in London', *Social and Cultural Geography,* Special issue: Masculinities and intersectionality, vol 10, no 8, pp 853–73.

Datta, K., McIlwaine, C.J., Evans, Y., Herbert, J., May, J. and Wills, J. (2010) 'Towards a migrant ethic of care? Negotiating care and caring among migrant workers in London's low pay economy', *Feminist Review,* vol 94, pp 93-116.

De Boreck, M. and Koen, V. (2000) *The soaring eagle: anatomy of the Polish take-off in the 1990s,* IMF Working Papers, Washington, DC: International Monetary Fund.

De Goede, M. (2003) 'Hawala discourses and the war on terrorist finance', *Environment and Planning D: Society and Space,* vol 21, no 5, pp 513-32.

De Goede, M. (2008) 'The politics of pre-emption and the war on terror in Europe', *European Journal of International Relations,* vol 14, no 1, pp 161-84.

De Haas, H. (2005) 'International migration, remittances and development: myths and facts', *Third World Quarterly,* vol 26, pp 1269-84.

De Haas, H. (2006) 'Migration, remittances and regional development in Southern Morocco', *Geoforum,* vol 37, pp 568-80.

De Haas, H. (2007) 'Turning the tide? Why development will not stop migration', *Development and Change,* vol 38, no 5, pp 819-41.

De Haas, H. (2010) 'Remittances, migration and development: policy options and policy illusions', in K. Hujo and N. Piper (eds) *South–south migration: implications for social policy and development*, Basingstoke and London: Palgrave Macmillan, pp 158-89.

De Montclos, M. (2003). 'A refugee diaspora – when the Somalis go west', in K. Koser (ed) *New African diasporas*, London: Routledge, pp 37-55.

DFEE (Department for Education and Employment) (2000) *Financial capability through personal financial education: guidance for schools*, London: DFEE.

DFID (Department for International Development) (2005) *UK remittance market profile*, Business Intelligence, London: DFID.

Dobson, J., Latham, A. and Salt, J. (2009) *On the move? Labour migration in times of recession*, Policy Network Paper, Barrow: Cadbury Trust.

Dore, R. (2000) *Stock market capitalism: welfare capitalism*, Oxford and New York: Oxford University Press.

Dore, R. (2002) 'Stock market capitalism and its diffusion', *New Political Economy*, vol 7, no1, pp 115-21.

Drakeford, M. and Sachdev, D. (2001) 'Financial exclusion and debt redemption', *Critical Social Policy*, vol 21, no 2, 209-30.

Dreze, J., Lanjouw, P. and Sharma, N. (1997) *Credit transactions in a north Indian village* (mimeo). Delhi: Delhi School of Economics.

Duvall, F. (2007) *EU ascension of Bulgaria and Romania: migration issues*, Briefing document, Oxford: COMPAS.

DWP (Department for Work and Pensions) (2009) *Family resources survey United Kingdom 2008–2009*, London: DWP.

DWP (Department for Work and Pensions) (2010) *Social fund reform: debt, credit and low income households*, London: DWP.

Dwyer, P.S. (2006) 'US money transmitters in the Brazilian *Doleiro* currency market', White paper prepared for the National Money Transmitters Association. Available from http://www.nmta.us/site/e107_docs/DoleiroPaper_FirstRelease.pdf (accessed January 2011).

Dymski, G. (1999) *The bank merger wave: the economic causes and social consequences of financial consolidation,* Armonk, NY: M.E. Sharpe.

Dymski, G. (2005) 'Financial globalization, social exclusion and financial crisis', *International Review of Applied Economics,* vol 19, no 4, pp 439-57.

Dymski, G. (2006) ' Editorial: Targets of opportunity in two landscapes of financial globalisation', *Geoforum*, vol 37, pp 307-11.

Dymski, G. (2010) 'Confronting the quadruple global crisis', *Geoforum,* vol 41, pp 837-40.

Dymski, G. and Li, W. (2004) 'Financial globalization and cross-border co-movements of money and populations: foreign bank offices in Los Angeles', *Environment and Planning A*, vol 36, no 2, pp 213-40.

Dymski, G. and Veitch, J. M. (1992) 'Race and the financial dynamics of urban growth: L.A. as Fay Wray', in G. Riposa and C. Dersch (eds) *City of Angels*, Dubuque, IA: Kendall/Hunt, pp 131-58.

Dymski, G. and Veitch, J. M. (1994) 'Taking it to the bank: credit, race, and income in Los Angeles', in R.D. Bullard, J.E. Grigsby and C. Lee (eds) *Residential segregation: the American legacy*, Los Angeles, CA: Centre for Afro-American Studies, University of California, pp 150-79.

Dymski, G. and Veitch, J.M. (1996) 'Financial transformation and the metropolis: booms, busts and banking in Los Angeles', *Environment and Planning A*, vol 28, 1233-60.

Edmonds, T. (2011) *Financial inclusion (exclusion)*, House of Commons Standard note, London: House of Commons.

Elliott, L. and Allen, K. (2011) 'Britain in grip of worst ever financial crisis Bank of England Governor fears', *The Guardian*, 6 December.

Elson, D. (1995) 'Male bias in macro economics: the case of structural adjustment', in D. Elson (ed) *Male bias in the development process*, Manchester: Manchester University Press.

Engbersen, G. (1995) 'The road to anomia? Poverty regimes and life chances', in B. Unger and F. van Waarden (eds) *Convergence or diversity?*, Aldershot: Avebury, pp 200-25.

Engbersen, G. (2001) 'The unanticipated consequences of panopticon Europe: residence strategies of illegal immigrants', in V. Guiraudon and C. Joppke (eds), *Controlling a new migration world*, London: Routledge, pp 222-46.

Engbersen, G. and van der Leun, J.P. (2001) 'The social construction of illegality and criminality', *European Journal on Criminal Policy and Research*, vol 9, no 1, pp 51-70.

Epstein, G.E. (2005) 'Introduction: financialization and the world economy,' in G. Epstein (ed) *Financialization and the world economy*, Cheltenham and Northampton: Edward Elgar, pp 3–16.

Erdemir, A. and Vasta, E. (2007) *Differentiating irregularity and solidarity: Turkish immigrants at work in London*, Working paper no 42, Oxford: COMPAS.

Eroǔlu, S. (2010) 'Informal finance and the urban poor: an investigation of rotating savings and credit associations in Turkey', *Journal of Social Policy*, vol 39, no 3, pp 461-81.

Erturk, F., Johal, L. and Williams, K. (2007) 'The democratisation of finance? Promises, outcomes and conditions', *Review of International Political Economy*, vol 14, no 4, pp 553-75.

Erturk, I., Froud, J., Johal, S., Leaver, A. and Williams, C. (2008) 'General introduction: Financialization, coupon pool and conjecture', in I. Erturk, J. Froud, S. Johal, A. Leaver and C. Williams (eds) *Financialization at work: key texts and commentary*, London: Routledge, pp 1-43.

Evans, Y., Wills, J., Datta, K., Herbert, J., McIlwaine, C. J., May, J., Araújo, J. O., França, A. C. and França, A. P. (2007) *Brazilians in London: a report for the Strangers into Citizens campaign*, London: School of Geography, Queen Mary, University of London.

Evergeti, V. and Zontini, E. (2006) 'Introduction: some critical reflections on social capital, migration and transnational families', *Ethnic and Racial Studies*, vol 29, no 6, pp 1025-39.

EUROSTAT (2009) *Key figures on Europe, 2009 edition* Luxembourg: Statistical Offices of the European Communities.

Faist, T. (2000a) *The volume and dynamics of international migration and transnational social spaces*. Oxford: Oxford University Press.

Faist, T. (2000b) 'Transnationalization in international migration: implications for the study of citizenship and culture', *Ethnic and Racial Studies*, vol 23, no 2, pp 189-222.

Faist, T. (2004) 'The migration-security nexus: international migration and security before and after 9/11', *Willy Brandt Series of Working Papers on International Migration and Ethnic Relations, 4/03*, Malmö, Sweden: Malmö University.

Faist, T. (2008) 'Migrants as transnational development agents: an inquiry into the newest round of the migration-development nexus', *Population, Space and Place*, vol 14, pp 21-42.

Farrant, M., MacDonald, A. and Sriskandarajah, D. (2006) 'Migration and development: opportunities and challenges for policymakers', IOM Migration Research Series no 22, Geneva: International Organisation for Migration.

Favell, A. (2008) 'The new face of East–West migration in Europe,' *Journal of Ethnic and Migration Studies*, vol 34, no 5, pp 701–16.

Financial World (2008) *Money on the move*, available at www.financialworld.co.uk/archive/2008/2008_11nov (accessed 13 November 2008).

Finch, T. and Goodhart, D. (2010) *Immigration under Labour*, London: Institute of Public Policy Research.

Fine, J., Leimbach, L., Jacobs, K., Doan, T., Sanchez, A. and Savner, S. (2005) 'Distributing prepaid cards through workers' centres: a gateway to asset building for low income households', unpublished paper.

Finlayson, A. (2008) 'Characterising New Labour: the case of the Child Trust Fund', *Public Administration*, vol 86, no 1, pp 95–110.

Finlayson, A. (2009) 'Financialisation, financial literacy and asset based welfare', *British Journal of Politics and International Relations*, vol 11, pp 400-21.

FITF (Financial Inclusion Taskforce) (2010) *Banking services and poorer households*, available at http://www.hm-treasury.gov.uk/d/fin_inclusion_taskforce_poorerhouseholds_dec2010.pdf.

Fitzgerald, D. (2000) *Negotiating extra-territorial citizenship: Mexican migration and the transnational politics of community*, Monograph Series No 2, La Jolla, Center for Comparative Immigration Studies, University of California, San Diego.

Fix, M., Papademetriou, D., Batalova, J., Terrazas, A., Yi Ying Lin, S., Mittelstadt, M. (2009) *Migration and the global recession*, Washington, DC: Migration Policy Institute.

Flynn, D. (2003) *Tough as old boots? Asylum, immigration and the paradox of New Labour policy*, JCWI Immigration Rights Discussion Series, London: Joint Council for the Welfare of Immigrants.

Flynn, D. (2005) 'New borders, new management: the dilemmas of modern immigration policies', *Ethnic and Racial Studies*, vol 28, no 3, pp 463-90.

Flynn, D. (2010) 'Where was the radical new cosmopolitanism', in T. Finch and D. Goodhart (eds) *Immigration under Labour*, London: Institute of Public Policy Research, pp 27-9.

Ford, J. and Rowlingson, K. (1995) 'Low-income households and credit: exclusion, preference and inclusion', *Environment and Planning A*, vol 28, pp 1345-60.

French, S. and Leyshon, A. (2004) 'The new, new financial system? Towards a conceptualization of financial re-intermediation', *Review of International Political Economy*, vol 11, no 2, pp 263-88.

French, S. and Leyshon, A. (2010) '"These f@#king guys": The terrible waste of a good crisis', *Environment & Planning A*, vol 42, no 11, pp 2549-59.

French, S., Leyshon, A. and Signoretta, P. (2008) '"All gone now": the material, discursive and political erasure of bank and building society branches in Britain', *Antipode*, vol 40, no 1, pp 79-101.

French, S., Leyshon, A. and Thrift, N. (2009) 'A very geographical crisis: the making and breaking of the 2007–2008 financial crisis', *Cambridge Journal of Regions, Economy and Society*, vol 2, no 2, pp 287–302.

French, S., Lai, K. and Leyshon, A. (2010) 'Banking on financial services', in N. Coe and A. Jones (eds) *The economic geography of the UK*, London: Sage.

Freud, C. and Spatafora, N. (2005) *Remittances: transaction costs, determinants, and informal flows*, Policy Research Working Paper no 3704, Washington, DC, World Bank.

Froud, J.,and Williams, K. (2007) 'Private equity and the culture of value extraction', *New Political Economy*, vol 12, no 3.

Froud, J., Leaver, A., Williams, K. and Zhang, W. (2007) 'The quiet panic about financial illiteracy', in L. Assassi, D. Wigan and A. Nesvetailova (eds) *Global finance in the new century: beyond deregulation*, London: Palgrave, pp 112–25.

FSA (Financial Services Authority) (2005) *Consumers' views of proof of identity checks,* London: FSA.

Fugfugosh, M.A. (2006) *Informal remittance flows and their implications for global security*, GCSP Brief no 11, Program on the Geopolitical Implications of Globalization and Transnational Security, Geneva: Geneva Centre for Security Policy.

Fuller, D. and Jonas, A.E.G. (2002) 'Institutionalising future geographies of financial inclusion: national legitimacy versus local autonomy in the British Credit Union movement', *Antipode*, vol 34, no 1, pp 85-110.

Fuller, D. and Jonas, A.E.G. (2003) 'Alternative financial spaces', in R. Lee, A. Leyshon and C. Williams (eds) *Alternative economic spaces: rethinking the 'economic' in economic geography*, London: Sage, pp 55-73.

Fuller, D. and Mellor, M. (2008) 'Banking for the poor: addressing the needs of financially excluded communities in Newcastle upon Tyne', *Urban Studies,* vol 45, no 7, pp 1506-24.

Garapich, M. (2008) 'The migration industry and civil society: Polish immigrants in the United Kingdom before and after EU enlargement', *Journal of Ethnic and Migration Studies*, vol 34, no 5, pp 735-52.

Geddes, A. (2000) 'Denying access: asylum seekers and welfare benefits in the UK', in M. Bommes and A. Geddes (eds) *Immigration and welfare: challenging the borders of the welfare state*, London and New York: Routledge, pp 132-45.

Geertz, C. (1962) 'The Rotating Credit Association: a 'middle rung' in development', *Economic Development and Cultural Change*, vol 10, no 3, pp 241-63.

Gercheva, S. (2007) 'Financial exclusion in Bulgaria', Varna, Bulguria: Finance and Credit Department, University of Economics of Varna.

Gibbs, J. (2010) *Financial inclusion among new migrants in Northern Ireland: report by ICAR in collaboration with Citizens Advice Belfast*, London: Runnymede Trust.

Gibson-Graham, J.K. (1996) *The end of capitalism (as we knew it): a feminist critique of political economy*, Oxford and Cambridge: Blackwell Publishers.

Gill, N. and Bialski, P. (2011) 'New friends in new places: network formation during the migration process among Poles in the UK', *Geoforum*, vol 42, pp 241-49.

Giusti, C. (2009) 'Poverty, immigration and Latinos in the US Texas Colinas', Forum on Public Policy.

Glick-Schiller, N., Basch, L. and Blanc-Szanton, C. (1992) 'Transnationalism: a new analytical framework for understanding migration', *Annals of the New York Academy of Sciences*, vol 645, pp 1-24.

Glossop, C. and Shaheen, F. (2009) *Accession to recession: A8 migration in Bristol and Hull*, London: Centre for Cities.

Gloukoviezoff, G. (2006) *Understanding and combating financial exclusion and overindebtedness in Ireland: a European perspective*, Dublin: The Policy Institute, Trinity College.

Goetz, A. and Gupta, R.S. (1996) 'Who takes the credit? Gender, power and control over loan use in rural credit programs in Bangladesh', *World Development,* vol 24, no 1, pp 45-63.

Gonzáles de la Rocha, M. (1991) 'Family, well-being, food consumption and survival strategies during Mexico's economic crisis', in M. Gonzáles de la Rocha and A. Escobar (eds) *Social responses to Mexico's economic crisis of the 1980s,* San Diego, CA: Centre for US-Mexican Studies, UCLA, pp 115-27.

Goodwin, G., Adelman, L., Middleton, S. and Ashworth, K. (2000) *Debt, money management and access to financial services: evidence from the 1999 PSE survey of Britain,* Centre for Research in Social Policy, Working paper no 8, Bristol: University of Bristol.

Gregson, N. and Lowe, N. (1994) *Servicing the middle classes: class, gender and waged work in contemporary Britain,* London: Routledge.

Guarnizo, L.E. (1997) 'The emergence of a transnational social formation and the mirage of return migration among Dominican transmigrants', *Identities*, vol 4, no 2, pp 281-322.

Guarnizo, L.E. (2002) 'The economics of transnational living,' *International Migration Review*, vol 36, no 2, pp 355-88.

Hagan, J.M. (1998) 'Social networks, gender, and immigrant incorporation: resources and constraints', *American Sociological Review,* vol 63, pp 55-67.

Hamnett, C. (2003) *Unequal city: London in the global arena*, London: Routledge.

Hannam, M. (2009) *Financial inclusion and equality,* Runnymede Trust's Financial Inclusion and Equality Conference, October 2009, London.

Harris, J. and De Renzio, P. (1997): 'The missing link or 'analytically missing': the concept of social capital', *Journal of International Development*, vol 9, no 7, pp 919-935.

Harvey, P., Pettigrew, N., Madden, R., Emmerson, C., Tetlow, G. and Wakefield, M. (2007) *Final evaluation of the Savings Gateway 2 pilot, main report*, London: Department for Education and Skills.

Helleiner, E. (2010) 'A Bretton Woods moment? The 2007-2008 crisis and the future of global finance', *International Affairs*, vol 86, no 3, pp 619-36.

Herbert, T. and Hopwood Road, F. (2006) *Banking benefits: CAB evidence on payment of benefits into bank accounts*, London: Citizens Advice.

Hernandez, E. and Coutin, S. B. (2006) 'Remitting subjects: migrants, money and states', *Economy and Society*, vol 35, no 2, pp 185-208.

Hernández-Coss, R. and Bun, C.N. (2007) 'The UK–Nigeria remittance corridor: challenges of embracing formal transfer systems in a dual financial environment', Working Paper 92, Washington DC: World Bank.

Hochschild A. (2000) 'Global care chains and emotional surplus value', in W. Hutton and A. Giddens (eds) *On the edge: living with global capitalism*, London: Jonathan Cape.

Hogarth, J., Anguelov, C. and Lee, J. (2004) 'Why don't households have a checking account?', *Journal of Consumer Affairs*, vol 38, no 1, pp 1-34.

Home Office (2008) *Bulgarian and Romanian accession statistics January to March 2008*, available at: http://www.workpermit.com/news/2007-08-21/uk/uk-a8-romanian-bulgarian-accession-statistics.htm (accessed 15 January 2010).

Home Office (2010) *Bulgarian and Romanian accession statistics January to March 2009*, available at: http://www.workpermit.com/news/2008-09-21/uk/uk-a8-romanian-bulgarian-accession-statistics.htm (accessed 17 March 2010).

Hondagneu-Sotelo, P. (2001) *Domestica: immigrant workers and their employers*. Berkeley, CA: University of California Press.

Hopkins, G. (2010) 'A changing sense of Somaliness: Somali women in London and Toronto', *Gender, Place and Culture*, vol 17, no 4, pp 519-38.

Horst, C. (2004) *Money and mobility: transnational livelihood strategies of the Somali diaspora*, Global Migration Perspectives no 9, Geneva: Global Commission on International Migration.

Hudson, D. (2007) 'Financialisation of the poorest? The case of remittances', Paper presented at the 48th ISA Annual Convention. Chicago, USA.

Hudson, D. (2008) 'Developing geographies of financialisation: banking the poor and remittance securitisation', *Contemporary Politics*, vol 14, no 3, pp 315-33.

Hudson, M., Phillips, J., Ray, K. and Barnes, H. (2007) *Social cohesion in diverse communities*. York: Joseph Rowntree Foundation, available at: www.jrf.org.uk/publications/social-cohesion-diverse-communities.

Hugo, S. (2010) 'Remittance sending costs', Paper presented at ICBI Money Transfers and Workers' Remittances Conference, June 2010, Barcelona.

IDS (Institute of Development Studies) Bulletin (2009) Special issue: *Policy responses to the global financial crisis*, vol 40, no 5.

IMF (International Monetary Fund) (2010) 'World Economic Update: restoring confidence without harming recovery', 7 July, available at: www.imf.org/external/pubs/ft/weo/2010/update/02/index.htm (accessed on 8 September 2010).

IOM (International Organisation for Migration) (2011) *World Migration Report 2010*, Geneva: IOM.

Ipsos MORI (2008) *Political monitor, recent trends: the most important issues facing Britain today*, available at: www.ipsos-mori.com/polls/trends/issues12.shtml (accessed 18 March 2008).

Isaacs, L. (2008) *Research on migrant remittances and linkage to broader access to financial services*, Report to UK Remittance Taskforce, London: Developing Markets Associates Limited.

Iskander, N. (2007) 'Informal work and protest: undocumented immigrant activism in France, 1996–2000', *British Journal of Industrial Relations,* vol 45, no 2, pp 309-34.

Itzigsohn, J. (2000) 'Immigration and the boundaries of citizenship: the institutions of immigrants' political transnationalism', *International Migration Review,* vol 34, no 4, pp 1126-53.

Jessop, B. (2000) *From Thatcherism to New Labour: neo-liberalism, workfarism, and labour market regulation*, Department of Sociology, Lancaster University, available at: http://www.comp.lancs.ac.uk/sociology/soc131rj.pdf (accessed 15 July 2011).

Joassart-Marcelli, P. and Stevens, P. (2010) 'Immigrant banking and financial exclusion in Greater Boston', *Journal of Economic Geography*, vol 10, pp 883-912.

Johnson, S. (1998) 'Microfinance north and south: contrasting current debates', *Journal of International Development,* vol 10, pp 799-809.

Johnson, S. (2004) 'Gender norms in financial markets: evidence from Kenya', *World Development*, vol 32, no 8, pp 1355-74.

Johnson, S. and Rogaly, B. (1997) *Microfinance and poverty reduction*, Oxford: Oxfam and London: Action Aid.

Jones, A.M. (2008) 'The rise of global work', *Transactions of the Institute of British Geographers*, vol 33, no 1, pp 12-26.

Jones, A.M. (2010) 'Immigration and the UK labour market in financial services: a case of conflicting policy challenges?', in M. Ruhs and B. Andersen (eds) *Who needs migrant workers? Labour shortages, immigration and public policy*, Oxford: Oxford University Press, pp 259-94.

Jones, G.A. and Datta, K. (1999) 'From self-help to self-finance: the changing focus of urban research and policy', in K.Datta and G.A. Jones (eds) *Housing and finance in developing countries*, London: Routledge, pp 3-25.

Jones, P.A. (1999) *Towards sustainable credit union development, report of a national research project*, Manchester: Association of British Credit Unions Ltd.

Jones, P.A. (2006) 'Giving credit where it's due: promoting financial inclusion through quality credit unions', *Local Economy*, vol 21, no 1, pp 36-48.

Jordan, B. and Duvell, F. (2002) *Irregular migration: the dilemmas of transnational mobility*, Cheltenham: Edward Elgar.

Kabeer, N. (2001) 'Conflicts over credit: re-evaluating the empowerment potential of loans to women in rural Bangladesh', *World Development*, vol 29, no 1, pp 63-84.

Kabeer, N. (2003) 'Wider social impacts of microfinance: concepts, methods and findings', *IDS Bulletin*, vol 34, no 4, pp 106-14.

Kantor, A. and Nystuen, J. (1982) 'Defacto redlining a geographic view', *Economic Geography*, vol 58, no 2, pp 309-28.

Kapur, D. (2003) *Remittances: the new development mantra*, G24 Discussion Paper Series, Research Papers for the Intergovernmental Group of Twenty-Four on International Monetary Affairs, UN: New York and Geneva.

Kelly, G. and Lissauer, R. (2000) *Ownership for all*, London: Institute of Public Policy Research.

Kelly, P. and Lusis, T. (2006) 'Migration and the transnational habitus: evidence from Canada and the Philippines', *Environment and Planning A*, vol 38, pp 831-47.

Kempson, E. (1994) *Outside the banking system: a review of households without a current account*, London: Social Security Advisory Committee.

Kempson, E. (1998) *Savings and ethnic minority households*, Personal Investment Authority Research Reports, London: Personal Investments Authority.

Kempson, E. and Finney, A. (2009) *Saving in lower-income households: a review of the evidence*, Bristol: Personal Finance Research Centre.

Kempson, E. and Paxton, W. (2003) 'Savings among people on low to moderate incomes: the barriers and how they might be overcome', in W. Paxton (ed) *Equal shares: building a progressive and coherent asset-based welfare policy*, London: Institute of Public Policy Research, pp 57-71.

Kempson, E. and Whyley, C. (1999) *Kept out or opted out? Understanding and combating financial exclusion*, Bristol: The Policy Press.

Kempson, E., McKay, S. and Collard, S. (2005) *Incentives to save: encouraging saving among low-income households*, Final report on the Savings Gateway pilot project, London: HM Treasury.

Kempson, E., Whyley, C., Caskey, J. and Collard, S. (2000) *In or out?*, Financial Services Authority Consumer Research 3, London: Financial Services Authority.

Kennickell, A., Starr-McCluer, M. and Surette, B. (2000) 'Recent changes in US family finances: Results from the 1998 Survey of Consumer Finances', *Federal Reserve Bulletin*, vol 86, no 1, pp 1-29.

Khan, O. (2008) *Financial inclusion and ethnicity: an agenda for research and policy action*. London: Runnymede Trust.

Khan, O. (2009) *Financial inclusion*, Runnymede Trust's Financial Inclusion and Equality Conference, October 2009, London.

Khan, O. (2010) *Why do assets matter? Assets, equality, ethnicity – building towards financial inlusion*, London: Runnymede Trust.

Khatib-Chahidi, J. (1995) 'Gold coins and coffee ROSCAs: coping with inflation the Turkish way in northern Cyprus', in S. Ardener and S. Burman (eds) *Money-go-rounds: the importance of rotating savings and credit associations for women*, Oxford and Washington DC: Berg, pp 241-62.

Kirkup, J. (2011) 'World facing worst ever financial crisis in history, Bank of England Governor says', *The Telegraph*, 7 October.

Kivisto, P. (2001), 'Theorizing transnational immigration: a critical review of current efforts', *Ethnic and Racial Studies*, vol 24, no 4, pp 549-77.

Koser, K. (2007) *International migration: a very short introduction*, Oxford: Oxford University Press.

Lacoste, J.P. (2001) *Savings strategies of poor women in Zimbabwe: a socio-economic perspective*, Paper presented at the international conference on Livelihood, Savings and Debt in a Changing World: Developing Sociological and Anthropological Perspectives, Wageningen, The Netherlands: University of Wageningen.

Landolt, P. (2001) 'Salvadoran economic transnationalism: embedded strategies for household maintenance, immigrant incorporation, and entrepreneurial expansion,' *Global Networks,* vol 1, no 3, pp 217-42.

Langley, P. (2007) 'Uncertain subjects of Anglo-American financialization', *Cultural Critique*, vol 65, pp 67–91.

Langley, P. (2008) *The everyday life of global finance: savings and credit in Anglo-America*, Oxford: Oxford University Press.

Lee, R., Clark, G., Pollard, J. and Leyshon, A. (2009) 'The remit of financial geography – before and after the crisis', *Journal of Economic Geography*, vol 9, pp 723-47.

Le Grand, J. and Nissan, D. (2000) *A capital idea: start-up grants for young people*, London: Fabian Society.

Levine, R. (1997) 'Financial development and economic growth: views and agendas', *Journal of Economic Literature*, vol XXXV, pp 688-726.

Levitt, P. (1998) 'Social remittances: migration driven local-level forms of cultural diffusion', *International Migration Review*, vol 32, no 94, pp 926-48.

Levitt, P. (2001) *The Transnational Villagers*, University of California Press: Los Angeles.

Levitt P. and Glick-Schiller, N. (2004) 'Conceptualising simultaneity: a transnational social field perspective on society', *International Migration Review*, vol 38, no 3, pp 1002-39.

Levitt, P. and Lamba-Nieves, D. (2011) 'Social remittances revisited', *Journal of Ethnic and Migration Studies*, vol 37, no 11, pp 1-22.

Leyshon, A. (2005) 'Introduction: diverse economies', *Antipode*, vol 37, no 5, pp 856-62.

Leyshon, A. and Thrift, N (1993) 'The restructuring of the UK financial services industry in the 1990s: a reversal of fortunes', *Journal of Rural Studies*, vol 9, pp 223-41.

Leyshon, A. and Thrift, N. (1994) 'Access to financial services and financial infrastructure withdrawal: problems and policies', *Area*, vol 26, pp 268-75.

Leyshon, A. and Thrift, N. (1995) 'Geographies of financial exclusion: Financial abandonment in Britain and the United States', *Transactions of the Institute of British Geographers*, vol 20, no 3, pp 312-41.

Leyshon, A. and Thrift, N. (1996) 'Financial exclusion and the shifting boundaries of the financial system', *Environment and Planning A,* vol 28, pp 1150-56.

Leyshon, A. and Thrift, N. (1997) *Money/space: geographies of monetary transformation*, London: Routledge.

Leyshon, A., Pratt, J. and Thrift, N. (1999) 'Inside/outside: geographies of financial inclusion and exclusion in Britain', *Urban Studies*.

Leyshon, A., Thrift, N. and Pratt, J. (1998) 'Reading financial services: texts, consumers and financial literacy, *Environment and Planning D,* vol 16, no 1, pp 29-55.

Leyshon, A., Burton, D., Knights, D., Alferoff, C. and Signoretta, P. (2004) 'Towards an ecology of retail financial services: understanding the persistence of door-to-door credit and insurance providers', *Environment and Planning A*, vol 36, pp 625-45.

Leyshon, A., Signoretta, P., Knights, D., Alferoff, C., Burton, D. (2006) 'Walking with moneylenders: the ecology of the UK home-collected credit industry', *Urban Studies*, vol 43, 161–86.

Li, W., Oberle, A. and Dymski, G. (2009) 'Global banking and financial services to immigrants in Canada and the US', *International Migration and Integration*, vol 10, pp 1-29.

Lie, J. (1995) 'From international migration to transnational diaspora', *Contemporary Sociology*, vol 24, no 4, pp 303-6.

Lindley, A. (2009) 'Between "dirty money" and "development capital": Somali money transfer infrastructure under global scrutiny', *African Affairs,* 108/433, pp 519-39.

Lindley, A. (2010) *The early morning phone call: Somali refugees' remittances*, New York: Berghahn Books.

Lodge, S. (2011) 'New junior ISAs given go-ahead for autumn', *FT.com*, March 25 2011.

Lukas, R.B. and Stark, O. (1985) 'Motivations to remit: Evidence from Botswana', *Journal of Political Economy,* vol 93, no 5, pp 901-18.

MAC (Migration Advisory Committee) (2008) *The labour market impact of relaxing restrictions on employment in the UK of nationals of Bulgarian and Romanian EU member states,* Migration Advisory Committee Report.

Maimbo, S. (2004) 'The regulation and supervision of informal remittance systems: emerging oversight strategies', Paper presented at the Seminar on Current Developments in Monetary and Financial Law, available at www.imf.org/external/np/leg/sem/2004/cdmfl/eng/maimbo.pdf.

Mandelson, P. (1997) *Labour's next steps: tackling social exclusion*, Fabian Pamphlet 581, London: The Fabian Society.

Marcelli, E., Williams, C.C. and Joassart, P. (2009) (eds) *Informal work in developed nations*, London: Routledge.

Margolis, M. (1998) *An invisible minority: Brazilians in New York City*, Massachusetts: Ally and Bacon.

Markova, P. (2009) 'The impact of the financial crisis on Bulgarian migrants, migrants in Europe as development actors: between hope and vulnerability', European Social Watch Report, available atwww.socialwatch.eu/wcm/Bulgaria.html (accessed 6 September 2010).

Markova, E. and Black, R. (2007) *East European immigration and community cohesion*, London: Joseph Rowntree Foundation.

Marshall, J.N. (2004) 'Financial institutions in disadvantaged areas: a comparative analysis of policies encouraging financial inclusion in Britain and the United States', *Environment and Planning A*, vol 36, pp 241-61.

Martin, P. (2009) *The recession and migration: alternative scenarios*, Working Paper 13, Oxford: International Migration Institute, James Martin 21st Century School, University of Oxford.

Martin, R. (1999) 'The new economic geography of money', in R. Martin (ed) *Money and the space economy*, Chichester: Wiley, pp 3-28.

Martin, R. (2002) *Financialisation of daily life*, Philadelphia: Temple University Press.

Massey, D., Alarcon, R., Durand, J. and Gonzalez. H. (1987) *Return to Aztlan: the social process of international migration from Western Mexico.* Berkeley and Los Angeles: University of California Press.

Massey, D., Arango, J., Hugo, G.L., Kouaouci, A., Pellegrino, A. and Taylor, J. (1993) 'Theories of international migration: a review and appraisal', *Population and Development Review*, vol 19, no 3, pp 431-66.

Massey, D., Arango, J., Hugo, G., Kouaouci, A., Pellegrino, A. and Taylor, J. (1998) *Worlds in motion: understanding international migration at the end of the millennium*, Oxford: Clarendon Press.

Matin, I. and Sinha, S. (1998) 'Informal credit transaction of microcredit borrowers', *IDS Bulletin*, vol 29, no 4.

Matin, I., Hulme, D. and Rutherford, S. (2002) 'Finance for the poor: from microcredit to microfinancial services', *Journal of International Development,* vol 14, pp 273-94.

Mawhinney, P. (2010) *Seeking sound advice: financial inclusion and ethnicity,* London: Runnymede Trust.

Maxwell, D. and Sodha, S. (2006) *Turning on the taps: next steps for CTFs,* Paper presented at Political Studies Conference, University of Reading, 6 April.

May, J., Datta, K., Evans, Y., Herbert, J., McIlwaine, C.J. and Wills, J. (2010) 'Travelling neoliberalism: Polish and Ghanaian migrant workers in London', in A. Smith, A. Stenning and K. Willis (eds) *Social justice and neoliberalism: global perspectives*, London: Zed, pp 61-89.

May, J., Wills, J., Datta, K., Evans, Y., Herbert, J. and McIlwaine, C.J. (2007) 'Keeping London working: global cities, the British state and London's migrant division of labour', *Transactions of the Institute of British Geographers,* vol 32, pp 151-67.

Mayoux, L. (1999) 'Questioning virtuous spirals: microfinance and women's empowerment in Africa', *Journal of International Development,* vol 11, pp 957-84.

Mayoux, L. (2005) *Women's empowerment through sustainable microfinance: rethinking best practice*, Discussion draft paper.

Mazzucato, V. (2006) 'Informal insurance arrangements in a transnational context: the case of Ghanaian migrants' networks', Paper presented at CSAE conference 'Reducing poverty and inequality: how can Africa be included?', Oxford University, 19-21 March 2006.

McDowell, L. (2009) 'Old and new European economic migrants: whiteness and managed migration policies', *Journal of Ethnic and Migration Studies,* vol 35, no 1, pp 19-36.

McGeehan, S. (2006) 'CDFIs – a coming of age?', *Local Economy*, vol 21, no 1, pp 84-90.

McIlwaine, C.J. (2009) 'Legal Latins? Webs of (ir)regularity among Latin American migrants in London', Working Paper no 4, Nottingham: Identity, Citizenship and Migration Centre, University of Nottingham.

McIlwaine, C.J. (2010) 'Transnational asset building among Latin Americans within Europe: exploring UK–Spain connections', Paper presented at the 8th European Urban and Regional Studies Conference, 15-17 September 2010.

McIlwaine, C.J. (forthcoming) 'Constructing transnational social spaces among Latin American onward migrants in Europe', *Cambridge Journal of Regions, Economy and Society*, doi: 10.1093/cjres/rsr041.

McIlwaine, C.J. and Moser, C. (2003) Poverty, violence and livelihood security in urban Colombia and Guatemala, *Progress in Development Studies*, vol 3, no 2, pp 113–30.

McKenzie, S. and Menjívar, C. (2011) 'The meanings of migration, remittances, and gifts: the views of Honduran women who stay', *Global Networks,* vol 11, no 1, pp 63-81.

McKay, S. and Winkelmann-Gleed, A. (2005) *Migrant workers in the east of England*, London: East of England Development Agency.

McKillop, D.G. and Wilson, J. (2003) 'Credit unions in Britain: a time for change', *Public Money and Management,* vol 23, pp 119-23.

McKillop, D.G., Ward, A.M. and Wilson, O.S. (2007) 'The development of credit unions and their role in tackling financial exclusion', *Public Money and Management*, vol 27, no 2, pp 37-44.

Menjívar, C. (2000) *Fragmented ties: Salvadoran immigrant networks in America,* Berkeley, CA: University of California Press.

Migration Watch (2009) *The invisible cost of immigration,* Briefings Paper Economics 1.23, available at http://www.migrationwatchuk.org/briefingpaper/document/157 (accessed 15 September 2011).

Milligan, M. (2009) *The welfare effects of international remittance income,* PhD dissertation, Department of Economics, University of New Mexico.

Mitton, L. (2008) *Financial inclusion in the UK: review of policy and practice,* York: Joseph Rowntree Foundation.

Mohan, H. (2000) *Structural adjustment: theory, practice and impacts,* London: Routledge.

Montgomerie, J. (2009) 'The pursuit of (past) happiness? Middle-class indebtedness and American financialisation', *New Political Economy,* vol 14, no 1, pp 1-24.

Morris, L. (2002) *Managing migration: civic stratification and migrants' rights,* London: Routledge.

Moser, C. (1998) 'The asset vulnerability framework: reassessing urban poverty reduction strategies', *World Development,* vol 26, no 1, pp 1-19.

Moser, C. (ed) (2007) *Reducing global poverty,* Washington DC: Brookings Institute.

Moser, C. (2008) 'Assets and livelihoods: a framework for asset-based social policy', in C. Moser and A. Dani (eds) *Assets, livelihoods and social policy: new frontiers of social policy,* Washington DC: World Bank, pp 43-81.

Mosley, P. and Steel, L. (2004) 'Microfinance, the labour market and social exclusion: a tale of three cities', *Social Policy and Administration,* vol 38, no 7, pp 721-43.

Muzvidziwa, V.N. (2010) 'Double-rootedness and networking among urban migrants in Zimbabwe', *Journal of Sociology Social Anthropology,* vol 1, no 1-2, pp 81-90.

NACAB (National Association of Citizens Advice Bureaux) (2005a) *Financial literacy: a guide to activities in the CAB service,* London: NACAB.

NACAB (2005b) *Front-line financial capability,* Interim Project Report (Feb-Apr 2005), London: NACAB.

Nee, C. and Sanders, J. (2001) 'Understanding the diversity of immigrant incorporation: a forms-of-capital model', *Ethnic and Racial Studies,* vol 24, no 3, pp 386-411.

Neef, R. (2002) 'Aspects of the informal economy in a transforming country: the case of Romania', *International Journal of Urban and Regional Research,* vol 26, no 2, pp 299-322.

NEF (New Economics Foundation) (2007) *Reconsidering UK community development finance,* London: New Economics Foundation.

NEF (2008) *Keeping Britain posted: how post office banking could save the network and combat financial exclusion,* Briefing: Financial Inclusion 1, Future Economy, London: New Economics Foundation.

Nelson, N. (1995) 'The Kiambu group: a successful women's ROSCA in Mathare Valley, Nairobi (1971–1990)', in S. Ardener and S. Burman (eds) *Money-go-rounds: the importance of rotating savings and credit associations for women,* Oxford and Washington DC: Berg, pp 49-70.

Nyberg-Sørensen, N., Van Hear, N. and Engberg-Pedersen, P. (2002a) 'The migration-development nexus: evidence and policy options: state-of-the-art overview', *International Migration*, vol 40, pp 3-43.

Nyberg-Sørensen, N., Van Hear, N. and Engberg-Pedersen, P. (2002b) 'The migration-development nexus: evidence and policy options', *International Migration*, vol 40, pp 49-71.

OECD (Organisation for Economic Development and Cooperation) (2005) *Improving financial literacy: analysis of issues and policies*, Paris: OECD Publishing.

OFT (Office of Fair Trading) (1999a) *Vulnerable consumers and financial services*. London, OFT.

OFT (1999b) *Qualitative research into ethnic minorities and financial services, Appendix 5: Vulnerable consumers and financial services*. London: OFT.

Olden, A. (1999) 'Somali refugees in London: oral culture in a western information environment', *Libri*, vol 49, pp 212-14.

Olejarova, D. with Mosley, P. and Alexeeva, E. (2003) 'Microfinance, social capital formation and political development in Russia and Eastern Europe', *IDS Bulletin*, vol 34, no 4, pp 115-20.

Olesen, H. (2002) 'Migration, return and development: an institutional perspective', *International Migration*, vol 40, no 5, pp 126-50.

ONS (Office of National Statistics) (2010) *Statistical Bulletin: labour market statistics*, available at: http://www.statistics.gov.uk/cci/nugget. asp?id=192 (accessed 26 October 2010).

ONS (2011) *Statistical Bulletin: labour market statistics*, available at: http://www.statistics.gov.uk/cci/nugget.asp?id=192 (accessed 19 February 2011).

Orozco, M. (2004) *The remittance marketplace: prices, policy and financial institutions*, Washington DC: Institute for the Study of International Migration, Georgetown University.

Orozco, M. (2005) 'Markets and financial democracy: the case for remittance transfers', *Journal of Payment Systems Law*, vol 1, no 2, pp 166-215.

Orozco, M. (2006) 'Between a rock and a hard place: migrant remittance senders, banking access and alternative products', Paper presented at the Illinois Bankers Association 3rd Symposium on Hispanic banking, Building New Markets, available at www.thedialogue. org/PublicationFiles/Banking%20Access%20and%20Alternative%20 Products.pdf.

Orozco, M. (2007) 'Migrants' foreign savings and asset accumulation', in C. Moser (ed) *Reducing global poverty: the case for asset accumulation*, Washington DC: Brookings Institute, pp 225-38.

Orozco, M. (2010) *Migration, remittances and assets in Bangladesh: considerations about their intersection and development policy recommendations*, Report commissioned by the IOM, Geneva: International Organisation for Migration.

Orozco, M. and Fedewa, R. (2005) *Regional integration? Trends and patterns of remittance flows within South East Asia*, Washington DC: Inter-American Dialogue.

Orozco, M. and Ferro, A. (2007) 'Worldwide trends in international remittances', *Migrant Remittances*, vol 4, no 5, pp 1-5.

Osborne, G. (2010) Budget speech, House of Commons, 22 June.

Padilla, B. (2011) 'Engagement policies and practices: Expanding the citizenship of the Brazilian diaspora', *International Migration*, vol 49, no 3, pp 10-29.

Papademetriou, D.G. and Terrazas, A. (2009) *Immigrants and the current economic crisis: research evidence, policy changes and implications*, Washington DC: Migration Policy Institute.

Paulson, A., Singer, A., Newberger, R. and Smith, J. (2006) *Financial access for immigrants: lessons from diverse perspectives*, Chicago: The Federal Reserve Bank of Chicago, The Brookings Institutional Reserve.

Paxton, W. (2003) *Equal shares: building a progressive and coherent asset-based welfare policy*, London: Institute of Public Policy Research.

Paxton, W., White, S. and Maxwell, D. (2006) *The citizen's stake: exploring the future of universal asset policies*, Bristol: The Policy Press.

Paxton, W. (2009) *Asset based welfare in the UK: new routes to social mobility?*, Paper presented at the International Seoul Welfare Forum, Seoul.

Payments Council (2009) *Key payment facts*, available at: http://www.paymentscouncil.org.uk/payment_advice/key_payment_facts/.

Pfau-Effinger, B. (2009) 'Varieties of undeclared work in European societies', *British Journal of Industrial Relations*, vol 47, no 1, pp 79-99.

Phillips, N. (2009) 'Migration as development strategy? The new political economy of dispossession and inequality in the Americas,' *Review of International Political Economy*, vol 16, no 2, pp 231-59.

Phillips, J. (2010) *Is microfinance an appropriate solution for financial exclusion in developed countries?*, Masters dissertation, Department of Geography, University of Cambridge.

Phillips, J. (forthcoming) *New transnational geographies of migrant entrepreneurship*, PhD thesis, School of Geography, Queen Mary, University of London.

Pieke, F., Van Hear, N. and Lindley, A. (2005) *Synthesis study: part of the report on informal remittance systems in Africa, the Caribbean and Pacific (ACP) countries*, Oxford: COMPAS (ESRC Centre on Migration, Policy and Society), University of Oxford.

Pieke, F., Van Hear, N. and Lindley, A. (2007) 'Beyond control? The mechanics and dynamics of "informal" remittances between Europe and Africa', *Global Networks*, vol 7, no 3, pp 348-66.

Piirainen, T. (1997) *Towards a new social order in Russia: transforming structures and everyday life*, Aldershot: Ashgate.

Piper, N. (2009) 'The complex interconnections of the migration-development nexus: a social perspective', *Population, Space and Place*, vol 15, pp 93-101.

Policis and DTI (2004) *The effect of interest rate controls in other countries*, London: Department for Trade and Industry, available at: www.bis.gov.uk/files/file53896.pdf (accessed 30 September 2011).

Pollard, J. (2003) 'Small firm finance and economic geography', *Journal of Economic Geography*, vol 3, pp 429-52

Pollard, J. and Samers, M. (2007) 'Islamic banking and finance: postcolonial political economy and the decentring of economic geography', *Transactions of the Institute of British Geography*, vol 32, pp 313-30.

Pond, C. (2009) 'Financial inclusion and financial capability: the next steps', Speech to the Inside Government Forum, London, 8 July.

Poros, M.V. (2001) 'The role of migrant networks in linking labour markets: the case of Asian Indians in New York and London', *Global Networks*, vol 1, no 3, pp 243-59.

Portes, A. (1998) 'Social capital: its origins and applications in modern sociology', *American Review of Sociology*, vol 24, no 1, pp 1-24.

Portes, A. (2003) 'Conclusion: theoretical convergencies and empirical evidence in the study of immigrant transnationalism', *International Migration Review*, vol 37, no 3, pp 874-92.

Potter, R.B. and Phillips, J. (2006) 'Both black and symbolically white: the 'Bajan-Brit' return migrant as post-colonial hybrid', *Ethnic and Racial Studies*, vol 29, no 5, pp 901-27.

Prabhakar, R. (2008) *The assets agenda: principles and policy*, Basingstoke: Palgrave.

Prabhakar, R. (2009) 'What is the future of the asset-based welfare?', *Public Policy Research,* vol 16, no 1, pp 51-6.

Prabhakar, R. (2010) 'Developing financial capability among the young through education and asset-based welfare', *Public Money and Management*, vol 30, no 5, pp 279-84.

Putnam, R. (1993) 'The prosperous community: social capital and public life', *American Prospect*, vol 4, no 13, pp 18-21.

Putnam, R (1995) 'Tuning in, tuning out: the strange disappearance of social capital in America', *Political Science and Politics,* vol 28, no 4, pp 664-83.

Putnam, R. (2000) *Bowling alone: the collapse and revival of American community*, New York: Simon and Schuster.

Putnam, R., Leonardi, R. and Nanetti, R. (1993) *Making democracy work: civic traditions in modern Italy*, Princeton: Princeton University Press.

Putzel, J. (1997) 'Accounting for the 'dark side' of social capital', *Journal of International Development,* vol 9, no 7, pp 939-49.

Rahim, N., Wan, K. and Franceschelli, M. (2009) 'Financial inclusion amongst new migrants in Northern Ireland: a literature review' London: ICAR (Information Centre about Asylum and Refugees).

Rahman, F. (2010) 'Opposition parties must be called to account on financial exclusion', *The Guardian*, 28 April.

Rakodi, C. (1999) 'A capital assets framework for analyzing household livelihood strategies: implications for poverty', *Development Policy Review,* vol 17, pp 315-42.

Ramsay, I. (2009) '"To heap distress upon distress?" Comparative reflections on interest rate ceilings', Draft paper for symposium in honour of Michael Trebilcock, University of Toronto, 1-2 October 2009.

Ratha, D. (2003) 'Workers' remittances: an important and stable source of external development finance', in *Global development finance 2003: striving for stability in development finance*, Washington DC: World Bank, pp 157-75.

Ratha, D., Mohapatra, S. and Plaza, S. (2008) 'Beyond aid: new sources and innovative mechanisms for financing development in sub-Saharan Africa', Policy Research Working Paper 4609, Migration and Remittances Team, Development Prospects Group, World Bank, Washington DC: World Bank.

Ratha, D. and Mohapatra, S. (2009) 'Revised outlook for remittance flows 2009–2011, *Migration and Development Brief 9,* Migration and Remittances Team, Development Prospects Group, World Bank, Washington DC: World Bank.

Ratha, D., Mohapatra, S. and Silwal, A. (2009) *Migration and Development Brief 10*, Washington DC: World Bank, available at: siteresources.worldbank. org/INTPROSPECTS/Resources/334934-1110315015165/ Migration&DevelopmentBrief10.pdf.

Reagan, S. and Paxton, W. (eds) (2001) *Asset-based welfare: international comparisons*, London: Institute of Public Policy Research.

Reagan, S. and Paxton, W. (2003) *Beyond bank accounts: full financial inclusion*, London: Institute of Public Policy Research.

Reingold, D.A. (1999) 'Social networks and the employment problem of the urban poor', *Urban Studies*, vol 36, pp 1907-32.

Rhine, S.L. and Greene, W.H. (2006) 'The determinants of being unbanked for US immigrants', *The Journal of Consumer Affairs*, vol 40, no 1, pp 21-40.

Richardson D.C. and Lennon B.L. (2001) *Teaching old dogs new tricks: the commercialization of credit unions*, Bethseda, MD, Microenterprise Best Practices.

Richmond, A. (1994) *Global apartheid*, Oxford: Oxford University Press.

Robinson, R. (2004) *Globalization, immigrants' transnational agency and economic development in their homelands*, Policy Paper, Canadian Foundation for the Americas, Ottawa, Ontario.

Roche, B. (2000) 'UK migration in a global economy', Presentation at the IPPR's Conference on the Future of Labour Migration into the UK, 11 September 2000, London. Available at http://m.ippr.org/events/54/5875/uk-migration-in-a-global-economy

Roche, B. and Rodrigues de Paula, L. (2008) 'The determinants of recent foreign bank penetration in Brazil', *CEPAL Review*, vol 79, pp 159-76.

Rogaly, B., Fisher, T. and Mayo, E. (1999) *Poverty, social exclusion and microfinance in Britain*, Oxford: Oxfam and London: New Economics Foundation.

Rogers, A., Anderson, B. and Clark, N. (2009) *Recession, vulnerable workers and immigration: background report*, Oxford: COMPAS, University of Oxford.

Rowlingson, K., Whyley, C. and Warren, T. (1999) *Wealth in Britain: a life-cycle perspective*, London: Policy Studies Institute.

Runnymede Trust (2009) *Financial inclusion and equality*, conference report, London: Runnymede Trust.

Rutherford, S. (1999) *The poor and their money: an essay about financial services for the poor*, Manchester: Institute of Development Studies, University of Manchester.

Rutherford, S. (2002) *Money talks: conversations with poor households in Bangladesh about managing money*, Finance and Development Research Programme Working Paper Series, No 45, Manchester: Institute of Development Policy and Management, University of Manchester.

Ruthven, O. (2002) 'Money mosaics: financial choice and strategy in a West Delhi squatter settlement', *Journal of International Development*, vol 14, pp 249-71.

Ryan, L., Sales, R., Tilki, M. and Siala, B. (2009) 'Family strategies and transnational migration: recent Polish migrants in London', *Journal of Ethnic and Migration Studies*, vol 35, no 1, pp 61-77.

Saini, A. (2007) 'First Solution's last stand', *BBC London*, 4 July.

Samers, M. (2005) 'The myopia of "diverse economies" or a critique of the "informal economy"', *Antipode*, vol 37, no 5, pp 875-86.

Sander, C. (2003) *Migrant remittances to developing countries, a scoping study: overview and introduction to issues for pro-poor financial services*, London: Bannock Consulting.

Sassen, S. (1991) *The global city: New York, London, Tokyo*, Princeton: Princeton University Press.

Sassen, S. (1994) 'The informal economy: between new developments and old regulations', *Yale Law Review*, vol 103, no 8, pp 2289-304.

Sassen, S. (2001) *The global city: New York, London, Tokyo*. 2nd edn, Princeton: Princeton University Press.

Scott, J.C. (1985) *Weapons of the weak: everyday forms of peasant resistance*, Yale University Press: New Haven.

Sherraden, M. (1991) *Assets and the poor: a new American welfare policy*, London: M.E. Sharpe.

Sigona, N. (2012) '"I have too much baggage": the impacts of legal status on the social worlds of irregular migrants', *Social Anthropology*, vol 20, no 1, pp 50-65.

Silvey, R. (008) 'Development and geography: anxious times, anaemic geographies and migration', *Progress in Human Geography*, vol 33, no 4, pp 507-15.

Simeonova, D. (2004) *The negative effects of securitizing immigration: the case of Bulgarian migrants to the EU*, available at: www.migrationonline.cz.

Simon, D. (2008) 'Neoliberalism, structural adjustment and poverty reduction strategies', in V. Desai and R.B. Potter (eds) *The companion to development studies*, London: Hodder Education, pp 86-91.

Sinha, S. and Matin, I. (1998) 'Informal credit transactions of micro-credit borrowers in rural Bangladesh', *IDS Bulletin*, vol 29, no 4, pp 66-80.

Sklair, L. (2002) 'The transnational capitalist class and global politics: deconstructing the corporate-state connection', *International Political Science Review*, vol 23, no 2, pp 159-74.

Smith, A. (2000) 'Employment restructuring and household survival in "post-communist transition": rethinking economic practices in Eastern Europe', *Environment and Planning A*, vol 32, pp 1759–80.

Somerville, W. and Sumption, M. (2009) *Immigration in the United Kingdom: recession and beyond*, London: Equality and Human Rights Commission and Migration Policy Institute.

Sparr, P. (ed) (1994) *Mortgaging women's lives: feminist critiques of structural adjustment*, London: Zed.

Spence, L. (2005) *Country of birth and labour market outcomes in London: an analysis of Labour Force Survey and Census Data*, London: GLA.

Spence, L. (2006) *A profile of Londoners by language: an analysis of the Labour Force Survey data by language*, London: GLA.

Spencer, S. (2010) 'Economic gain, political cost', in T. Finch and D. Goodhart (eds) *Immigration under Labour*, London: Institute of Public Policy Research, pp 19-20.

Spencer, S. (2011) *The migration debate*, Bristol: The Policy Press.

Sporten, D., Valentine, G. and Nielsen, K.B. (2006) 'Post-conflict identities: practices and affiliations of Somali asylum seeker children', *Children's Geographies,* vol 4, no 2, pp 203-17.

Srinivasan, S. (1995) 'ROSCAs among South Asians in Oxford', in S. Ardener and S. Burman (eds) *Money-go-rounds: the importance of rotating savings and credit associations for women*, Oxford and Washington DC: Berg, pp 199-208.

Stack, C. (1974) *All our kin: strategies for survival in a Black community*, New York: Harper and Row.

Stenning, A., Smith, A., Rochovská, A. and Swiatek, D. (2010a) 'Credit, debt and everyday financial practices: low income households in two postsocialist cities', *Economic Geography,* vol 86, no 2, pp 119-45.

Stenning, A., Smith, A., Rochovská, A. and Swiatek, D. (2010b) *Domesticating neo-liberalism: spaces of economic practice and social reproduction in post-Socialist cities*, Oxford: Wiley Press.

Stewart, K. and Hills, J. (2005) 'Introduction', in J. Hills and K. Stewart (eds) *A more equal society? New Labour, poverty, inequality and exclusion*, Bristol: The Policy Press.

Stookey, S. (2006) *Financial services segregation: improving access to financial services for recent Latino immigrants*, Inter-American Development Bank.

Summerfield, H. (1995) 'A note on ROSCAs among northern Somali women in the United Kingdom', in S. Ardener and S. Burman (eds) *Money-go-rounds: the importance of rotating savings and credit associations for women,* Oxford and Washington DC: Berg, pp 209-16.

Sumption, M. (2009) *Social networks and Polish immigration to the UK*, Economics of Migration Working Paper no 5, London: Institute of Public Policy Research.

Sumption, M. (2010) 'Foreign workers and immigrant integration: emerging from the recession in the UK', in D.G. Papademetriou, M. Sumption, A. Terrazas, with C. Burket, S. Loyal, A. Ferrero-Turrión (eds) *Migration and immigrants two years after the financial collapse: where do we stand?*, Washington, DC: Migration Policy Institute.

Sumption, M. and Sommerville, W. (2010) *The UK's new Europeans: progress and challenges five years after ascension*, London: Equality and Human Rights Commission.

Sward, J. with Skeldon, R. (2009) 'Migration and the financial crisis: how will the economic downturn affect migrants?', *Briefing no 17*, Brighton: Development Research Centre on Migration, Globalisation and Poverty, University of Sussex.

Taylor, M. (2011) *The long term impacts of financial capability: evidence from the British Household Panel Survey*, Report prepared for the Consumer Financial Education Body, London: CFEB.

Taylor, M., Jenkins, S. and Sacker, A. (2009) *Financial capability and wellbeing: evidence from the British Household Panel Survey*, London: Financial Services Authority.

The Economist (2009) 'Remittances: trickle-down economics', 19 February.

Thiel, V. (2006) *Doorstep robbery: why the UK needs a fair lending law*, London: New Economics Foundation.

Thiel, V. and Nissan, S. (2008) *UK CDFIs: from thriving to surviving: realising the potential for community development finance*, London: New Economics Foundation.

Thrift, N.J. and Leyshon, A. (1992) 'In the wake of money. The city of London and the accumulation of value', in L. Budd and S. Whimster (eds) *Global finance and urban living: a study of metropolitan change*, London: Routledge, pp 282-311.

Toxopeus, H.S. and Lensink, R. (2007) *Remittances and financial inclusion in development*, Research paper no 2007/49, World Institute for Economics Development Research, United Nations University.

Toynbee Hall (2005) *Banking the unbanked: a snapshot*, London: Toynbee Hall.

Toynbee Hall (2008) *From access to inclusion: an evaluation of the role of Basic Bank Accounts in promoting financial inclusion*, London: Toynbee Hall.

Transact (National Forum for Financial Inclusion) (2008) *Newsletter*, London: Toynbee Hall.

Treasury (1999) *Access to financial services: PAT 14*. London, HM Treasury.

Treasury (2001a) *Saving and assets for all: the modernisation of Britain's tax and benefit system number 8*, London: HM Treasury.

Treasury (2001b) *Delivering saving and assets: the modernisation of Britain's tax and benefit system number 9*, London: HM Treasury.

Treasury (2004) *Promoting financial inclusion*. London: HM Treasury.

Treasury (2007a) *Financial inclusion: an action plan for 2008-2011*, Norwich: Office of Public Sector Information.

Treasury (2007b) *Financial inclusion: the way forward*. Norwich: Office of Public Sector Information.

Treasury (2007c) *Financial capability: the government's long term approach*, Norwich: Office of Public Sector Information.

UN (United Nations) (2006) *Building inclusive financial sectors for development*, New York: United Nations.

UNDP (United Nations Development Programme) (2009) *Overcoming barriers: human mobility and development*, Global Human Development Report, Basingstoke and New York: Palgrave Macmillan.

Van Hear, N. (2004) 'Refugee diasporas or refugees in diaspora', in M. Ember, C.R. Ember and I. Skoggard (eds) *Encyclopedia of diasporas: immigrant and refugee cultures around the world*, vol I: Overviews and topics, New York: Kluwer Academic/Plenum Publishers, pp 580-92.

Van Hear, N. and Sørensen, N. (eds) (2003) *The migration-development nexus*, Geneva: International Organisation for Migration.

Van Hear, N., Brubaker, R. and Bessa, T. (2009) *Managing mobility for human development: the growing salience of mixed migration*, UN Development Programme Human Development Reports Research paper 2009/02, New York, UNDP.

Van Liempt, I. (2011) '"And then one day they all moved to Leicester": the relocation of Somalis from the Netherlands to the UK explained', *Population, Space and Place,* vol 17. no 3, pp 254-266.

Vargas-Silva, C. (2011) 'Long-term international migration flows to and from the UK', Migration Observatory Briefing, available at: www.migrationobservatory.ox.ac.uk.

Vass, P. (2007) 'Solving financial exclusion needs joined up government', *Public Money and Management*, vol 27, no 2, pp 3-4.

Vasta, E. (2006) 'The paper market: "borrowing" and "renting" of identity documents', Paper presented at Paper Tigers or Tiger Papers: The Paper Regime of Modern Societies workshop, Oxford University.

Vasta, E. (2008) 'The paper market: "borrowing" and "renting" of identity documents', COMPAS Working Paper, WP-08-03, Oxford: Oxford University.

Vershinina, N., Barrett, R. and Meyer, M. (2011) 'Forms of capital, intra-ethnic variation and Polish entrepreneurs in Leicester', *Work, Employment and Society*, vol 25, no 1, pp 101-17.

Vertovec, S. (2004) 'Migrant transnationalism and modes of transformation', *International Migration Review*, vol 38, no 3, pp 970-1001.

Vertovec, S. (2007) 'Super-diversity and its implications', *Ethnic and Racial Studies*, vol 30, no 6, pp 1024-54.

Vertovec, S. and Cohen, R. (1999) *Migration, diasporas and transnationalism*, Aldershot: Edward Elgar.

Vleck, W. (2006) 'Development v. terrorism – migrant remittances or terrorist financing?', *Work Package 2 – securitization beyond borders: exceptionalism inside the EU and impact on policing beyond borders.* Challenge Working Paper, European Foreign Policy Unit, London School of Economics and Political Science.

Vonderlack, R. and Schreiner, M. (2001) *Women, microfinance and savings: lessons and proposal*, St Louis, MO: Centre for Social Development, Washington University in St Louis.

Wallace, C. (2002) 'Household strategies: their conceptual relevance and analytical scope in social research', *Sociology*, vol 36, no 2, pp 275-92.

Wallace, A. and Quilgars, D. (2005) *Homelessness and financial exclusion: a literature review*, York: Centre for Housing Policy, University of York.

Watson, M. (2009) 'Planning for a future of asset-based welfare? New Labour, financialized economic agency and the housing market', *Planning, Practice & Research*, vol 24, no 1, pp 41–56.

Wearden, G. (2009) 'UK faces worse recession than US and Europe IMF warns', *The Guardian*, 18 March.

Williams, T. (2007) 'Empowerment of whom and for what? Financial literacy education and the new regulation of consumer financial services', *Law and Policy*, vol 29, no 2, pp 226-56.

Willis, K. and Yoeh, B. (2002) 'Gendering transnational communities: a comparison of Singaporean and British migrants in China', *Geoforum*, vol 33, pp 553-65.

Wills, J., Datta, K., Evans, Y., Herbert, J., May, J. and McIlwaine, C.J. (2010) *Global cities at work: new migrant divisions of labour*, London: Pluto Press.

Wimaladharma, J., Pearce, D. and Stanton, D. (2004) 'Remittances: the new development finance?', *Small Enterprise Development*, vol 15, no 1, pp 12-19.

World Bank (2005) *Global development finance 2005*, Washington DC: World Bank.

World Bank (2008) *Migration and remittances factbook 2008*, Washington DC: World Bank.

World Bank (2011) *Migration and remittances factbook 2011,* Washington DC.: World Bank.

Wright, K. and Black, R. (2011) 'International migration and the downturn: assessing the impacts of the global financial downturn on migration, poverty and human well-being', *Journal of International Development*, vol 23, no 4, pp 555-64.

www.dahabshiil.com

www.geldnaarhius.nl

www.hm-treasury.gov.uk

www.moneyadviceservice.org

www.natwest.com

www.remesas.org

www.sendepenger.no

www.sendmoneyhome.org

www.westernunion.com

Yujuico, E. (2009) 'All modes lead to home: assessing the state of the remittance art', *Global Networks,* vol 9, no 1, pp 63-81.

Zontini, E. (2004) 'Immigrant women in Barcelona: coping with the consequences of transnational lives', *Journal of Ethnic and Migration Studies,* vol 30, no 6, pp 1113-44.

Index

Page references for notes are followed by n